CliffsAP®

5 Biology Practice Exams

CliffsAP®

5 Biology Practice Exams

by

Phillip E. Pack, Ph.D.

Wiley Publishing, Inc.

About the Author

Phillip E. Pack, Ph.D., taught AP Biology for eleven years. He is currently Professor of Biology at Woodbury University in Burbank, California. He teaches courses in biology, human biology, botany, field botany, environmental studies, and evolution, and co-teaches various interdisciplinary courses, including Energy & Society (with architecture faculty) and Natural History of California & Nature Writing (with English faculty).

To Mary and Megan

Publisher's Acknowledgments

Editorial

Acquisitions Editor: Greg Tubach

Project Editor: Kelly D. Henthorne

Technical Editor: Maria Furci

Production

Proofreader: Susan Moritz

Wiley Publishing, Inc. Composition Services

CliffsAP® 5 Biology Practice Exams

Published by:
Wiley Publishing, Inc.
111 River Street
Hoboken, NJ 07030-5774
www.wiley.com

Copyright © 2006 Bobrow Test Preparation Services

Published by Wiley, Hoboken, NJ
Published simultaneously in Canada

Library of Congress Cataloging-in-Publication Data

Pack, Phillip E.
  CliffsAP 5 biology practice exams / by Phillip E. Pack.-- 1st ed.
    p. cm. -- (CliffsAP)
    ISBN-13 978-0-471-77027-5
    ISBN-10 0-471-77027-2
1. Biology—Examinations—Study guides. I. Title: II. Title: CliffsAP five biology
practice exams. III. Series.
  QH316.P33 2006
  570.76--dc22

                        2006008779

Printed in the United States of America

10 9 8 7 6 5 4 3 2 1

1O/SQ/QW/QW/IN

WILEY

Table of Contents

Introduction

How You Should Use This Book

The Advanced Placement Program is designed to encourage students to take challenging courses in high school and receive college credit for their efforts. Many high schools offer classes especially designed for the AP program, but any course or program of study, whatever it is called, is appropriate as preparation for taking the AP exam if the content is college level. This book helps you to prepare for the Advanced Placement Examination in Biology by giving you five practice exams that are similar in content and format to actual AP exams. Taking these practice exams helps to improve your AP exam in three ways:

- You become aware of the topics you understand and the topics for which you need additional study.

- You learn more about each topic. Following each exam is a complete list of answers and explanations for each exam question. The explanations act as a study guide, providing you with a review of the material and helping you understand the concept tested by the question.

- You become more familiar with the format of the AP exam. Questions on the AP exam are presented in various ways. By taking the practice exams in this book you become more proficient at reading exam questions and determining the correct answer.

A companion book is also available. *CliffsAP Biology,* also by Phillip E. Pack, provides a detailed but compact review of each of the major topics. The review of each topic is followed by multiple-choice and essay questions specific to the topic. Complete answers and explanations are provided. In addition, a separate section provides a review of each of the 12 AP labs with relevant multiple-choice and essay questions. One practice exam is also provided. Altogether, the book provides almost 400 multiple-choice questions and 50 essay questions. All the questions in both books are unique. There is little overlap of questions among the practice tests of this book or between the questions of both books. Each question is designed to evaluate your understanding of a different aspect of a principle, a concept, or a word in the vocabulary of biology.

Format

The AP exam in biology consists of two parts. The first part is a 100-question multiple-choice test. You have 80 minutes to complete this section. The second part of the exam consists of four free-response, or essay, questions. First, you are given a 10-minute reading period to read the four questions, organize your thoughts, and record notes or create an outline on provided paper. Then you have 90 minutes to write your essay response to all four questions. The multiple-choice section counts for 60 percent of the exam, and the essay section counts for the remaining 40 percent. The exam is administered in May of each year along with AP exams in other subjects.

Section I	Multiple Choice	100 questions	80 minutes	60%
Section II	Reading Period		10 minutes	
	Writing Period	4 questions	90 minutes	40%

Grading

Exams are graded on a scale of 1 to 5, with 5 being best. Most colleges will accept a score of 3 or better as a passing score. If you receive a passing score, colleges will give you college credit (applied toward your bachelor's degree), advanced placement (you can skip the college's introductory course in biology and take an advanced course), or both. You should check with the biology department at the colleges you're interested in to determine how they award credit for the exam.

The distribution of student scores for some recent AP exams in biology are as follows.

	Exam Grade	Percentage of Students		
		2003	2004	2005
Extremely well qualified	5	17.9	18.9	18.2
Well qualified	4	18.6	20.2	20.1
Qualified	3	22.4	21.9	22.9
Possibly qualified	2	26.1	24.6	23.3
No recommendation	1	14.9	14.4	15.5
Mean Score (1 to 5)		2.98	3.05	3.02

The multiple-choice section is designed with a balance of easy and difficult questions to produce a mean score of 50 out of 100 (on one recent test, the actual mean was 55 percent). Essay questions are also designed to obtain a 50 percent mean score, but scores vary significantly with individual questions and from year to year. On the 2005 exam, mean scores ranged from 2.78 to 4.88 (out of a possible 10 points) for the four questions. Clearly, both sections of the exam are difficult. They are deliberately written that way so that the full range of students' ability can be measured. In spite of the exam difficulty, however, 61 percent of the students taking the exam in 2005 received a score of 3 or better. Therefore, the AP exam is difficult, but most (prepared) students do well.

What's on the Exam

The multiple-choice section of an AP exam is written with a certain number of questions from each area in biology. Generally, each of the major topics is represented by the percentages given in the following table. These same percentages were used to choose the questions for the five exams in this book. Since there are 100 questions on the exam, a topic with a 7 percent representation, such as chemistry, means there will be 7 questions for that topic. However, many questions address topics in more than one area, so the number of questions per topic may be higher than indicated here.

Area I.	Molecules and Cells		25%
	Topic 1:	Chemistry	7%
	Topic 2:	Cells	6%
	Topic 3:	Photosynthesis	4%
	Topic 4:	Respiration	4%
	Topic 5:	Cell Division	4%

Area II.	**Genetics and Evolution**		**25%**
	Topic 6:	Heredity	8%
	Topic 7:	Molecular Genetics	9%
	Topic 8:	Evolution	8%
Area III.	**Organisms and Populations**		**50%**
	Topic 9:	Five-Kingdom Survey	8%
	Topic 10:	Plants	12%
	Topic 11:	Animal Structure and Function	10%
	Topic 12:	Animal Reproduction and Development	6%
	Topic 13:	Animal Behavior	4%
	Topic 14:	Ecology	10%

Hints for Taking the Multiple-Choice Section

In the AP exam, questions for the multiple-choice section are provided in a booklet. While reading the questions in the booklet, feel free to cross out answers you know are wrong or underline important words. After you've selected the answer from the various choices, you carefully fill in bubbles, labeled A, B, C, D, or E, on an answer sheet. Mark only your answers on the answer sheet. Since unnecessary marks can produce machine-scoring errors, be sure to fill in the bubbles carefully and erase errors and stray marks thoroughly.

Some specific strategies for answering the multiple-choice questions follow.

1. **Don't let easy questions mislead you.** The multiple-choice questions range from easy to difficult. On one exam, 92 percent of the candidates got the easiest question right, but only 23 percent got the hardest question right. Don't let the easy questions mislead you. If you come across what you think is an easy question, it probably is. Don't suspect that it's a trick question.

2. **Budget your time by skipping hard questions.** You have 80 minutes to answer 100 questions, 48 seconds per question. If you come across a hard question that you can't answer quickly, skip it, and mark the question to remind you to return to it if time permits. If you can eliminate some of the answer choices, mark those also so that you can save time when you return. It's important to skip a difficult question, even if you think you can eventually figure it out, because for each difficult question you spend three minutes on, you could have answered three easy questions. If you have time at the end of the test, you can always go back. If you don't have time, at least you will have had the opportunity to try all the questions. Also, if you don't finish the test, don't be overly concerned. Since the test is designed to obtain a mean score of 50 percent, it is not unusual for a student to leave some answers blank.

3. **Make only educated guesses.** If you're not sure of the answer to a question, don't guess unless you can make an "educated" guess. You make an educated guess when you can reduce the answer to two or three choices. If you get an answer right, you receive one point. If you leave it blank, you receive no points. *However, for each wrong answer, one-fourth point is deducted from your score.*

4. **Avoid wrong answer penalties.** One-fourth point is deducted for each wrong answer. The one-fourth point deduction for wrong answers adjusts for random guessing. Since each question has five choices, there is a one-in-five chance that you can *randomly* select the correct answer. If you choose five answers randomly for five questions, probability predicts that you will guess one correct answer and four wrong answers. Your total score for the five guesses would be $1 - \frac{1}{4} - \frac{1}{4} - \frac{1}{4} - \frac{1}{4} = 0$. By deducting one-fourth point for each of the wrong answers, your total score would be zero. That's reasonable because you really didn't know any of the answers. But if you can reduce your choices to two or three, the odds are in your favor that the number of questions you get right will exceed the number of points deducted. That's also reasonable, because you knew some of the answer choices were wrong.

5. **Carefully answer reverse multiple-choice questions.** In a typical multiple-choice question, you need to select the choice that is true. On the AP exam, you will find many reverse multiple-choice questions where you need to select the *false* choice. These questions usually use the word "EXCEPT" in sentences such as "All of the following are true EXCEPT . . ." or "All of the following occur EXCEPT. . . ." A reverse multiple-choice question is more difficult to answer than regular multiple-choice questions because it requires you to know four true pieces of information about a topic before you can eliminate the false choice. It is equivalent to correctly answering five true-false questions to get one point; and if you get one of the five wrong, you get them all wrong. Reverse multiple-choice questions are also difficult because half way through the question you can forget that you're looking for the false choice. To avoid confusion, do the following: After reading the opening part of the question, *read each choice and mark a* T *or an* F *next to each one to identify whether it is true or false.* If you're able to mark a *T* or an *F* for each one, then the correct answer is the choice marked with an *F*. Sometimes you won't be sure about one or more choices, or sometimes you'll have two choices marked *F*. In these cases, you can concentrate on the uncertain choices until you can make a decision.

Hints for Taking the Essay Section

There are four questions on the essay section of the test. One of the questions is taken from Area I (molecules and cells), one from Area II (genetics and evolution), and two from Area III (organisms and populations). One of the four questions will also evaluate your ability to design experiments or to analyze experimental results. Each of the four questions can earn a maximum of 10 points. The 40 points on this section of the exam counts as 40 percent of your total test score.

The essay questions are provided in a green (or lavender) booklet. During the 10-minute reading period, read the questions thoroughly, circling key words. Next, write a brief outline using key words to organize your thoughts. When the writing period begins, begin writing your answer on the answer sheets that are provided separately. If for some reason you don't write an outline, go back and re-read the question half way through writing your answer. Make sure that you're still answering the question. It's easy to get carried away, and by the end of your response, you might be answering a different question.

Strategies for answering the essay questions follow.

1. **Don't approach the essay section with apprehension.** Most students approach the essay section of the exam with more anxiety than they have when approaching the multiple-choice section. However, in terms of the amount of detail in the knowledge required, the essay section is easier. On essay questions, *you* get to choose what to write. You can get an excellent score without writing every relevant piece of information. Besides, you don't have time to write an entire book on the subject. A general answer that addresses the question with a limited number of specifics will get a good score. Additional details may (or *may not*) improve your score, but the basic principles are the most important elements for a good score. In contrast, a multiple-choice question focuses on a very narrow and specific body of knowledge, which you'll either know or you won't. The question doesn't let you select from a range of correct information. This isn't true for the essay questions.

2. **Give specific information in your answer.** You need to give specific information for each essay question. Don't be so general that you don't really say anything. Give more than just terminology with definitions. You need to use the terminology to explain biological processes. It's the combination of using the proper terminology and explaining processes that will convince an AP exam reader that you understand the answer. Give some detail when you know it—names of processes, names of structures, names of molecules—and then tell how they're related. The reader is looking for specific information. If you say it, you get the points. You don't have to say everything, however, to get the maximum 10 points.

3. **Answer each part of an essay question separately.** Many of the AP essay questions ask several related questions. A single question, for example, might have two or three parts, each requesting specific information. You should answer each part of the question in a separate paragraph. This will help the reader recognize each part of your answer. Some questions are formally divided into parts, such as a, b, c, d. Again, answer these questions separately, in paragraphs labeled a, b, c, and d.

4. **Answer all parts of an essay question.** When you answer the essay questions, it is extremely important that you give a response for each part of the question. Don't overload the detail on one part at the expense of saying nothing in another part because you ran out of time. Each part of the question is apportioned a specific number of points. If you give abundant information on one part and nothing on the remaining parts, you receive only the maximum

number of points allotted to the part you completed. In a four-part question, that's often only 2.5 points. You won't get any extra points above the maximum 2.5, even if what you write is Nobel-prize quality.

5. **Budget your time.** You have 90 minutes for four questions, about 23 minutes each. Just as it's most important to answer all parts of a question, it's best to respond to all the essay questions rather than to answer two or even three of them extremely well, with no response on the last one or two. You'll probably know *something* about every question, so be sure you get that information written for each question. If you reach the last question with five minutes remaining, for example, use that time to write as much information as possible. One or two points is a lot better than zero.

6. **Don't worry if you make a factual error.** What if you write something that is incorrect? The AP exam readers look for correct information. They search for key words and phrases and award points when they find them. If you use the wrong word to describe a process, or identify a structure with the wrong name, there is no formal penalty (unlike the deduction for guessing on the multiple-choice test). If you're going to get any points, however, you need to write correct information.

7. **Don't be overly concerned about grammar, spelling, punctuation, or penmanship.** The AP exam readers don't penalize for incorrect grammar, spelling, or punctuation or for poor penmanship. They are interested in *content*. However, if your grammar, spelling, or penmanship impairs your ability to communicate, then the readers cannot recognize the content, and your score will suffer.

8. **Don't write a standard essay.** Don't spend your time writing a standard essay with introduction, support paragraphs, and conclusion. Just dive right into your outline and answer the question directly. On the other hand, your essay response cannot be an outline; it must have complete sentences written in paragraph form.

9. **Drawings can improve your score.** Drawings and diagrams may sometimes add up to 1 point to your essay score. But the drawings must be explained in your essay, and the drawings must be labeled with supporting information. If not, the AP exam reader will consider them doodles, and you will get no additional points.

10. **Pay attention to direction words.** A direction word is the first word in an essay question that tells you how to answer the question. The direction word tells you what you need to say about the subject matter that follows. Here are the most common direction words found on the AP exam:

   - *Discuss* means to consider or examine various aspects of a subject or problem.
   - *Describe* means to characterize or give an account in words.
   - *Define* means to give a precise meaning for a word or phrase.
   - *Explain* means to clarify or make understandable.
   - *Compare* means to discuss two or more items with an emphasis on their *similarities*.
   - *Contrast* means to discuss two or more items with an emphasis on their *differences*.

There are also specialized direction words for the laboratory essays. These words include *design* (an experiment), *calculate* (a value), and *construct* and *label* (a graph). These words have specific meanings for laboratory analyses and are discussed separately in the following section.

Laboratory Essay Questions

The College Board provides 12 laboratory exercises for use in AP Biology courses. Completing these labs, or similar labs that your teacher may substitute, provides the laboratory experience typical of a first-year college course in biology. One essay question and approximately 10 percent of the multiple-choice questions are based on these lab exercises.

The laboratory essay question is usually one of two types.

1. **Experimental analysis.** In this type of essay question, you are given some experimental data and asked to interpret or analyze the data. The question usually includes several parts, each requesting specific interpretations of the data. In addition, you are usually asked to prepare a graphic representation of the data. Graph paper is provided. Guidelines for preparing a graph are given in the following section.

2. **Experimental design.** This type of essay question asks you to design an experiment to answer specific questions about given data or an experimental situation. Guidelines for designing an experiment are given later in this introduction.

Although the data or situation in both of these types of questions will be somewhat different from those you encountered in your AP labs, you will be able to draw from your AP lab experience to analyze data or design experiments.

How to Graph Data

The laboratory question in the essay part of the AP exam will often ask you to create a graph using data provided in the question. Include the following in your graph.

1. **Label each axis.** Indicate on each axis what is being measured and in what unit of measurement. For example "Time (minutes)," "Distance (meters)," and "Water Loss (ml/m^2)" are appropriate labels.

2. **Provide values along each axis at regular intervals.** Select values and spacing that will allow your graph to fill as much of the graphing grid as possible.

3. **Use the x-axis for the independent variable and the y-axis for the dependent variable.** The dependent variable is the value you are measuring as a result of an independent variable imposed by the experiment. If the graph is plotting the progress of an event, then time is the independent variable, and the data you collect that measures the event (such as weight change, distance traveled, or carbon dioxide released) is the dependent variable.

4. **Connect the plotted points.** Usually, straight lines are used to connect the points. Smooth curves are also used, but that usually implies knowledge about intermediate points not plotted or a mathematical equation that fits the experimental results. If the question asks you to make predictions beyond the data actually graphed, extrapolate, or extend, the plotted line with a different line form (for example, dotted or dashed).

5. **In graphs with more than one plot, identify each plot.** If you plot more than one set of data on the same graph, identify each plot with a short phrase. Alternatively, you can draw the points of each plot with different symbols (for example, circles, squares, or triangles) or connect the plotted points using different kinds of lines (solid line, dashed line, or dash-dot line) and then identify each kind of symbol or line in a legend.

6. **Provide a title for the graph.** Your title should be brief but descriptive.

How to Design an Experiment

The laboratory essay question may ask you to design an experiment to test a given hypothesis or to solve a given problem. In most cases, the question will ask you not only to design an experiment but also to discuss expected results. Since the form of these questions can vary dramatically, it is not possible to provide a standard formula for preparing your answer. However, the following list provides important elements that you should include in your answer if they are appropriate to the question.

1. **Identify the independent and dependent variables.** The independent variable is the variable you are manipulating to see how the dependent variable changes.

   ■ You are investigating how the crustacean *Daphnia* responds to changes in temperature. You expose *Daphnia* to temperatures of 5°C, 10°C, 15°C, 20°C, and 30°C. You count the number of heartbeats/sec in each case. Temperature is the independent variable (you are manipulating it), and number of heartbeats/sec is the dependent variable (you observe how it changes in response to different temperatures).

   ■ You design an experiment to investigate the effect of exercise on pulse rate and blood pressure. The physiological conditions (independent variable, or variable you manipulate) include sitting, exercising, and recovering at various intervals following exercise. You make two kinds of measurements (two dependent variables) to evaluate the effect of the physiological conditions—pulse rate and blood pressure.

2. **Describe the experimental treatment.** The experimental treatment (or treatments) is the various values that you assign to the independent variable. The experimental treatments describe how you are manipulating the independent variable.

   ■ In the *Daphnia* experiment, the different temperature values (5°C, 10°C, 15°C, 20°C, and 30°C) represent five experimental treatments.

   ■ In the experiment on physiological conditions, the experimental treatments are exercise and recovery at various intervals following exercise.

3. **Identify a control treatment.** The control treatment, or control, is the independent variable at some normal or standard value. The results of the control are used for comparison with the results of the experimental treatments.

   - In the *Daphnia* experiment, you choose the temperature of 20°C as the control because that is the average temperature of the pond where you obtained the culture.

   - In the experiment on physiological conditions, the control is sitting, when the subject is not influenced by exercising.

4. **Use only one independent variable.** Only one independent variable can be tested at a time. If you manipulate two independent variables at the same time, you cannot determine which is responsible for the effect you measure in the dependent variable.

   - In the physiological experiment, if the subject also drinks coffee in addition to exercising, you cannot determine which treatment, coffee or exercise, causes a change in blood pressure.

5. **Random sample of subjects.** You must choose the subjects for your experiments randomly. Since you cannot evaluate every *Daphnia,* you must choose a subpopulation to study. If you choose only the largest *Daphnia* to study, it is not a random sample, and you introduce another variable (size) for which you cannot account.

6. **Describe the procedure.** Describe how you will set up the experiment. Identify equipment and chemicals to be used and why you are choosing to use them. If appropriate, provide a labeled drawing of the setup.

7. **Describe expected results.** Use graphs to illustrate the expected results, if appropriate.

8. **Provide an explanation of the expected results in relation to relevant biological principles.** The results you give are your expected results. Describe the biological principles that led you to make your predictions.

   - In the experiment on physiological conditions, you expect blood pressure and pulse rate to increase during exercise in order to deliver more O_2 to muscles. Muscles use the O_2 for respiration, which generates the ATP necessary for muscle contraction.

Must-Know Essay Questions

Some AP Biology teachers try to predict which essay questions will be on the next AP test. For example, reviewing old AP exams might reveal some questions that haven't been asked in a while. A new scientific discovery, or research that receives a Nobel prize, might suggest an AP question. Unfortunately, guessing questions in this way is very unreliable.

Here is a better way. Questions on the essay section of the AP exam generally address fundamental principles or processes in biology. Here is a list of the most important principles—the ones on which questions keep reappearing on AP exams. Being able to answer these questions is an absolute requirement for being prepared. So, at the very least, know this material. Sample responses to questions on these topics appear in the answer sections following each practice exam in this book. Additional responses appear at the end of each topic section in the companion *CliffsAP Biology*.

1. Section 2: Cells: Cell structure, especially structure and function of the plasma membrane
2. Section 3: Photosynthesis: Photosynthesis and chloroplasts
3. Section 4: Respiration: Respiration and mitochondria
4. Section 5: Cell Division: Mitosis and meiosis
5. Section 7: Molecular Genetics: DNA structure and replication
6. Section 7: Molecular Genetics: Protein synthesis
7. Section 8: Evolution: Natural selection
8. Section 8: Evolution: Speciation
9. Section 10: Plants: Reproduction in flowering plants
10. Section 10: Plants: Plant tropisms and hormones (especially auxin)
11. Section 11: Animal Structure and Function: Nerve transmission
12. Section 11: Animal Structure and Function: Muscle contraction
13. Section 12: Animal Reproduction and Development: Menstrual cycle
14. Section 14: Ecology: Succession
15. Section 14: Ecology: Biogeochemical cycles

There's no guarantee that questions on these topics will appear on your AP exam, but these topics appear so often that you should be prepared. In any case, the multiple-choice section of the exam will certainly include questions on these topics. So you can't lose by focusing on these areas.

Some Final Suggestions

Each of the exams in this book is followed by an answer key for the multiple-choice questions, a scoring template for the exam, explanations for the multiple-choice questions, and scoring standards for the free-response questions (often called a rubric).

To get the full benefit of simulating a real AP exam, set aside at least three hours for each of the 5 exams. Begin the multiple-choice section and after 80 minutes, stop and move on to the essay section. Spend 10 minutes outlining your answers to each essay question and then allow yourself 90 minutes to write out your full answers. By using the actual times that the real AP exam allows, you will learn if the time you spend on each multiple-choice and each essay question is appropriate.

When you're done taking the exam, score your exam using the multiple-choice answers that follow the exam and the free-response scoring standards that follow the multiple-choice answer explanations. Then, go back and answer any multiple-choice questions that you were unable to complete in the allotted 80 minutes. When you are done, read all of the multiple-choice explanations, even those for questions you got right. The explanations are thorough and provide you with information and suggestions. Even if you know the answers, reviewing the provided explanations is good review.

Although you've heard it so many times, practice *will* improve your test performance (although it's unlikely to make you perfect). So be sure to complete all the tests and review all the answers. Good luck.

Answer Sheet for Practice Exam 1

1 Ⓐ Ⓑ Ⓒ Ⓓ Ⓔ	26 Ⓐ Ⓑ Ⓒ Ⓓ Ⓔ	51 Ⓐ Ⓑ Ⓒ Ⓓ Ⓔ	76 Ⓐ Ⓑ Ⓒ Ⓓ Ⓔ
2 Ⓐ Ⓑ Ⓒ Ⓓ Ⓔ	27 Ⓐ Ⓑ Ⓒ Ⓓ Ⓔ	52 Ⓐ Ⓑ Ⓒ Ⓓ Ⓔ	77 Ⓐ Ⓑ Ⓒ Ⓓ Ⓔ
3 Ⓐ Ⓑ Ⓒ Ⓓ Ⓔ	28 Ⓐ Ⓑ Ⓒ Ⓓ Ⓔ	53 Ⓐ Ⓑ Ⓒ Ⓓ Ⓔ	78 Ⓐ Ⓑ Ⓒ Ⓓ Ⓔ
4 Ⓐ Ⓑ Ⓒ Ⓓ Ⓔ	29 Ⓐ Ⓑ Ⓒ Ⓓ Ⓔ	54 Ⓐ Ⓑ Ⓒ Ⓓ Ⓔ	79 Ⓐ Ⓑ Ⓒ Ⓓ Ⓔ
5 Ⓐ Ⓑ Ⓒ Ⓓ Ⓔ	30 Ⓐ Ⓑ Ⓒ Ⓓ Ⓔ	55 Ⓐ Ⓑ Ⓒ Ⓓ Ⓔ	80 Ⓐ Ⓑ Ⓒ Ⓓ Ⓔ
6 Ⓐ Ⓑ Ⓒ Ⓓ Ⓔ	31 Ⓐ Ⓑ Ⓒ Ⓓ Ⓔ	56 Ⓐ Ⓑ Ⓒ Ⓓ Ⓔ	81 Ⓐ Ⓑ Ⓒ Ⓓ Ⓔ
7 Ⓐ Ⓑ Ⓒ Ⓓ Ⓔ	32 Ⓐ Ⓑ Ⓒ Ⓓ Ⓔ	57 Ⓐ Ⓑ Ⓒ Ⓓ Ⓔ	82 Ⓐ Ⓑ Ⓒ Ⓓ Ⓔ
8 Ⓐ Ⓑ Ⓒ Ⓓ Ⓔ	33 Ⓐ Ⓑ Ⓒ Ⓓ Ⓔ	58 Ⓐ Ⓑ Ⓒ Ⓓ Ⓔ	83 Ⓐ Ⓑ Ⓒ Ⓓ Ⓔ
9 Ⓐ Ⓑ Ⓒ Ⓓ Ⓔ	34 Ⓐ Ⓑ Ⓒ Ⓓ Ⓔ	59 Ⓐ Ⓑ Ⓒ Ⓓ Ⓔ	84 Ⓐ Ⓑ Ⓒ Ⓓ Ⓔ
10 Ⓐ Ⓑ Ⓒ Ⓓ Ⓔ	35 Ⓐ Ⓑ Ⓒ Ⓓ Ⓔ	60 Ⓐ Ⓑ Ⓒ Ⓓ Ⓔ	85 Ⓐ Ⓑ Ⓒ Ⓓ Ⓔ
11 Ⓐ Ⓑ Ⓒ Ⓓ Ⓔ	36 Ⓐ Ⓑ Ⓒ Ⓓ Ⓔ	61 Ⓐ Ⓑ Ⓒ Ⓓ Ⓔ	86 Ⓐ Ⓑ Ⓒ Ⓓ Ⓔ
12 Ⓐ Ⓑ Ⓒ Ⓓ Ⓔ	37 Ⓐ Ⓑ Ⓒ Ⓓ Ⓔ	62 Ⓐ Ⓑ Ⓒ Ⓓ Ⓔ	87 Ⓐ Ⓑ Ⓒ Ⓓ Ⓔ
13 Ⓐ Ⓑ Ⓒ Ⓓ Ⓔ	38 Ⓐ Ⓑ Ⓒ Ⓓ Ⓔ	63 Ⓐ Ⓑ Ⓒ Ⓓ Ⓔ	88 Ⓐ Ⓑ Ⓒ Ⓓ Ⓔ
14 Ⓐ Ⓑ Ⓒ Ⓓ Ⓔ	39 Ⓐ Ⓑ Ⓒ Ⓓ Ⓔ	64 Ⓐ Ⓑ Ⓒ Ⓓ Ⓔ	89 Ⓐ Ⓑ Ⓒ Ⓓ Ⓔ
15 Ⓐ Ⓑ Ⓒ Ⓓ Ⓔ	40 Ⓐ Ⓑ Ⓒ Ⓓ Ⓔ	65 Ⓐ Ⓑ Ⓒ Ⓓ Ⓔ	90 Ⓐ Ⓑ Ⓒ Ⓓ Ⓔ
16 Ⓐ Ⓑ Ⓒ Ⓓ Ⓔ	41 Ⓐ Ⓑ Ⓒ Ⓓ Ⓔ	66 Ⓐ Ⓑ Ⓒ Ⓓ Ⓔ	91 Ⓐ Ⓑ Ⓒ Ⓓ Ⓔ
17 Ⓐ Ⓑ Ⓒ Ⓓ Ⓔ	42 Ⓐ Ⓑ Ⓒ Ⓓ Ⓔ	67 Ⓐ Ⓑ Ⓒ Ⓓ Ⓔ	92 Ⓐ Ⓑ Ⓒ Ⓓ Ⓔ
18 Ⓐ Ⓑ Ⓒ Ⓓ Ⓔ	43 Ⓐ Ⓑ Ⓒ Ⓓ Ⓔ	68 Ⓐ Ⓑ Ⓒ Ⓓ Ⓔ	93 Ⓐ Ⓑ Ⓒ Ⓓ Ⓔ
19 Ⓐ Ⓑ Ⓒ Ⓓ Ⓔ	44 Ⓐ Ⓑ Ⓒ Ⓓ Ⓔ	69 Ⓐ Ⓑ Ⓒ Ⓓ Ⓔ	94 Ⓐ Ⓑ Ⓒ Ⓓ Ⓔ
20 Ⓐ Ⓑ Ⓒ Ⓓ Ⓔ	45 Ⓐ Ⓑ Ⓒ Ⓓ Ⓔ	70 Ⓐ Ⓑ Ⓒ Ⓓ Ⓔ	95 Ⓐ Ⓑ Ⓒ Ⓓ Ⓔ
21 Ⓐ Ⓑ Ⓒ Ⓓ Ⓔ	46 Ⓐ Ⓑ Ⓒ Ⓓ Ⓔ	71 Ⓐ Ⓑ Ⓒ Ⓓ Ⓔ	96 Ⓐ Ⓑ Ⓒ Ⓓ Ⓔ
22 Ⓐ Ⓑ Ⓒ Ⓓ Ⓔ	47 Ⓐ Ⓑ Ⓒ Ⓓ Ⓔ	72 Ⓐ Ⓑ Ⓒ Ⓓ Ⓔ	97 Ⓐ Ⓑ Ⓒ Ⓓ Ⓔ
23 Ⓐ Ⓑ Ⓒ Ⓓ Ⓔ	48 Ⓐ Ⓑ Ⓒ Ⓓ Ⓔ	73 Ⓐ Ⓑ Ⓒ Ⓓ Ⓔ	98 Ⓐ Ⓑ Ⓒ Ⓓ Ⓔ
24 Ⓐ Ⓑ Ⓒ Ⓓ Ⓔ	49 Ⓐ Ⓑ Ⓒ Ⓓ Ⓔ	74 Ⓐ Ⓑ Ⓒ Ⓓ Ⓔ	99 Ⓐ Ⓑ Ⓒ Ⓓ Ⓔ
25 Ⓐ Ⓑ Ⓒ Ⓓ Ⓔ	50 Ⓐ Ⓑ Ⓒ Ⓓ Ⓔ	75 Ⓐ Ⓑ Ⓒ Ⓓ Ⓔ	100 Ⓐ Ⓑ Ⓒ Ⓓ Ⓔ

Practice Exam 1

Section I (Multiple-Choice Questions)

Time: 80 minutes

100 questions

Directions: Each of the following questions or statements is followed by five possible answers or sentence completions. Choose the one best answer or sentence completion.

1. A scientist chemically analyzes the plasma membrane of a cell. He determines that it is an animal cell because he finds that it contains

   A. cholesterol molecules
   B. phospholipids
   C. proteins
   D. cellulose
   E. chitin

2. During interphase, chromosomes are not visible because

   A. they condense and form small circular bodies
   B. they move into the cytoplasm and attach to ribosomes
   C. they attach to the nuclear envelope
   D. they move into the cytoplasm to form the endoplasmic reticulum
   E. they unwind for replication and transcription

3. The plant cells responsible for increases in the length of roots are located in the

   A. apical meristem
   B. vascular cambium
   C. cork cambium
   D. secondary xylem
   E. primary phloem

4. Natural selection occurs for all of the following reasons EXCEPT:

   A. Resources are limited.
   B. Traits are inherited.
   C. There is variation in traits among individuals in a population.
   D. Individuals change in order to adapt.
   E. Individuals compete for resources.

5. In the hydrological cycle, plants transfer most of their water to the environment through

   A. photosynthesis
   B. respiration
   C. denitrification
   D. nitrification
   E. transpiration

6. Asci, perithecia, and hyphae characterize which of the following groups?

   A. algae
   B. bacteria
   C. cyanobacteria
   D. slime molds
   E. fungi

7. Which of the following correctly describes DNA polymerase activity?

   A. It can operate in either the $3' \rightarrow 5'$ or $5' \rightarrow 3'$ direction.
   B. It can initiate DNA replication.
   C. It operates continuously without interruption on either DNA strand.
   D. It can copy a mutation from the template strand to the replicate strand.
   E. It requires no other enzymes to assemble DNA.

GO ON TO THE NEXT PAGE

8. During photosynthesis, the pH *inside* a thylakoid

   A. decreases as O_2 enters the thylakoid
   B. decreases as H^+ accumulates inside the thylakoid from photolysis
   C. only decreases in the dark
   D. is always greater than the pH of the stroma
   E. decreases as ATP is generated across the thylakoid membrane

9. Seeds are produced by all of the following EXCEPT:

   A. ferns
   B. angiosperms
   C. gymnosperms
   D. flowering plants
   E. conifers

10. The Krebs cycle occurs

    A. in the matrix
    B. in the stroma
    C. in the cytoplasm
    D. between the crista membrane and the mitochondrial membrane
    E. outside the thylakoids

11. Which of the following describes a correct order of events for the germination and early growth of a dicotyledon seedling?

    A. cotyledon digestion → imbibition → root growth → shoot growth
    B. imbibition → cotyledon digestion → root growth → shoot growth
    C. imbibition → root growth → shoot growth → cotyledon digestion
    D. root growth → shoot growth → imbibition → cotyledon digestion
    E. root growth → imbibition → shoot growth → cotyledon digestion

12. Compared to a person who is physically unfit, a person who is fit

    A. pumps a smaller volume of blood with each heart beat
    B. takes longer to reach a maximum heart rate
    C. delivers the same amount of oxygen to the circulatory system with each heart beat
    D. requires more oxygen for the same amount of muscle contraction
    E. is more likely to skip heart beats

13. Both cyclic and noncyclic photophosphorylation

    A. require H_2O
    B. generate NADP
    C. generate oxygen
    D. generate PGAL
    E. generate ATP

14. All of the following involve membrane transport by passive or active transport processes EXCEPT the

    A. large intestine
    B. postsynaptic membranes of a neuron
    C. loop of Henle
    D. alveolus
    E. urethra

15. Which of the following is a characteristic that differentiates the domains Archaea and Bacteria? Of the two domains,

    A. only members of Archaea have a nuclear envelope
    B. only members of Archaea have a circular chromosome
    C. only members of Bacteria have peptidoglycans in their cell walls
    D. only members of Bacteria have membrane-enclosed organelles
    E. only members of Bacteria have plasma membranes with lipids

16. All of the following are true about energy in an ecosystem EXCEPT:

    A. Energy flows in one direction: from producers to primary consumers, to secondary consumers, to tertiary consumers.
    B. Most of the energy transferred out of one trophic level is lost before passing into the next higher trophic level.
    C. The ultimate source of most energy entering an ecosystem is the sun.
    D. Heat generated by organisms represents a loss of energy to the ecosystem.
    E. Energy is recycled in an ecosystem.

17. During development of an embryo, a cleavage refers to

    A. a cell division
    B. the disposal of embryonic waste products
    C. the merging of two adjacent cells
    D. the formation of the neural groove
    E. the invagination of cells to form the gastrula

18. New alleles appear in an isolated population as a result of

    A. genetic drift
    B. natural selection
    C. mutation
    D. nonrandom mating
    E. a small population size

19. Sugar and CO_2 are dissolved in water to make soft drinks. Which of the following is the solute?

    A. only the water
    C. only the CO_2
    B. only the sugar
    D. both the sugar and the CO_2
    E. both the sugar and the water

20. Which of the following would most likely provide examples of *mitotic* cell divisions?

    A. cross section of muscle tissue
    B. cross section of an anther
    C. longitudinal section of a shoot tip
    D. endosperm of a dormant seed
    E. cross section of a leaf

21. All of the following support the endosymbiotic theory that ancestors of mitochondria and chloroplasts were once independent, free-living prokaryotes EXCEPT:

    A. Mitochondria and chloroplasts divide independently of the eukaryotic host cell by a process similar to binary fission.
    B. Mitochondria and chloroplasts carry on protein synthesis separately from the eukaryotic host cell.
    C. Mitochondria and chloroplasts have ribosomes that more closely resemble those of bacteria than of eukaryotic cells.
    D. Mitochondria and chloroplasts function independently of the eukaryotic host cell.
    E. Mitochondria, chloroplasts, and bacteria have a single, circular chromosome without histones or proteins.

22. The electrons that leave chlorophyll and are passed to the electron transport chain in photosynthesis are replaced by electrons from

    A. light
    B. H_2O
    C. NADH
    D. NADPH
    E. oxygen

23. The most fit individual in a population is defined as

    A. the strongest individual
    B. the individual with an appearance most attractive to the opposite sex
    C. the individual who produces the greatest number of fertile offspring
    D. the individual who is able to acquire the most food
    E. the individual who lives the longest

24. Which of the following connects the two hemispheres of the brain?

    A. anterior pituitary
    B. medulla oblongata
    C. optic chiasma
    D. corpus callosum
    E. cerebral cortex

25. Which of the following animal structures provides a function that most closely resembles the function of plasmodesmata in plants?

    A. tight junctions
    B. gap junctions
    C. blastopores
    D. synaptic clefts
    E. desmosomes

26. Which of the following nutrients most commonly limits plant growth?

    A. calcium
    B. carbon
    C. nitrogen
    D. phosphorus
    E. potassium

GO ON TO THE NEXT PAGE

27. All of the following structures or mechanisms have contributed to the ability of plants to make the transition from water to land EXCEPT:

   A. a cuticle
   B. a vascular system
   C. seasonal dormancy
   D. wind pollination
   E. flagellated sperm

28. Which of the following reactions occurs in the forward direction during the Krebs cycle but in the reverse direction during fermentation?

   A. pyruvate $\leftrightarrow$ acetyl CoA
   B. pyruvate $\leftrightarrow$ lactate
   C. pyruvate $\leftrightarrow$ ethanol
   D. $NAD^+ + H^+ + 2e^- \leftrightarrow NADH$
   E. $ADP + P_i \leftrightarrow ATP$

29. A typical virus, without modification by mutation, can usually infect

   A. any cell in a wide variety of species
   B. any cell, but only in a single species
   C. only specific kinds of cells in a single species or in closely related species.
   D. only cells with protein coats
   E. only bacteriophages

30. Which of the following is found within the unfertilized, mature embryo sac of a flowering plant?

   A. the egg
   B. the microspore mother cell
   C. the endosperm
   D. the fruit
   E. the seed

31. All of the following are necessary for a DNA virus to complete a lytic cycle EXCEPT:

   A. chromosomes of the host cell
   B. replication enzymes of the host cell
   C. ribosomes of the host cell
   D. amino acids of the host cell
   E. nucleotides of the host cell

32. Energy extracted by cellular respiration can originate from

   I. carbohydrates
   II. fats
   III. proteins

   A. I only
   B. II only
   C. III only
   D. I and II only
   E. I, II, and II

33. Two atoms with strongly unequal electronegativity would most likely form

   A. an ionic bond
   B. a hydrogen bond
   C. a polar covalent bond
   D. a nonpolar covalent bond
   E. a radioactive molecule

34. In the final steps of photosynthesis, glyceraldehyde-3-phosphate (G3P or PGAL), the energy-rich product of the Calvin cycle, is used to make

   A. ATP
   B. $NADP^+$
   C. NADPH
   D. Glucose
   E. O_2

35. A biologist is examining chromosomes from various people. She observes many different cells, including cells with extra X chromosomes. When she counts the number of Barr bodies, she is likely to find all of the following EXCEPT:

   A. no Barr bodies in an XO individual (Turner syndrome)
   B. one Barr body in an XX individual
   C. one Barr body in an XY individual
   D. two Barr bodies in an XXX individual
   E. three Barr bodies in an XXXX individual

36. All deuterostomes

   A. are bilateral
   B. are segmented
   C. possess a coelum
   D. have one gut opening
   E. have spiral cleavages during embryonic development

37. The final electron acceptor for oxidative phosphorylation is

  A. NAD^+
  B. NADH
  C. ATP
  D. O_2
  E. H_2O

38. All of the following are associated with microtubules EXCEPT:

  A. centrioles
  B. basal bodies
  C. muscle contraction
  D. separation of chromosomes into chromatids
  E. motion of flagella

39. White matter in the central nervous system is associated with

  A. multinucleated neurons
  B. myelinated axons of neurons
  C. areas involved in speech
  D. motor neurons
  E. sensory neurons

40. Cell types of phloem tissue include

  A. sieve tube members and companion cells
  B. tracheids and vessel elements
  C. tracheids and companion cells
  D. fibers and sclereids
  E. fibers and companion cells

Questions 41–42 refer to the following.

Female mosquitoes are bloodsucking insects that find their hosts by locating sources of carbon dioxide and lactic acid.

41. Which of the following describes the method used by mosquitoes to find their hosts?

  A. Kinesis
  B. Taxis
  C. Migration
  D. Habituation
  E. Pheromones

42. All of the following contribute to the effectiveness of both carbon dioxide and lactic acid as a signal for mosquitoes to locate hosts EXCEPT:

  A. The atmosphere contains large amounts of carbon dioxide.
  B. The largest sources of both carbon dioxide and lactic acid are large animals.
  C. Plants do not produce both carbon dioxide and lactic acid.
  D. Mammals produce carbon dioxide as a product of aerobic respiration.
  E. Mammals produce lactic acid as a product of the anaerobic respiration.

Questions 43–44 refer to the following.

Female Belding's ground squirrels are social animals that sound alarm calls to warn members of their extended family of the approach of a predator. The alarm-call behavior benefits the group as a whole but is a risk to the caller because the alarm call attracts the attention of the predator.

43. A squirrel that produces an alarm call is displaying which of the following?

  A. dominance
  B. territoriality
  C. agonistic behavior
  D. submissive behavior
  E. altruistic behavior

44. A squirrel that produces an alarm call is twice as likely to be eaten by predators as noncallers. Which of the following explains why this behavior is adaptive?

  A. It increases the number of offspring that the caller can personally leave to the next generation.
  B. It increases the inclusive fitness of the caller.
  C. A squirrel is more likely to attract a mate while sounding an alarm call.
  D. Squirrels that produce alarm calls produce more offspring.
  E. Alarm call behavior is not adaptive.

GO ON TO THE NEXT PAGE

Directions: The following questions consist of a phrase or sentence. Each question is preceded by five lettered choices. Select the one lettered choice that best matches the phrase or sentence. Each lettered choice may be used once, more than once, or not at all.

Questions 45–49 refer to the following processes.

    A. transcription
    B. transduction
    C. transformation
    D. translocation
    E. transpiration

45. Absorption and assimilation of DNA by bacteria from the environment.

46. Carried out by RNA polymerase.

47. End product is a polypeptide.

48. Genetic variation introduced into bacteria by viruses.

49. Transfer of DNA between nonhomologous chromosomes.

Questions 50–53 refer to the following structures.

    A. Ganglion
    B. Flame cell
    C. Crop
    D. Hemocoel
    E. Spiracle

50. Associated with the respiratory system of insects.

51. Associated with the circulatory system of insects and mollusks.

52. Associated with the excretory system of flatworms (Platyhelminthes).

53. Associated with the digestive system of birds, insects, and annelid worms.

Questions 54–57 refer to the following ratios.

    A. 3:1
    B. 1:2:1
    C. 9:3:3:1
    D. 1:1:1:1
    E. 4:0

For the genetic cross $Aa \times Aa$, identify for F_1 offspring

54. the phenotypic ratio if inheritance was by complete dominance.

55. the genotypic ratio if inheritance was by complete dominance.

56. the phenotypic ratio if inheritance was by incomplete dominance.

57. the genotypic ratio if inheritance was by incomplete dominance.

Questions 58–61 refer to the following.

    A. Parasitism
    B. Commensalism
    C. Mutualism
    D. Interspecific competition
    E. Intraspecific competition

58. Lichens.

59. Mycorrhizae.

60. Tapeworms live, eat, and reproduce inside the human digestive tract, robbing the host of nutrients.

61. In deserts, where water is scarce, individuals of creosote bush rarely grow more closely than five meters from each other.

Questions 62–67 refer to the following molecules.

    A. amino acids
    B. nucleotides
    C. fatty acids
    D. glucose molecules
    E. four interconnected carbon rings

62. Many polysaccharides are made of these.

63. Enzymes are made of these.

64. DNA is made of these.

65. Starch is made of these.

66. Triglycerides contain these.

67. Steroids contain these.

Questions 68–71 refer to the following.

    A. Sponges
    B. Cnidaria
    C. Platyhelminthes
    D. Annelida
    E. Chordata

68. Members of this group have radial symmetry.

69. Members of this group possess a coelum and are segmented.

70. Members of this group have a notochord during all or part of their life cycle.

71. Members of this group have no uniform body symmetry.

Questions 72–76 refer to the following structures.

    A. Epididymis
    B. Prostate gland
    C. Seminal vesicles
    D. Testes
    E. Vas deferens

72. Produces sperm.

73. Produces testosterone.

74. Secretes mucus to provide a liquid medium for the sperm and secretes fructose to provide energy for the sperm.

75. Site of final maturation and storage of sperm.

76. Tube through which sperm move to the urethra.

Questions 77–79 refer to the following pedigree.

Circles indicate females, and squares indicate males. A horizontal line connecting a male and female indicates that these two individuals produced offspring. Offspring are indicated by a descending vertical line that branches to the offspring. A filled circle or filled square indicates that the individual has a particular trait, in this case, hemophilia. Hemophilia is inherited as a sex-linked, recessive allele.

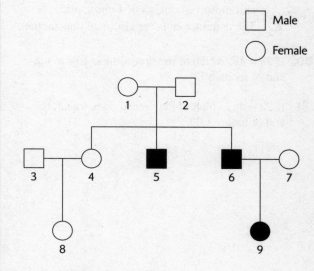

    A. $X^N X^N$
    B. $X^N X^n$
    C. $X^n X^n$
    D. $X^N Y$
    E. $X^n Y$

77. Identify the genotype for individual 6.

78. Identify the genotype for individual 1.

79. Identify the genotype for individual 9.

GO ON TO THE NEXT PAGE

Questions 80–81 refer to the following figure.

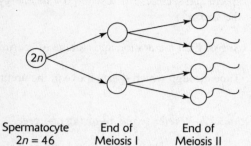

Spermatocyte	End of	End of
$2n = 46$	Meiosis I	Meiosis II

A. Each cell has 46 chromosomes; each chromosome consists of 2 chromatids.

B. Each cell has 46 chromosomes; each chromosome consists of 1 chromatid.

C. Each cell has 23 chromosomes; each chromosome consists of 2 chromatids.

D. Each cell has 23 chromosomes; each chromosome consists of 1 chromatid.

E. The daughter cells are clones of one another.

80. If $2n = 46$, which of the preceding is true at the end of meiosis I?

81. If $2n = 46$, which of the preceding is true at the end of meiosis II?

Questions 82–84 refer to the following.

The diagram that follows shows a mucus cell, a specialized cell of the intestines that secretes mucus, a glycoprotein substance that protects the lining of the intestines

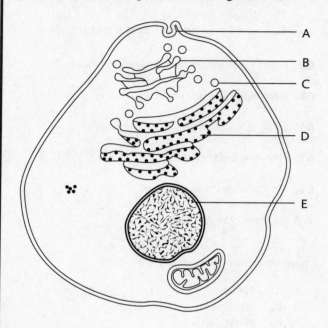

82. Site of glycoprotein synthesis.

83. Site of glycoprotein modification in preparation for export from the cell.

84. Site of exocytosis.

Directions: Questions that follow involve data from experiments or laboratory analyses. In each case, study the information provided. Then choose the one best answer for each question.

Questions 85–89 refer to the following.

Fifteen plants were divided into three groups of five plants each. Each group was placed under the environmental condition listed below; all other conditions were identical. The amount of water loss per m^2 of leaf surface was then measured at 10 minute intervals and the average for each group plotted in the following graph.

Treatment A: high humidity, no wind
Treatment B: normal humidity, no wind
Treatment C: normal humidity, wind (from a fan)

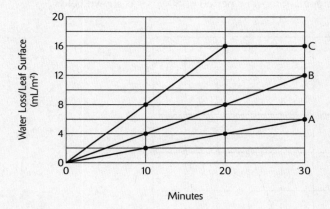

85. Which of the following was an experimental control?

  A. Treatment A
  B. Treatment B
  C. Treatment C
  D. Treatments A and C
  E. There is no control.

86. Which of the following was the dependent variable?

  A. Treatment A
  B. Treatment B
  C. Treatments A, B, and C
  D. time
  E. water loss

87. What was the *rate* of water loss in Treatment A?

  A. 0.1 mL/m^2/minute
  B. 0.2 mL/m^2/minute
  C. 4 mL/m^2/minute
  D. 5 mL/m^2/minute
  E. 6 mL/m^2/minute

88. How much water did Treatment C lose in the time interval from 20 to 30 minutes?

  A. 0 mL/m^2
  B. 16 mL/m^2
  C. 20 mL/m^2
  D. 30 mL/m^2
  E. unable to determine from graph

89. Which of the following could have been responsible for the amount of water lost in Treatment C between 20 and 30 minutes?

  A. The temperature decreased.
  B. The humidity decreased.
  C. The light intensity decreased.
  D. The light intensity increased.
  E. The stomata closed.

Questions 90–92 refer to the following.

The graph that follows shows the number of individuals in a population, N, at periods of time, t.

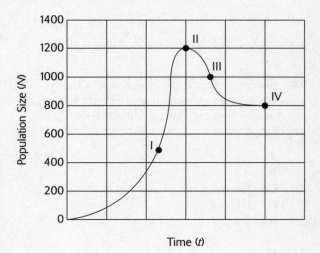

  A. I, only
  B. II, only
  C. III, only
  D. IV, only
  E. II and IV

GO ON TO THE NEXT PAGE

90. At what point or points of the graph does the intrinsic rate of growth for the population approximate exponential growth?

91. At what point or points of the graph is the intrinsic rate of growth equal to zero?

92. At what point or points of the graph is the intrinsic rate of growth negative?

93. What is the carrying capacity of the environment for this population?

A. 400
B. 600
C. 800
D. 1000
E. 1200

Questions 94–97 refer to the following.

Two color morphs of a beetle are controlled by a single gene with two alleles. The *B* allele produces black beetles and is dominant over the *b* allele which produces brown beetles. The life cycle of this beetle is one year, and each year the population is replaced by its descendents. Data for one large population over a period of 50 years is shown below.

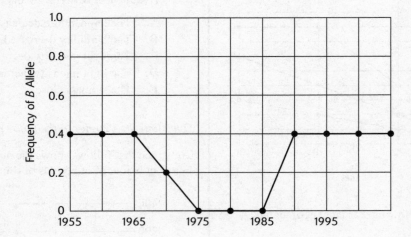

94. Assuming that the population was in Hardy-Weinberg equilibrium from 1955 to 1965, what was the frequency of the *b* allele during this period?

A. 0
B. 0.2
C. 0.4
D. 0.6
E. 0.8

95. From 1955 to 1965, what was the percentage of black beetles?

A. 4 percent
B. 16 percent
C. 48 percent
D. 64 percent
E. 84 percent

96. Which of the following is most likely responsible for the change in allele frequencies from 1965 to 1975?

A. selection against the brown-colored beetle
B. selection against the black-colored beetle
C. mutation
D. genetic drift
E. gene flow

97. Which of the following is most likely responsible for the change in allele frequencies from 1985 to 1990?

A. selection against the black-colored beetle
B. selection against the brown-colored beetle
C. mutation
D. genetic drift
E. gene flow

Questions 98–100 refer to the following.

The graph below shows the blood pressure as a function of distance from the heart in the systemic circuit. Area I begins at the heart and Area VII ends at the heart.

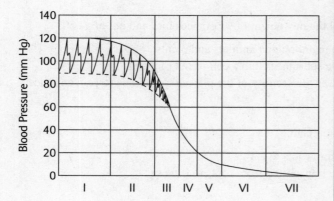

98. The blood pressure in area I is described as

    A. 105

    B. 110

    C. 120

    D. 120/85

    E. 120/90

99. The crests of the up and down fluctuations in area I are referred to as

    A. the capillary pressure

    B. the diastolic pressure

    C. the systolic pressure

    D. high blood pressure

    E. atrial fibrillation

100. According to the graph, the blood pressure in area VII indicates that

    A. the blood pressure is zero

    B. the blood is not moving

    C. there is no oxygen remaining in this part of the systemic circuit

    D. there is no blood in this area of the systemic circuit

    E. the blood pressure measurements cannot be made in this area of the systemic circuit

GO ON TO THE NEXT PAGE

Section II (Free-Response Questions)

Reading Time: 10 minutes (for organizing your thoughts and outlining your answers)
Writing Time: 90 minutes

1. A major function of the plasma membrane is to control the movement of substances into and out of a cell.

   A. Compare and contrast the structure of the plasma membrane in animals and plants.
   B. Describe **three** mechanisms that cells use to move substances into a cell or out of a cell.
   C. Describe **one** mechanism by which a virus bypasses the security of the plasma membrane to gain entrance into a cell.

2. Plants have evolved numerous adaptations for survival on land.

   A. Describe how plants are able to transport water from roots to leaves.
   B. Describe the property of water that allows it to be transported from roots to leaves.
   C. Explain why plants lose water from leaves.
   D. Describe how plants limit water loss from leaves.

3. In order for cells to carry out cellular respiration, there must be a mechanism for oxygen delivery and carbon dioxide removal.

   A. Explain how oxygen is delivered to cells in the human body.
   B. Explain how carbon dioxide is carried away from cells.
   C. Identify the need for oxygen and the source for carbon dioxide in the human body.

4. The kernels of an ear of corn are individual seeds. Each seed consists of an embryo surrounded by endosperm. Various genes control the color and texture of the endosperm. One of these genes is for endosperm color, where the Y allele produces yellow endosperm, while y produces white endosperm. For another gene, the S allele produces starchy endosperm, while s produces sweet endosperm. Traits for both of these genes are expressed by complete dominance.

   A female flower, artificially pollinated with pollen from another plant, developed an ear of corn with 440 kernels with the following characteristics.

Yellow endosperm	= 330 kernels	Y = yellow
White endosperm	= 110 kernels	y = white
Starchy endosperm	= 220 kernels	S = starchy
Sweet endosperm	= 220 kernels	s = sweet

   For each of the following, you may use Punnett squares to support your answer.

   A. What were the genotypes of the parents with respect to endosperm color?
   B. What were the genotypes of the parents with respect to starchy/sweet?
   C. What were the genotypes of the parents with respect to both traits?
   D. Calculate the dihybrid *genotypic* frequencies for the F_1 offspring.
   E. Calculate the dihybrid *phenotypic* frequencies for the F_1 offspring.
   F. Why was it necessary to artificially pollinate the female flower?

Answer Key for Practice Exam 1

Section I (Multiple-Choice Questions)

1. A	26. C	51. D	76. E
2. E	27. E	52. B	77. E
3. A	28. D	53. C	78. B
4. D	29. C	54. A	79. C
5. E	30. A	55. B	80. C
6. E	31. A	56. B	81. D
7. D	32. E	57. B	82. D
8. B	33. A	58. C	83. B
9. A	34. D	59. C	84. A
10. A	35. C	60. A	85. B
11. B	36. C	61. E	86. E
12. B	37. D	62. D	87. B
13. E	38. C	63. A	88. A
14. E	39. B	64. B	89. E
15. C	40. A	65. D	90. A
16. E	41. B	66. C	91. E
17. A	42. A	67. E	92. C
18. C	43. E	68. B	93. C
19. D	44. B	69. D	94. D
20. C	45. C	70. E	95. D
21. D	46. A	71. A	96. B
22. B	47. D	72. D	97. E
23. C	48. B	73. D	98. E
24. D	49. D	74. C	99. C
25. B	50. E	75. A	100. A

Scoring Your Practice Exam

Section I (Multiple-Choice Questions)

Number of questions you answered correctly: _____ × 1 = _____

Number of questions you answered wrong: _____ × ¼ = _____ *

Number of questions you left unanswered: _____ × 0 = ___0___

TOTAL for Section I (0–100 points): = _____ **

(subtract number wrong from number correct)

Round to nearest whole number.

** *If less than zero, enter zero.*

Section II (Free-Response Questions)

For each correct and relevant piece of information you include in your answers to the free-response questions, you earn one point. Refer to the scoring standards that follow the multiple-choice explanations.

Score for essay 1 (0–10 points): _____

Score for essay 2 (0–10 points): _____

Score for essay 3 (0–10 points): _____

Score for essay 4 (0–10 points): _____

Combined Score (Sections I + II)

Total for Section I (from above): _____ × 0.6 = _____

(60% of 100 points = 60 points maximum)

Total for Section II (from above): _____ × 1.0 = _____

(100% of 40 points = 40 points maximum)

Combined Score (Add Sections I and II)_____

(0–100 points possible)

Probable AP Grade	
61–100	5
47–60	4
39–46	3
30–38	2
0–29	1

Answers and Explanations for Practice Exam 1

1. **A.** Only the plasma membranes of animal cells contain cholesterol. Phospholipids and proteins are common to membranes of all organisms. Cellulose is the major component of the cell *walls* of plants. Chitin is the major component of the cell *walls* of fungi.

2. **E.** A chromosome is one long DNA molecule with proteins. It is only visible in its condensed state when it prepares for mitosis or meiosis. When the cell is not dividing (that is, during interphase), the chromosome is unwound and actively doing what DNA is supposed to do—replicating or serving as a template for transcription in the production of RNA.

3. **A.** The plant cells responsible for elongation of roots and shoots are the cells in the apical meristem. In the apical meristem, meristematic cells divide and elongate, providing for growth in these areas. In contrast, the vascular cambium contributes to growth in the girth, or diameter, of a root or shoot.

4. **D.** In natural selection, individuals do not change because they "want to" or "have to" adapt in order to survive. They have either inherited the genes that produce advantageous adaptations that allow them to successfully compete for resources, or they have not inherited those genes and do not survive. It is not a choice for an individual to make.

5. **E.** Transpiration is responsible for most water lost by plants. Respiration produces a small amount of water (at the end of oxidative phosphorylation) that can be used for photosynthesis or lost through transpiration during the day. Photolysis in photosynthesis uses a small amount of water to generate electrons and H^+, releasing O_2 to the atmosphere. Relatively speaking, most water acquired by plants is eventually transpired.

6. **E.** These structures are associated with ascomycetous fungi. Ascomycetes produce spore sacs called asci. Each ascus contains eight haploid ascospores. Numerous asci are grouped together within a fruiting body called a perithecium. The mass of filaments that makes up a fungus is the mycelium. Each individual filament is a hypha. (The life cycle of an ascomycetous fungus, *Sordaria fimicola,* is described in AP lab #3.)

7. **D.** Although DNA polymerase has error-checking and repair capabilities, an existing mutation (such as a nucleotide substitution, deletion, or insertion) in a template strand is likely to be copied to the complementary strand that the DNA polymerase assembles. DNA polymerase can operate only on a DNA template in its $3´ \rightarrow 5´$ direction, assembling a $5´ \rightarrow 3´$ complementary strand. It cannot initiate replication; rather, it requires RNA primase to attach short segments of RNA nucleotides before the DNA polymerase can begin. As a result, DNA polymerase can operate continuously on one DNA strand ($3´ \rightarrow 5´$) toward the replication fork but only in short segments away from the replication fork on the second DNA strand ($5´ \rightarrow 3´$). These short segments made from the second DNA strand are later joined by DNA ligase. Clearly, DNA replication is a group effort, requiring various enzymes. It should also be noted that there are many different DNA polymerases in most cells, with at least three of them required for genome replication in eukaryotic cells.

8. **B.** Inside the thylakoid membrane, hydrogen ions (H^+, essentially protons) accumulate as photolysis splits water H_2O ($H_2O \rightarrow 2H^+ + ½ O_2 + 2e^-$). As H^+ increases, acidity increases. But remember, increasing H^+ and increasing acidity are associated with *decreasing* pH. Whenever you get a test question that references pH or acid/base, make a clarification to yourself by writing words such as "more acidic" next to the test-question phrase "pH decreases." The last answer choice is the opposite of what happens—pH inside the thylakoid actually increases (becomes less acidic) as ATP is generated. The only time pH decreases (more acidic) is when photosynthesis occurs, when light is present to drive the light reactions and photolysis. The pH inside the thylakoid is less (more acidic, about pH = 5) than the pH in the stroma (about pH = 8).

9. **A.** Ferns produce spores. Angiosperms (flowering plants) and gymnosperms (including conifers) produce seeds.

10. **A.** The Krebs cycle (citric acid cycle) occurs in the matrix. The cristae membranes enclose the matrix, separating the matrix and the Krebs cycle reactions within it from the outer compartment region formed between the cristae and the mitochondrial outer membrane. In contrast, the electron transport chain and oxidative phosphorylation operate in the cristae, while H^+ concentrates in the narrow region between the cristae and the outer mitochondrial membrane. ATP is generated as H^+ moves down the proton gradient (up the pH gradient) through ATP syntheses in the cristae.

11. B. Imbibition, the absorption of water, is the first requirement for germination. If other conditions are met (such as temperature, light cues, fire cues, and the completion of a required dormancy), then energy is generated by the digestion of the endosperm or cotyledon. Energy generation is usually followed by root growth, followed by shoot growth.

12. B. A relatively fit person pumps a greater volume of blood and more oxygen with each heart beat and, as a result, takes longer to reach a maximum heart rate.

13. E. ATP is generated from ADP + P; during both cyclic and noncyclic photophosphorylation. Only noncyclic photophosphorylation requires H_2O and generates NADP, oxygen, and PGAL.

14. E. Movement of urine through the urethra is by bulk flow. Passive and active transport processes involve movement of substances across a (plasma) membrane, examples of which are: passive and active transport of water, vitamins, and electrolytes across the lining of the large intestine; passive transport of neurotransmitters across the postsynaptic membrane of a neuron; passive and active transport of ions and water across the loop of Henle; and passive transport of O_2 and CO_2 across blood vessel and alveolar membranes.

15. C. Only bacteria have peptidoglycans in their cell walls. Archaea have cell walls that contain substances distinct from peptidoglycans, cellulose, and chitin.

16. E. Energy cannot be recycled. It is transferred in one direction along the food chain with about 90% lost during each transfer. Energy must continually be added to the ecosystem through the metabolic activities of autotrophs, mostly by photosynthesis.

17. A. Cleavages are rapid cell divisions without cell growth that occur in the early development of an embryo.

18. C. Mutations produce new alleles. New alleles may also be introduced through gene flow (immigration), but because the population in this question is isolated, this cannot be the source. Genetic drift, occurring most often in small populations, natural selection, and nonrandom mating do not introduce new alleles. These mechanisms only change the relative frequencies of existing alleles in the population.

19. D. Substances (sugar and CO_2 in this question) that dissolve in another substance (water in this case) are solutes. The substance that they are added to (the water) is the solvent.

20. C. Growing parts of an organism are good places to find mitosis. The apical meristems at the root and shoot tips of plants have cells that are actively dividing by mitosis. In animals, mitotic divisions are visible in the early (blastula stage) development of embryos. In contrast, a good place to observe *meiosis* is in a cross section of a plant anther, where haploid pollen cells are being produced.

21. D. Mitochondria and chloroplasts do not function independently from the eukaryotic host cell. Some of the ancestral mitochondria and chloroplast genes are now located in the genome of the host cell. Thus, respiration and photosynthesis cannot occur without the manufacture of necessary enzymes by the host genome.

22. B. In photolysis, H_2O is broken down into $2H^+ + \frac{1}{2}O_2 + 2e^-$. The 2 electrons ($2e^-$) are used to replace the electrons in chlorophyll molecules that are energized by light photons and used in the electron transport chain of photophosphorylation.

23. C. The definition of fitness is the relative number of offspring that an individual leaves to the next generation (or in the case of inclusive fitness, the number of genes left to the gene pool). Being the strongest, most attractive, most able to acquire food, or being able to live the longest may or may not help an individual produce offspring. The bottom line for fitness is producing offspring.

24. D. The corpus callosum contains association neurons that connect the two hemispheres of the brain.

25. B. Plasmodesmata in plant cells allow the passage of materials between cells. The gap junctions in animal cells allow a similar function. In contrast, tight junctions seal the spaces between cells to prevent the movement of material in these spaces, while desmosomes act as anchors to hold cells together.

26. C. Nitrogen is the most common limiting nutrient to plant growth. The ingredient of largest proportion in most fertilizers is a nitrogen compound. Carnivorous plants, such as the Venus flytrap, typically grow in soils that are nitrogen deficient but supplement their nutritional needs by extracting nitrogen from insects.

27. **E.** Flagellated sperm require water for swimming to an egg. Plants with flagellated male gametes are limited to survival on wet or damp areas. The transition from water to land is marked by plant adaptations that help obtain or conserve water. These adaptations include: a cuticle that reduces desiccation; a vascular system that provides a mechanism to transfer water from the ground to leaves high in a tree; wind pollination that removes the water requirement for fertilization; and dormancy that provides a shutdown of metabolism during seasonal periods when water is not available.

28. **D.** The reaction $NAD^+ + H^+ + 2e^- \rightarrow NADH$ occurs in the Krebs cycle as energy from pyruvate is used to attach the electrons and protons to NAD^+. The result is NADH, a molecule to be used in oxidative phosphorylation (where the reverse of this reaction occurs), if oxygen is present, to generate 3 ATPs. The reverse of this reaction also occurs during anaerobic reactions. In the absence of oxygen, the Krebs cycle and oxidative phosphorylation cannot occur and no NAD^+ is released from NADH. In order to at least continue with glycolysis, where a net of 2 ATPs is generated, the NADH is converted back to NAD^+ during alcohol or lactic acid fermentation, allowing glycolysis to continue.

29. **C.** Viruses are specific cell parasites, usually limited to infecting specific kinds of cells in a single species or narrow range of closely related species. To cause disease, viruses must evade the immune system of the host and must recognize receptor molecules on the plasma membrane of the target cell. As receptor molecules on plasma membranes vary from cell to cell and from species to species, a virus can only cause disease when it possesses the specific genetic information to overcome the defenses mounted by the host cells. However, viruses mutate frequently, and a virus that previously could infect only birds may acquire the ability to infect humans as a result of a mutation.

30. **A.** The most common embryo sac in angiosperms contains the egg with two adjacent cells (synergids) at the micropyle end (where the pollen tube enters), three cells at the opposite end (antipodal cells), and two polar nuclei in the center for a total of eight nuclei. The egg will be fertilized by one of the sperm cells to form a zygote that will become the embryo. The endosperm will develop from the two polar nuclei after they have been fertilized by the second sperm cell. The embryo and endosperm together become the seed, and the integuments become the seed coat. The ovary wall and sometimes other flower structures contribute to the formation of the fruit that encloses the seed.

31. **A.** In a lytic cycle, a DNA virus does not necessarily need access to the host chromosome. During a lysogenic cycle, however, the viral DNA joins with the host DNA. In contrast, RNA retroviruses, such as HIV, must incorporate into the DNA of the host in order to replicate.

32. **E.** Carbohydrates, fats, and proteins, or their derivatives, can each be used in the Krebs cycle. Polysaccharide and disaccharide carbohydrates are broken down into the monomer glucose (or another monomer which can be converted to glucose). Glucose, through glycolysis, produces pyruvate, which enters the Krebs cycle. Proteins are broken down into amino acids, which can be converted to pyruvate, acetyl CoA, or intermediaries in the Krebs cycle. Fats can be used to generate PGAL or Acetyl CoA.

33. **A.** Electronegativity is a measure of how strong the attraction that an atom has for an electron is. Two very unequal electronegativities, such as chlorine (very high electronegativity of 3.16) and sodium (very low at 0.93), indicate that the chlorine atom will strongly pull on an electron and sodium will easily give one up. As a result, chlorine gains an electron to become a negative ion, and sodium gives up an electron to become a positive ion. The resulting two oppositely charged ions attract one another to form an ionic molecule (NaCl in this example) with an ionic bond. When two atoms have electronegativities that are close in value, the atoms will form covalent bonds.

34. **D.** The Calvin-Benson cycle generates two molecules of PGAL for every 6 CO_2 molecules that enter the cycle. Two molecules of PGAL can be used to make one glucose, fructose, or similar monosaccharide.

35. **C.** Regardless of the number of X chromosomes in a human cell, only one X chromosome is active. If both X chromosomes were to be active, then the X-chromosome genes in the normal female condition (XX) would supply twice the activity of these genes than the normal male condition (XY) with just one X chromosome. As a result, a mechanism to allow activity in only one X chromosome evolved for the X—Y sex inheritance pattern in mammals. All extra X chromosomes, regardless of the number, become inactive Barr bodies.

36. C. A coelum is a fluid-filled body cavity that develops from the mesoderm germ layer and surrounds the digestive tract. It occurs in all deuterostomes (Echinodermata and Chordata), as well as in all protostomes (Mollusca, Annelida, Arthropoda). Not all deuterostomes are bilateral (Echinodermata are radial), they are not segmented, they have two gut openings, and cleavages are radial (in protostomes cleavages are spiral).

37. D. Without oxygen, the electrons passing through the electron transport chain of oxidative phosphorylation have nowhere to go. The chemical equilibrium forces the reactions to stop or reverse and ATP is no longer generated. Anaerobic reactions may begin (producing much less ATP), but for most animals, without oxygen as the final electron acceptor in oxidative phosphorylation, cells will die.

38. C. Microtubules are found in centrioles, basal bodies, flagella, and cilia. Microtubules form the spindle that functions to separate the chromosomes during mitosis and meiosis. In contrast, the protein fibers of muscle cells include actin, a micro*filament*.

39. B. Neurons in the central nervous system (brain and spinal cord) whose axons have myelin sheaths comprise the white matter. Myelin sheaths speed the transmission of nerve impulses.

40. A. There are two kinds of phloem cells—sieve tube members, through which organic solutes are translocated, and companion cells that support the metabolism of the sieve tube members. Companion-cell support is necessary because sieve tube members lack nuclei.

41. B. Mosquitoes seeking food follow the plume of CO_2 and lactic acid to the source, an animal. This is taxis, or a directed movement in response to a stimulus. Because the stimulus is in the wind, it is more specifically called anemotaxis.

42. A. Following a plume of CO_2 and lactic acid will lead the mosquito to an animal, because animals produce CO_2 by aerobic respiration and lactic acid by anaerobic respiration. Carbon dioxide makes up a very small percentage of the atmosphere (about 0.03 percent, but rising), and the CO_2 exhaled by an animal (at about 4.5 percent) is over a hundred times greater than that background level. Skin temperature and humidity also guide the mosquito to a specific spot on the host.

43. E. Altruistic behavior is risky behavior that increases the safety of other animals. Altruistic behavior by parents to protect their young is common.

44. B. Altruistic behavior by a female Belding ground squirrel decreases her safety but increases the safety of squirrels in her extended family. By increasing the survival of her sisters and aunts, she increases her inclusive fitness, the sum of her direct fitness (from her own offspring) and the fitness she gains by increasing the survival of her genes that occur in her relatives.

45. C. Transformation describes the process by which bacteria and other cells import from their environment DNA which causes a change in genotype and phenotype. Note that transformation also describes the process in which a normal animal cell becomes cancerous.

46. A. Transcription, the process of assembling RNA nucleotides by using a DNA template, is carried out by RNA polymerase.

47. D. Translation is the process, carried out by ribosomes, by which amino acids are assembled into a polypeptide. Translation occurs in three stages: initiation, elongation, and termination. Initiation occurs when the ribosome attaches to the start codon (AUG) on the mRNA followed by the attachment of a tRNA to the second binding site (or P site) of the ribosome. Elongation is the process of adding tRNAs with their amino acids, one by one, and assembling the amino acids into a polypeptide. The elongation process includes a tRNA binding to the first binding site (or A site), a coupling of the amino acids attached to the tRNAs in the two binding sites, the release of the tRNA from the second binding site, and the *translocation* of the tRNA in the first binding site to the second binding site. The termination concludes the translation process when the ribosome encounters a "stop" codon. Note that translocation has other meanings: the transfer of DNA between nonhomologous chromosomes and the movement of organic materials through phloem tissue in plants.

48. B. Transduction describes the process in which a bacteriophage acquires a segment of a bacterial chromosome during an infection and carries that segment to the chromosome of a subsequent host bacterium.

49. D. Translocation describes the transfer of DNA between nonhomologous chromosomes. For example, there are two causes of Down syndrome: one is trisomy 21, where three copies of chromosome 21 are inherited, and the other is a 14, 21 translocation. In a person with 14, 21 translocation Down syndrome, there are two copies of chromosome 21 and two copies of chromosome 14 for a normal genome number of 46 chromosomes. But one chromosome 14 has a piece of chromosome 21 attached, so the genome effectively has three copies of this chromosome 21 piece, resulting in Down syndrome. See answer to question 47 for other meanings of translocation.

50. E. Spiracles are the openings of tubes (tracheae) in the exoskeletons of insects. Spiracles provide a passageway for air into and out of the insect and allow for gas exchange of O_2 and CO_2.

51. D. Insects and mollusks have an open circulatory system with a hemocoel, an internal, blood-filled cavity that bathes tissues with an oxygen- and nutrient-carrying fluid called hemolymph.

52. B. Flame cells of flatworms contain cilia that pull water (and sometimes wastes) into a system of ducts that exit the body at openings (nephridiopores) on the outer surfaces of their bodies.

53. C. Crops are used in the digestive systems of birds, insects, and annelid worms to physically break down, moisten, or store food before the food moves on for digestion.

54. A. The probabilities for the offspring in the cross $Aa \times Aa$ are ¼ *AA*, ½ *Aa*, and ¼ *aa*. In complete dominance, *A* is dominant to *a* and both *AA* and *Aa* genotypes have the dominant phenotype (trait). Only the *aa* genotype has the recessive phenotype. Therefore, ¾ of the offspring have the dominant phenotype, ¼ have the recessive phenotype, and the ratio is 3:1.

55. B. This is the same as question 54, except the question wants the *genotypic* ratio. Since the offspring genotypes are ¼ *AA*, ½ *Aa*, and ¼ *aa*, the ratio is 1:2:1.

56. B. In incomplete dominance, the three genotypes, *AA*, *Aa*, and *aa*, each have a different phenotype. For example, if *AA* produces red carnations and *aa* produces white carnations, the heterozygote, *Aa*, would produce pink carnations. Since each genotype produces a different phenotype, the genotypic and phenotypic ratios are the same: 1:2:1.

57. B. See answer for question 56.

58. C. A lichen is a mutualistic relationship between an alga and a fungus. The alga supplies sugars it makes by photosynthesis to the fungus. In return, the fungus provides minerals, water, a place to attach, and protection from herbivores and ultraviolet radiation.

59. C. A mycorrhiza is a mutualistic relationship between a fungus and the roots of a plant. The fungus helps increase the absorption of water and minerals by the roots, while the plant provides sugars to the fungus.

60. A. A tapeworm in the human digestive tract is an example of parasitism. The tapeworm benefits by absorbing food digested by the intestinal tract of the human host, who, in turn, is hurt by the loss of its nutrients.

61. E. This is an example of intraspecific competition, in particular, competition for water. Creosote bush seedlings that germinate too close to adult individuals die because they are unable to obtain adequate amounts of water with their immature root systems.

62. D. Polysaccharides are carbohydrates that are polymers of a monosaccharide, most often glucose.

63. A. Enzymes are proteins and proteins are polymers of amino acids.

64. B. DNA is a polymer of nucleotides.

65. D. Starch is a specific kind of polysaccharide whose monomer is glucose. In starch, the bond between glucose monomers is an α-glycosidic link. In contrast, the glucose monomers in the plolysaccharide cellulose have a β-glycosidic link.

66. C. A triglyceride consists of three fatty acids bonded to a glycerol molecule.

67. E. Steroids, such as testosterone and cholesterol, have four carbon rings. Each ring shares one side of its hexagon or pentagon ring with an adjacent ring.

68. B. Cnidaria (also called coelenterates) consist of hydrozoans, jellyfish, sea anemones, and corals. All have radial symmetry.

69. D. The only segmented animals with a coelum are those in the group Annelida (segmented worms such as earthworms).

70. E. A defining characteristic of Chordata is the appearance of a notochord during embryonic development. In most Chordata, the notochord is replaced by bone during subsequent development.

71. A. Sponges do not have any uniform body symmetry.

72. D. Sperm are produced in the seminiferous tubules within the two testes.

73. D. Testosterone is produced by the interstitial cells surrounding the seminiferous tubules within the two testes.

74. C. The seminal vesicles secrete into the vas deferens fructose for sperm nourishment, a fluid to suspend the sperm, and prostaglandins, hormones that stimulate uterine contractions in the female.

75. A. Sperm complete their final stages of development in the epididymis. Sperm are stored there until ejaculation. Note that the prostate gland secretes a milky, slightly acidic fluid into the urethra.

76. E. Sperm pass from each testis into the vas deferens, a tube the empties into the urethra.

77. E. Because individual 6 is a male, his sex-chromosome makeup is XY. Since the gene is linked to the X chromosome, there are only two possibilities: $X^N Y$ with the normal N allele expressing the dominant trait and $X^n Y$ with the n allele expressing the recessive trait. Because the square that represents individual 6 is filled, he expresses the recessive trait and must be $X^n Y$. No alleles for this gene occur on the Y chromosome.

78. B. Individual 1 is female and XX. There are three possibilities for the X-linked gene: $X^N X^N$, $X^N X^n$, and $X^n X^n$. The phenotypes expressed by these three genotypes would be, respectively, the normal trait, a carrier expressing the normal trait, and the recessive trait. Because the circle that represents individual 1 is not filled, she does not express the recessive trait and so she is either $X^N X^N$ or $X^N X^n$. She has two sons, offspring 5 and 6, who must be $X^n Y$ (see answer to Question 77). Since the Y chromosome must come from her mate, she must have donated the recessive allele, X^n, to her sons. Therefore, she is $X^N X^n$.

79. C. Individual 9 is a female and XX. In order for her to express the recessive trait, she must have two copies of the recessive allele, n. Therefore, she must be $X^n X^n$.

80. C. A diploid cell with $2n = 46$ has 46 chromosomes, each with 2 chromatids. At the beginning of meiosis, each chromosome consists of 2 chromatids. In anaphase I the two members of each pair of homologous chromosomes move to opposite poles. Each daughter cell formed at the end of meiosis I (interphase II) will be haploid with $n = 23$ (23 chromosomes, each with two chromatids). During the second division of meiosis, at anaphase II, the 2 chromatids of each chromosome separate and move to opposite poles. The daughter cells that result will be $n = 23$ (23 chromosomes, each with 1 chromatid).

81. D. See explanation for question 80.

82. D. A glycoprotein is a protein with a carbohydrate attached. After amino acids are assembled into a protein by ribosomes bound to the rough endoplasmic reticulum (rough ER), the endoplasmic reticulum attaches the carbohydrate. From there, the glycoprotein is shuttled by a transport vesicle to a Golgi apparatus where it is further modified for export. The modified glycoprotein is packaged in another vesicle that transports it to the plasma membrane. The vesicle fuses with the membrane, releasing the contents from the cell.

83. B. The function of the Golgi apparatus is to modify proteins and lipids. The modified molecules are then packaged in vesicles that may travel to the plasma membrane, merge with it, and release the modified molecules to the outside. Some vesicles may remain in the cell for other purposes. Some lysosomes originate in this fashion.

84. A. Exocytosis occurs when a vesicle merges with the plasma membrane and releases its contents to the other side.

85. B. A control is an independent variable at some normal or standard value. Data from the control treatment are compared to the data from the experimental treatments. In this experiment, there are two independent variables. The first is the environmental condition—humidity, wind, and no humidity with no wind (control). The second independent variable is time.

86. E. The dependent variable is expressed by the data collected, in this case, water loss.

87. **B.** Water loss at different times is represented by the vertical distance from the x-axis. The *rate* of water loss, or the amount of water lost per unit of time, is represented by the slope of the line connecting the data points. The slope for a straight line is given by $\Delta y/\Delta x$, or the change in a y distance divided by accompanying change in the x distance. For the entire line representing treatment A on the graph, $\Delta y/\Delta x$ is $6/30 = 1/5 = 0.2$ mL/m^2/minute.

88. **A.** During the interval from 20 to 30 minutes, treatment C is represented by a horizontal line with a constant water loss value of 16 mL/m^2. The total water loss at 20 minutes was 16, and the total water loss at 30 minutes was still 16. So the water loss for this interval was zero.

89. **E.** The water loss for treatment C during the first 20 minutes was very high. The wind was apparently responsible for this high rate of transpiration. As a result, the stomata closed to prevent further desiccation. Light intensity and temperature were the same for all treatments, so that these variables were not responsible for the differences observed between the treatments.

90. **A.** The intrinsic rate of growth, the maximum growth rate, occurs anywhere along the curve where it is J-shaped. Only point I occurs in this area.

91. **E.** Growth rate is zero when the plot of population growth produces a horizontal line or a point with a horizontal tangent, as in points II and IV. At these locations, the change in N divided by the change in t is equal to zero ($\Delta N/\Delta t = 0$).

92. **C.** Growth rate is negative at point III. The slope of the tangent at this point is negative.

93. **C.** The carrying capacity is the maximum population size that can be sustained by the environment. This appears at point IV.

94. **D.** The ordinate (vertical axis) of the graph represents p, the frequency of the dominant allele B. The frequency of q, the recessive allele, is calculated from $p + q = 1$, or $q = 1 - p = 1 - 0.4 = 0.6$.

95. **D.** The frequency of phenotypes is calculated using the equation $p^2 + 2pq + q^2 = 1$. Black-colored beetles, the dominant trait, is expressed by both p^2 and $2pq$. So $p^2 + 2pq = (0.4)^2 + (2)(0.4)(0.6) = 0.16 + 0.48 = 0.64 = 64\%$.

96. **B.** For the 10-year period from 1965 to 1975, there was a dramatic shift in the frequencies of p and q. When p became 0, q became fixed at 1.0. Selection (perhaps a disease) against the black phenotype (both BB and Bb phenotypes) is the most likely cause. Genetic drift is usually significant only in small populations (this is a large population), and a sudden bottleneck resulting from some catastrophic event would not likely have eliminated all the black beetles (representing 64 percent of the population).

97. **E.** The change in p from 1985 to 1990 can best be explained by gene flow. Immigrants carrying the dominant allele, B, entered the population. This implies that the selection pressure against the black-colored beetles (perhaps a disease) was removed sometime between 1975 and 1985.

98. **E.** Blood pressure is a report of systolic and diastolic pressures. Systolic pressure is generated with each contraction of the ventricles, and diastolic pressure is the pressure between these contractions. In area I of this graph, the blood pressure is 120/90, read as "120 over 90."

99. **C.** For each rise and fall of blood pressure between the contraction of the ventricles, the crests (maximum values) represent the systolic pressure, and the troughs (minimum values) represent the diastolic pressures.

100. **A.** The blood pressure is zero in region VII, but the blood continues to move due to the contraction of nearby muscles. Backflow of blood is prevented by valves in veins that permit the movement of the blood in only the forward direction.

Section II (Free-Response Questions)

Scoring Standards for the Essay Questions

To score your answers, award your essay points using the standards given below. For each item listed below that matches the content and vocabulary of a statement or explanation in your essay, add the indicated number of points to your essay score (to the maximum allowed for each section). Scores for each essay question range from 0 to 10 points.

Question 1 (10 points maximum)

A. structure of the plasma membrane (*4 points maximum*)

    1 pt: In both animals and plants, the membrane consists of proteins embedded in a double layer of phospholipids.

    1 pt: Animals have cholesterol molecules in the membrane; plants do not.

    1 pt: Phospholipids are orientated with hydrophobic heads to the outside, hydrophilic tails to the inside of the membrane.

    1 pt: Carbohydrates attached to phospholipids and proteins are called glycolipids and glycoproteins, respectively.

B. mechanisms of transport across the membrane (*4 points maximum*)

    1 pt: Transport proteins use ATP to move materials by active transport.

    1 pt: Channel proteins move hydrophilic substances by passive transport (or facilitated diffusion).

    1 pt: Vesicular transport by exocytosis occurs when vesicles fuse with the membrane to release contents to the outside.

    1 pt: Vesicular transport by endocytosis occurs when the membrane engulfs substances outside the cell, resulting in the formation of a vesicle inside the membrane.

    1 pt: Channel proteins called aquaporins facilitate the transport of water across the plasma membrane.

    1 pt: Oxygen, carbon dioxide, and other nonpolar molecules diffuse across the plasma membrane by diffusion, unassisted by membrane proteins.

C. mechanisms viruses use to penetrate plasma membranes (*4 points maximum*)

    1 pt: Bacteriophage DNA is injected into the host cell through protein tails.

    1 pt: Proteins of bacteriophage tails recognize and bind to the plasma membrane of host cells, allowing penetration of the tail into the membrane.

    1 pt: Virus recognizes and binds to receptor molecules on plasma membrane surface of host cell.

    1 pt: Receptor molecules on host plasma membrane are specific to host cell and usually serve transport, signaling, or other necessary function for host cell.

    1 pt: Virus enters cell by receptor-mediated endocytosis.

    1 pt: Receptor-mediated endocytosis occurs when specific molecules (including those of viruses) bind to receptor molecules that are concentrated in coated pits.

    1 pt: The coated pits of receptor-mediated endocytosis are areas with a high concentration of proteins on the inside of the plasma membrane that will become the outside of the formed vesicle.

    1 pt: Virus may enter host cell with or without its capsid.

    1 pt: Envelopes of enveloped viruses merge with plasma membrane of host.

    1 pt: Envelopes of enveloped viruses are obtained from host membrane as viruses bud from host cell.

Question 2 (10 points maximum)

A. transportation of water (*4 points maximum*)

    1 pt: Water can be transported short distances by osmosis and capillary action.

    1 pt: Most water is transported through xylem tissue by the mechanics of cohesion-tension theory.

    1 pt: Transpiration is the evaporation of water from leaves.

    1 pt: Transpiration drives the movement of water by building negative pressure (tension) in the xylem.

    1 pt: The movement of water from roots to leaves is bulk flow resulting from the heating action of the sun.

B. property of water (*1 point maximum*)

    1 pt: Water is pulled through the xylem because of the cohesion of water that results from hydrogen bonding between water molecules.

C. why leaves loose water (*3 points maximum*)

    1 pt: Stomata are holes in leaves through which water is lost.

    1 pt: Transpiration is the loss of water from leaves through stomata.

    1 pt: Stomata must be open to allow gas exchange for carbon dioxide for photosynthesis.

    1 pt: Stomata must be open to allow gas exchange for oxygen for respiration.

D. how plants limit water loss (*4 points maximum*)

    1 pt: The cuticle provides a waxy layer to prevent water loss.

    1 pt: The cuticle provides a shiny surface to reflect solar radiation.

    1 pt: Stomata may be sunken to reduce the evaporative effect of wind.

    1 pt: Leaves may bear hairs that reduce the evaporative effect of wind.

    1 pt: Leaves may bear white hairs that reduce leaf albedo and that increase solar reflection.

    1 pt: For CAM plants, stomata may close during the day and open at night.

    1 pt: Leaves may have a vertical orientation to minimize solar radiation.

    1 pt: Leaves may be small to reduce surface area exposure to solar radiation.

    1 pt: Plants may be summer deciduous to minimize water loss during hot, dry periods.

Question 3 (10 points maximum)

A. how oxygen is delivered to cells (*6 points maximum*)

    1 pt: Contraction of the diaphragm and intercostal muscles increases the volume of the lungs, lowering the pressure of gases inside, causing higher pressure gases outside the body to rush in. Relaxation of the muscles forces gases out.

    1 pt: Movement of oxygen from outside the body to the lungs is by bulk flow.

    1 pt: The pathway of gases from outside to inside is: nose, pharynx, larynx, trachea, bronchus, alveolus.

    1 pt: The alveolus is a sac-like chamber densely surrounded by capillaries.

    1 pt: Oxygen in the inhaled air diffuses into the moisture covering the lining of the alveolus, across the alveolar and capillary walls, into the blood, and into red blood cells.

    1 pt: Oxygen attaches to hemoglobin molecules inside red blood cells, a maximum of four O_2 molecules per hemoglobin.

1 pt: Red blood cells transport oxygen throughout the body by bulk flow.

1 pt: In capillaries, hemoglobin releases oxygen, and oxygen diffuses out of the red blood cells, into the blood, across capillary wall, and across plasma membrane of body cells.

1 pt: Oxygen released by hemoglobin increases with increases of any of the following: partial pressure of CO_2, temperature, acidity.

B. how carbon dioxide is carried away (*4 points maximum*)

1 pt: Most carbon dioxide is transported in blood plasma as bicarbonate ion (HCO_3^-).

1 pt: HCO_3^- formation occurs by enzymatic action of carbonic anhydrase on CO_2 and H_2O within the red blood cell. HCO_3^- diffuses out of the red blood cell into the plasma.

1 pt: Some carbon dioxide binds to hemoglobin (carbaminohemoglobin) inside the red blood cell.

1 pt: A small amount of carbon dioxide is carried in the plasma as a dissolved gas.

C. need of oxygen; source of carbon dioxide (*2 points maximum*)

1 pt: Oxygen is required for the final electron acceptor of oxidative phosphorylation. If oxygen is absent, oxidative phosphorylation and the Krebs cycle stop.

1 pt: Carbon dioxide originates as a product from aerobic respiration when pyruvate is converted to acetyl CoA and a product of the Krebs cycle.

Question 4 (10 points maximum)

A. genotypes of parents for endosperm color (*2 points maximum*)

1 pt: *Yy* and *Yy* (or *Yy* × *Yy*)

1 pt: Punnett square that shows $Yy \times Yy \rightarrow \frac{1}{4}\ YY + \frac{1}{2}\ Yy + \frac{1}{4}\ yy$

B. genotypes of parents for starchy/sweet (*2 points maximum*)

1 pt: *SS* and *Ss* (or *SS* × *Ss*)

1 pt: Punnett square that shows $SS \times Ss \rightarrow \frac{1}{2}\ SS + \frac{1}{2}\ Ss$

C. genotypes of parents with respect to both traits (*1 point maximum*)

1 pt: *YySS* and *YySs* (or *YySS* × *YySs*)

D. genotypic frequencies (*3 points maximum*)

2 pts: The frequencies listed below or a ratio of 1:2:1:1:2:1 with supporting calculations, as below.

YYSS = ⅛ or 1

YySS = ¼ or 2

yySS = ⅛ or 1

YYSs = ⅛ or 1

YySs = ¼ or 2

yySs = ⅛ or 1

1 pt: for a 4×2 Punnett square with *YS, Ys, yS,* and *ys* on the left and *YS* and *yS* on the top or 2×4 Punnett square with *YS* and *yS* on the left and *YS, Ys, yS,* and *ys* on the top (shown below).

	YS	Ys	yS	ys
YS	YYSS	YYSs	YySS	YySs
yS	YySS	YySs	yySS	yySs

P   YySS   ×   YySs

gametes   YS, yS   YS, Ys,
                        yS, ys

F_1

| genotypic frequencies | phenotypic frequencies |

YYSS = 1
YySS = 2   } 6 yellow-starchy
YYSs = 1
YySs = 2

yySS = 1   } 2 white-starchy
yySs = 1

or

1 pt: for work showing calculations using fractions, as follows:

YYSS $= \frac{1}{4} \times \frac{1}{2} = \frac{1}{8}$

YySS $= \frac{1}{2} \times \frac{1}{2} = \frac{1}{4}$

yySS $= \frac{1}{4} \times \frac{1}{2} = \frac{1}{8}$

YYSs $= \frac{1}{4} \times \frac{1}{2} = \frac{1}{8}$

YySs $= \frac{1}{2} \times \frac{1}{2} = \frac{1}{4}$

yySs $= \frac{1}{4} \times \frac{1}{2} = \frac{1}{8}$

E. hybrid phenotypic frequencies (*3 points maximum*)

1 pt: yellow-starchy $= \frac{3}{4}$

1 pt: white-starchy $= \frac{1}{4}$

1 pt: same as **D,** except phenotypes given (see figure above)

YYSS $= \frac{1}{4} \times \frac{1}{2} = \frac{1}{8}$ = yellow-starchy

YySS $= \frac{1}{2} \times \frac{1}{2} = \frac{1}{4}$ = yellow-starchy

yySS $= \frac{1}{4} \times \frac{1}{2} = \frac{1}{8}$ = white-starchy

YYSs $= \frac{1}{4} \times \frac{1}{2} = \frac{1}{8}$ = yellow-starchy

YySs $= \frac{1}{2} \times \frac{1}{2} = \frac{1}{4}$ = yellow-starchy

yySs $= \frac{1}{4} \times \frac{1}{2} = \frac{1}{8}$ = white-starchy

F. why artificial pollination (*1 point maximum*)

1 pt: Artificial pollination insures that all of the pollen are from the same father.

Answer Sheet for Practice Exam 2

1 Ⓐ Ⓑ Ⓒ Ⓓ Ⓔ	26 Ⓐ Ⓑ Ⓒ Ⓓ Ⓔ	51 Ⓐ Ⓑ Ⓒ Ⓓ Ⓔ	76 Ⓐ Ⓑ Ⓒ Ⓓ Ⓔ
2 Ⓐ Ⓑ Ⓒ Ⓓ Ⓔ	27 Ⓐ Ⓑ Ⓒ Ⓓ Ⓔ	52 Ⓐ Ⓑ Ⓒ Ⓓ Ⓔ	77 Ⓐ Ⓑ Ⓒ Ⓓ Ⓔ
3 Ⓐ Ⓑ Ⓒ Ⓓ Ⓔ	28 Ⓐ Ⓑ Ⓒ Ⓓ Ⓔ	53 Ⓐ Ⓑ Ⓒ Ⓓ Ⓔ	78 Ⓐ Ⓑ Ⓒ Ⓓ Ⓔ
4 Ⓐ Ⓑ Ⓒ Ⓓ Ⓔ	29 Ⓐ Ⓑ Ⓒ Ⓓ Ⓔ	54 Ⓐ Ⓑ Ⓒ Ⓓ Ⓔ	79 Ⓐ Ⓑ Ⓒ Ⓓ Ⓔ
5 Ⓐ Ⓑ Ⓒ Ⓓ Ⓔ	30 Ⓐ Ⓑ Ⓒ Ⓓ Ⓔ	55 Ⓐ Ⓑ Ⓒ Ⓓ Ⓔ	80 Ⓐ Ⓑ Ⓒ Ⓓ Ⓔ
6 Ⓐ Ⓑ Ⓒ Ⓓ Ⓔ	31 Ⓐ Ⓑ Ⓒ Ⓓ Ⓔ	56 Ⓐ Ⓑ Ⓒ Ⓓ Ⓔ	81 Ⓐ Ⓑ Ⓒ Ⓓ Ⓔ
7 Ⓐ Ⓑ Ⓒ Ⓓ Ⓔ	32 Ⓐ Ⓑ Ⓒ Ⓓ Ⓔ	57 Ⓐ Ⓑ Ⓒ Ⓓ Ⓔ	82 Ⓐ Ⓑ Ⓒ Ⓓ Ⓔ
8 Ⓐ Ⓑ Ⓒ Ⓓ Ⓔ	33 Ⓐ Ⓑ Ⓒ Ⓓ Ⓔ	58 Ⓐ Ⓑ Ⓒ Ⓓ Ⓔ	83 Ⓐ Ⓑ Ⓒ Ⓓ Ⓔ
9 Ⓐ Ⓑ Ⓒ Ⓓ Ⓔ	34 Ⓐ Ⓑ Ⓒ Ⓓ Ⓔ	59 Ⓐ Ⓑ Ⓒ Ⓓ Ⓔ	84 Ⓐ Ⓑ Ⓒ Ⓓ Ⓔ
10 Ⓐ Ⓑ Ⓒ Ⓓ Ⓔ	35 Ⓐ Ⓑ Ⓒ Ⓓ Ⓔ	60 Ⓐ Ⓑ Ⓒ Ⓓ Ⓔ	85 Ⓐ Ⓑ Ⓒ Ⓓ Ⓔ
11 Ⓐ Ⓑ Ⓒ Ⓓ Ⓔ	36 Ⓐ Ⓑ Ⓒ Ⓓ Ⓔ	61 Ⓐ Ⓑ Ⓒ Ⓓ Ⓔ	86 Ⓐ Ⓑ Ⓒ Ⓓ Ⓔ
12 Ⓐ Ⓑ Ⓒ Ⓓ Ⓔ	37 Ⓐ Ⓑ Ⓒ Ⓓ Ⓔ	62 Ⓐ Ⓑ Ⓒ Ⓓ Ⓔ	87 Ⓐ Ⓑ Ⓒ Ⓓ Ⓔ
13 Ⓐ Ⓑ Ⓒ Ⓓ Ⓔ	38 Ⓐ Ⓑ Ⓒ Ⓓ Ⓔ	63 Ⓐ Ⓑ Ⓒ Ⓓ Ⓔ	88 Ⓐ Ⓑ Ⓒ Ⓓ Ⓔ
14 Ⓐ Ⓑ Ⓒ Ⓓ Ⓔ	39 Ⓐ Ⓑ Ⓒ Ⓓ Ⓔ	64 Ⓐ Ⓑ Ⓒ Ⓓ Ⓔ	89 Ⓐ Ⓑ Ⓒ Ⓓ Ⓔ
15 Ⓐ Ⓑ Ⓒ Ⓓ Ⓔ	40 Ⓐ Ⓑ Ⓒ Ⓓ Ⓔ	65 Ⓐ Ⓑ Ⓒ Ⓓ Ⓔ	90 Ⓐ Ⓑ Ⓒ Ⓓ Ⓔ
16 Ⓐ Ⓑ Ⓒ Ⓓ Ⓔ	41 Ⓐ Ⓑ Ⓒ Ⓓ Ⓔ	66 Ⓐ Ⓑ Ⓒ Ⓓ Ⓔ	91 Ⓐ Ⓑ Ⓒ Ⓓ Ⓔ
17 Ⓐ Ⓑ Ⓒ Ⓓ Ⓔ	42 Ⓐ Ⓑ Ⓒ Ⓓ Ⓔ	67 Ⓐ Ⓑ Ⓒ Ⓓ Ⓔ	92 Ⓐ Ⓑ Ⓒ Ⓓ Ⓔ
18 Ⓐ Ⓑ Ⓒ Ⓓ Ⓔ	43 Ⓐ Ⓑ Ⓒ Ⓓ Ⓔ	68 Ⓐ Ⓑ Ⓒ Ⓓ Ⓔ	93 Ⓐ Ⓑ Ⓒ Ⓓ Ⓔ
19 Ⓐ Ⓑ Ⓒ Ⓓ Ⓔ	44 Ⓐ Ⓑ Ⓒ Ⓓ Ⓔ	69 Ⓐ Ⓑ Ⓒ Ⓓ Ⓔ	94 Ⓐ Ⓑ Ⓒ Ⓓ Ⓔ
20 Ⓐ Ⓑ Ⓒ Ⓓ Ⓔ	45 Ⓐ Ⓑ Ⓒ Ⓓ Ⓔ	70 Ⓐ Ⓑ Ⓒ Ⓓ Ⓔ	95 Ⓐ Ⓑ Ⓒ Ⓓ Ⓔ
21 Ⓐ Ⓑ Ⓒ Ⓓ Ⓔ	46 Ⓐ Ⓑ Ⓒ Ⓓ Ⓔ	71 Ⓐ Ⓑ Ⓒ Ⓓ Ⓔ	96 Ⓐ Ⓑ Ⓒ Ⓓ Ⓔ
22 Ⓐ Ⓑ Ⓒ Ⓓ Ⓔ	47 Ⓐ Ⓑ Ⓒ Ⓓ Ⓔ	72 Ⓐ Ⓑ Ⓒ Ⓓ Ⓔ	97 Ⓐ Ⓑ Ⓒ Ⓓ Ⓔ
23 Ⓐ Ⓑ Ⓒ Ⓓ Ⓔ	48 Ⓐ Ⓑ Ⓒ Ⓓ Ⓔ	73 Ⓐ Ⓑ Ⓒ Ⓓ Ⓔ	98 Ⓐ Ⓑ Ⓒ Ⓓ Ⓔ
24 Ⓐ Ⓑ Ⓒ Ⓓ Ⓔ	49 Ⓐ Ⓑ Ⓒ Ⓓ Ⓔ	74 Ⓐ Ⓑ Ⓒ Ⓓ Ⓔ	99 Ⓐ Ⓑ Ⓒ Ⓓ Ⓔ
25 Ⓐ Ⓑ Ⓒ Ⓓ Ⓔ	50 Ⓐ Ⓑ Ⓒ Ⓓ Ⓔ	75 Ⓐ Ⓑ Ⓒ Ⓓ Ⓔ	100 Ⓐ Ⓑ Ⓒ Ⓓ Ⓔ

CUT HERE

CUT HERE

Practice Exam 2

Section I (Multiple-Choice Questions)

Time: 80 minutes

100 questions

Directions: Each of the following questions or statements is followed by five possible answers or sentence completions. Choose the one best answer or sentence completion.

1. In the biogeochemical cycle for carbon, carbon passes from inorganic to organic form through the process of

    A. ammonification
    B. cellular respiration
    C. decay
    D. photosynthesis
    E. transpiration

2. Growth that stops when an organism becomes an adult is called

    A. asexual
    B. heterotrophic
    C. embryonic
    D. determinant
    E. eukaryotic

3. During which phase of the cell cycle do chromosomes replicate?

    A. anaphase
    B. telophase
    C. metaphase
    D. prophase
    E. interphase

4. Which of the following processes produces pyruvate?

    A. glycolysis
    B. oxidative phosphorylation
    C. Krebs cycle
    D. alcohol fermentation
    E. lactic acid fermentation

5. In which of the following areas of the brain do speech, conscious thinking, and control of skeletal muscles occur?

    A. cerebellum
    B. medulla oblongata
    C. optic chiasma
    D. corpus callosum
    E. cerebral cortex

6. All of the following products form as a result of a condensation or dehydration reaction EXCEPT:

    A. proteins
    B. disaccharides
    C. polysaccharides
    D. steroids
    E. triglycerides

7. Which of the following events is believed to be the earliest step toward the origin of a living cell?

    A. the development of RNA-like molecules with enzymatic functions
    B. the appearance of oxygen in the atmosphere
    C. the development of photosynthesis
    D. the development of respiration
    E. the development of DNA in protected pools of water

GO ON TO THE NEXT PAGE

8. Cellular activities that occur during the G_1, G_2, and M checkpoints control whether or not subsequent phases of the cell cycle will be completed. These checkpoint activities do not control cell division in

A. fetal cells
B. liver cells
C. cancer cells
D. nerve cells
E. embryonic stem cells

9. A researcher is observing a cell through a microscope. She determines that it is a plant cell because she observes a

A. mitochondrion
B. lysosome
C. centriole
D. central vacuole
E. nucleus

10. Which of the following would most likely provide examples of *meiotic* cell divisions?

A. cross section of muscle tissue
B. cross section of an anther
C. longitudinal section of a shoot tip
D. endosperm of a dormant seed
E. cross section of a leaf

11. All of the following occur during photosynthesis EXCEPT:

A. Light absorption occurs in the thylakoid membranes.
B. Oxygen is generated during photolysis.
C. CO_2 concentrates inside the thylakoid.
D. ATP is generated as protons move from inside the thylakoid to the stroma.
E. Glucose is produced in the stroma.

12. The amount of energy *lost* during the transfer of energy from one trophic level of a pyramid of energy to the next higher trophic level is, on average, about

A. 90%
B. 75%
C. 60%
D. 50%
E. 25%

13. The structure of the seed and seedling that stores food for the embryo and seedling is called the

A. apical meristem
B. plumule
C. hypocotyl
D. cotyledon
E. coleoptile

14. All of the following provide evidence for the support of evolution EXCEPT:

A. Many shrubs in Southern California and South Africa possess thick, shiny leaves and are well adapted to fire, characteristics well suited to their Mediterranean-type habit, yet the plants of Southern California and South Africa are not closely related.
B. Closely related species share higher percentages of DNA than species more distantly related.
C. Tails and gill arches appear during the development of human embryos.
D. Whales do not have hind legs, but small, nonfunctional bones that resemble leg and foot bones are present.
E. Acquired characteristics, such as the dwarf-like appearance in bonsai that results when trees are closely pruned, can be passed on to offspring.

15. Which of the following processes convert NADH to NAD^+?

A. glycolysis and Krebs cycle
B. glycolysis and alcohol fermentation
C. Krebs cycle and oxidative phosphorylation
D. Krebs cycle and alcohol fermentation
E. alcohol fermentation, lactic acid fermentation, and oxidative phosphorylation

16. When water evaporates from the surface of a pond, what happens to the remaining liquid water?

A. The surface water cools.
B. The surface water warms.
C. The surface water temperature remains unchanged.
D. The amount of energy stored in water molecules remaining in the pond increases.
E. The pH of the remaining water decreases.

17. Cell types of xylem tissue include

    A. tracheids and vessel elements
    B. tracheids and companion cells
    C. sieve tube members and companion cells
    D. parenchyma and chlorenchyma
    E. fibers and companion cells

18. Assuming there is no crossing over and that *R* and *T* assort independently, which of the following would be true for sperm of the individual with the genotype *RrTt?*

    A. all *RrTt*
    B. ¼ *RRTT* + ½ *RrTt* + ¼ *rrtt*
    C. ½ *Rr* + ½ *Tt*
    D. ½ *RT* + ½ *rt*
    E. ¼ *RT* + ¼ *Rt* + ¼ *rT* + ¼ *rt*

19. Which of the following structures would be found in a prokaryotic cell?

    A. endoplasmic reticulum
    B. ribosome
    C. Golgi apparatus
    D. nuclear envelope
    E. flagellum with microtubules in a "9 + 2" arrangement

20. The heart sounds associated with the pumping of the heart originate from the

    A. closing of the heart valves
    B. contraction of heart muscle
    C. relaxation of heart muscle
    D. blood movement in the pulmonary circuit
    E. P wave that depolarizes the atria

21. Various organisms recycle dead organisms, fallen branches and leaves, or other organic material. All of the following groups contain organisms that recycle these kinds of materials EXCEPT:

    A. detritivores
    B. scavengers
    C. cyanobacteria
    D. bacteria
    E. fungi

22. Which of the following is a complete description of the nuclei in a pollen tube?

    A. one sperm nucleus, only
    B. one tube nucleus, only
    C. two tube nuclei, only
    D. two sperm nuclei, only
    E. two sperm nuclei and one tube nucleus

23. Why are most animal cells, regardless of species, relatively small and about the same size?

    A. Small cells avoid excessive osmosis and subsequent lysis.
    B. Small cells have a small surface-to-volume ratio.
    C. Small cells have a large surface-to-volume ratio.
    D. Small cells require less energy.
    E. Small cells fit together more tightly

24. Which of the following is most likely to promote the formation of two species in which only one species existed before?

    A. the separation of the population into two reproductively isolated groups
    B. a mutation in one individual that provides an advantage over other individuals
    C. a catastrophic event that reduces the population size to 50 individuals
    D. the introduction of individuals of the same species from a different population
    E. the introduction of a disease to which many individuals are susceptible

25. Which of the following plant hormones inhibit growth?

    A. abscisic acid
    B. auxin
    C. cytokinin
    D. ethylene
    E. gibberellin

GO ON TO THE NEXT PAGE

26. Which of the following is true about evolution?

   A. Natural selection is random.

   B. Natural selection is survival of the strongest.

   C. Natural selection occurs when individuals compete for survival.

   D. Individuals evolve when environmental pressures are strong.

   E. Individuals must change in order to survive.

27. All of the following may be functions of proteins in the plasma membrane EXCEPT:

   A. transport of substances across the membrane

   B. catalysis of substances inside the cell

   C. transmission of a signal received from a hormone outside the cell into chemical activity inside the cell

   D. formation of junctions between the cell membranes of two adjacent cells

   E. replication of DNA

28. Which of the following is an example of external fertilization?

   A. pollen released into the environment

   B. eggs and sperm of frogs released into the surrounding water

   C. double fertilization in flowering plants

   D. embryonic development in an external maternal pouch, as in a marsupial

   E. seeds of viviparous plants that germinate while still attached to the parent plant

29. Which of the following best describes how a small change in genotype can produce a large change in phenotype?

   A. the deletion of a single nucleotide in a DNA sequence that codes for a major protein

   B. the deletion of a single nucleotide in an mRNA sequence that codes for a major protein

   C. a change in a gene that controls the timing of growth during development

   D. a mutation in a gene that codes for cytochrome proteins

   E. a mutation in a gene that codes for a ribosomal protein

30. How are members of the domains Archaea and Eukarya (eukaryotes) similar? Members of both domains have

   A. one or more nuclear envelopes

   B. histones associated with their chromosomes

   C. membrane-enclosed mitochondria

   D. membrane-enclosed Golgi bodies

   E. flagella or cilia with a "9 + 2" arrangement of microtubules

31. All of the following contribute to a reduction of water loss from plant leaves EXCEPT:

   A. a thick cuticle

   B. stomata that occur in depressions in the leaf surface

   C. a vertical leaf orientation

   D. hairs on the surface of leaves

   E. the green color of chlorophyll

32. For an X-linked gene, the trait associated with the recessive allele

   A. will appear in males more frequently than in females

   B. will appear in females more frequently than in males

   C. will appear in males and females with equal frequencies

   D. cannot appear in any males

   E. cannot appear in any females

33. All of the following processes generate ATP from ADP EXCEPT:

   A. oxidative phosphorylation

   B. glycolysis

   C. Krebs cycle

   D. Calvin cycle

   E. cyclic photophosphorylation

34. Two molecules with the same molecular formula have different biological effects. This can best be explained if

   A. one of the molecules has a greater molecular weight

   B. both of the molecules have carbon chains that are unbranched

   C. the two molecules are isomers

   D. the two molecules are isotopes

   E. the two molecules are inorganic

35. In tall trees, most water and solutes move through the vascular system of a plant by

   A. diffusion
   B. osmosis
   C. bulk flow
   D. active transport
   E. passive transport

36. The pathway that best describes the production of a glycoprotein from manufacture to export is

   A. smooth endoplasmic reticulum → Golgi apparatus → plasma membrane
   B. rough endoplasmic reticulum → Golgi apparatus → plasma membrane
   C. rough endoplasmic reticulum → lysosome → plasma membrane
   D. nucleus → smooth endoplasmic reticulum → plasma membrane
   E. nucleus → rough endoplasmic reticulum → plasma membrane

37. Which of the following processes requires oxygen?

   A. glycolysis
   B. oxidative phosphorylation
   C. Krebs cycle
   D. alcohol fermentation
   E. lactic acid fermentation

38. A climax community

   A. remains unchanged even after a dramatic climate shift
   B. is likely to be gradually replaced by another community
   C. is usually short-lived and quickly replaced by another community
   D. will be replaced by another community if some catastrophic event occurs
   E. contains a small biomass relative to other communities that may occupy the same region

39. A biochemist analyzes the composition of DNA extracted from cells of an unknown species. In reviewing his data, all of the percentages for DNA base composition appear reasonable EXCEPT:

   A. adenine = 28%
   B. thymine = 28%
   C. uracil = 0%
   D. adenine + thymine = 56%
   E. adenine + cytosine = 45%

40. In which of the following structures does the breakdown of substances occur by transferring hydrogen to oxygen to form H_2O_2 (hydrogen peroxide)?

   A. lysosome
   B. peroxisome
   C. endoplasmic reticulum
   D. chloroplast
   E. mitochondrion

41. High-fructose corn syrup (HFCS) is a sweetener derived from corn starch and often added to soft drinks. Which of the following reactions would most likely be involved in the production of HFCS? ($n > 100$ and denotes a polymer)

   A. $(glucose)_n$ → polysaccharide
   B. glucose → fructose + glucose
   C. glucose → fructose
   D. starch → $(fructose)_n$
   E. fructose → glucose

42. All of the following are associated with members of a species with a K-selected life history strategy EXCEPT:

   A. They have few offspring.
   B. They have a long life.
   C. They require a long period of time to reach reproductive maturity.
   D. There is little or no parental care.
   E. Population growth approximates the logistic growth model.

43. The plant cells responsible for increases in the girth, or diameter, of roots and shoots are located in the

   A. apical meristem
   B. vascular cambium
   C. endodermis
   D. secondary xylem
   E. primary phloem

44. Which one structure among the following influences the activities of the others?

   A. adrenal cortex
   B. anterior pituitary
   C. ovary
   D. testis
   E. thyroid

GO ON TO THE NEXT PAGE

45. All of the following are true about crossing over EXCEPT:

    A. Crossing over occurs during meiosis.

    B. Crossing over contributes to genetic variation among the daughter cells.

    C. Crossing over results in nondisjunction.

    D. Crossing over occurs during prophase I.

    E. Crossing over provides for the exchange of DNA between nonsister chromatids.

46. For which of the following values of r, the intrinsic growth rate, will population growth be exponential?

    I. $r = 0.001$

    II. $r = 0.1$

    III. $r = 1$

    A. I only

    B. II only

    C. III only

    D. I, II, and III

    E. none of these

Questions 47–49 refer to the genetic code, in which "words" are "codes" for amino acids.

47. How many "letters" make up a "word" of the genetic code?

    A. 1

    B. 2

    C. 3

    D. 4

    E. 6

48. How many different "words" are there in the genetic code?

    A. 3

    B. 6

    C. 61

    D. 64

    E. more than 100

49. How many of the "words" in the genetic code are codes for amino acids?

    A. 3

    B. 6

    C. 61

    D. 64

    E. more than 100

Question 50 refers to the following.

The figure that follows illustrates chromosome 3 for humans, chimpanzees, gorillas, and orangutans (left to right). Boxes 1 and 4 outline banding patterns that are nearly identical for all four species, but differences between species occur in boxes 2 and 3.

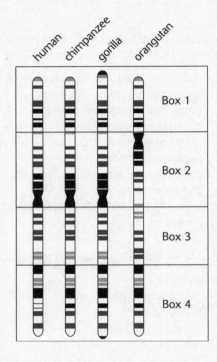

50. What is the most likely explanation for the differences in boxes 2 and 3?

    A. chromosomal deletion

    B. chromosomal addition

    C. chromosomal translocation

    D. chromosomal inversion

    E. chromosomal nondisjunction

Questions 51–52 refer to the following.

A piece of potato is dropped into a beaker of pure water.

51. Which of the following describes the initial condition when the potato enters the water?

    A. The water potential of the pure water is negative.

    B. The water potential of the pure water is positive.

    C. The water potential of the potato is negative.

    D. The water potential of the potato is positive.

    E. The water potential of the potato is zero.

52. Which of the following describes the activity after the potato is immersed in the water?

    A. Water moves from the potato into the surrounding water.

    B. Water moves from the surrounding water into the potato.

    C. Potato cells plasmolyze.

    D. Solutes in the water move into the potato.

    E. There is no movement of water into or out of the potato.

GO ON TO THE NEXT PAGE

Directions: The following questions consist of a phrase or sentence. Each question is preceded by five lettered choices. Select the one lettered choice that best matches the phrase or sentence. Each lettered choice may be used once, more than once, or not at all.

Questions 53–56 refer to the following.

    A.   competitive exclusion principle
    B.   intraspecific competition
    C.   realized niche
    D.   resource partitioning
    E.   character displacement

53. A researcher combined cultures of two species of paramecium. All individuals of one of the species died after 20 days.

54. Five closely related species of warblers (birds) eat insects in the same spruce tree. Each species searches for food in a different area of the tree or hunts for food in a unique manner.

55. Two species of barnacles live on rocks in the intertidal zone. Each species can occupy the entire intertidal zone in the absence of the other species. When both are present, one species occupies the lower two-thirds of the zone, while the other species occupies the upper one-third of the zone.

56. When two species of finches live on different islands, the average depth of their beaks is 10 mm. When the two species live together on the same island, the average beak depth for one species is 8 mm and for the other it is 12 mm.

Questions 57–59 refer to the following.

    A.   adaptive radiation
    B.   coevolution
    C.   convergent evolution
    D.   divergent evolution
    E.   parallel evolution

57. The North American pocket gopher, the Eurasian mole rat, and the Australian marsupial mole belong to different families but are all burrowing mammals with enlarged forelimbs and small eyes and feed underground.

58. There are more that 500 species of *Drosophila* fruit flies on the Hawaiian Islands.

59. The saddleback carapaces (shells) of tortoises on certain Galápagos islands allow the animals to reach high into the vegetation to obtain food. *Opuntia* cactuses on these same islands grow tall and tree-like with fleshy pad-like stems beyond the reach of the tortoises.

Questions 60–63 refer to the following.

In the following four questions, long hair in rabbits (*A*) is dominant to short hair (*a*), and black color (*B*) is dominant to brown (*b*).

    A.   0
    B. $\frac{1}{16}$
    C. $\frac{1}{4}$
    D. $\frac{1}{2}$
    E. $\frac{3}{4}$

60. The probability that the cross $Aa \times Aa$ will produce offspring with the genotype *aa*.

61. The probability that the cross $AaBb \times AaBb$ will produce offspring with the genotype *aabb*.

62. The probability that the cross $AaBB \times AaBb$ will produce offspring with the genotype *Aabb*.

63. The probability that the cross $Bb \times Bb$ will produce rabbits that have black hair.

Questions 64–67 refer to the following.

    A.   angiosperms
    B.   bryophytes
    C.   gymnosperms
    D.   lichens
    E.   ferns

64. There are generally no specialized tissues to transport water, but water is required for flagellated sperm.

65. The sporophyte represents the dominant generation in this spore-producing group.

66. This produces seeds, but ovules do not develop within an ovary.

67. Two fertilizations are required to produce a single seed.

Questions 68–71 refer to the following.

    A. imprinting
    B. habituation
    C. insight
    D. trial-and-error
    E. classical conditioning

68. A young, inexperienced bear travels from a remote region and wanders into a campsite for the first time and discovers many containers. He approaches each container, smells it, and breaks it open. After tasting the contents, the bear either eats all of it or discards it. What kind of behavior is the bear demonstrating?

69. An experienced bear uses his sense of smell to discover food in a parked vehicle. What kind of behavior is he demonstrating?

70. What kind of behavior is demonstrated by a bear who breaks into a vehicle that contains no food?

71. Bear canisters are specially designed food containers that bears are unable to open. After trying a few times to open a canister, an experienced bear will soon ignore all canisters. What kind of behavior is the bear demonstrating when he ignores the canisters?

Questions 72–75 refer to the following.

    A. mRNA
    B. tRNA
    C. rRNA
    D. DNA polymerase
    E. RNA polymerase

72. carries the genetic instructions to the ribosome for forming a polypeptide chain

73. carries an amino acid to the site of polypeptide formation

74. creates a copy of the genetic information

75. creates in the nucleus a product that is active in the cytoplasm

Questions 76–79 refer to the following.

    A. neutrophils
    B. interferons
    C. antibiotics
    D. cytotoxic T cells
    E. plasma B cells

76. cells that produce antibodies in response to foreign substances or foreign cells

77. cells that become killer cells in response to infected cells of the body

78. phagocytic cells that engulf and destroy foreign invaders

79. secretions from virus-infected cells that stimulate neighboring cells to protect themselves

Questions 80–82 refer to the following.

    A. The ionic charge would change.
    B. The pH would decrease.
    C. The pH would increase.
    D. An isotope of the atom would be created.
    E. The atom would change to an atom of a different element.

80. What would be the effect on an atom if the number of *protons* of the atom were changed?

81. What would be the effect on an atom if the number of *neutrons* of the atom were changed?

82. What would be the effect on an atom if the number of *electrons* of the atom were changed?

GO ON TO THE NEXT PAGE

Directions: Questions that follow involve data from experiments or laboratory analyses. In each case, study the information provided. Then choose the one best answer for each question.

Questions 83–87 refer to the following diagram that illustrates the hormonal regulation of the menstrual cycle.

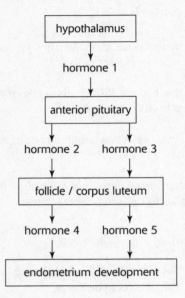

83. If GnRH is gonadotropin-releasing hormone, FSH is follicle-stimulating hormone, and LH is luteinizing hormone, then hormones 2 and 3 in the diagram are

    A. GnRH and LH
    B. FSH and LH
    C. FSH and estrogen
    D. LH and estrogen
    E. estrogen and progesterone

84. Hormones 4 and 5 are

    A. GnRH and progesterone
    B. LH and FSH
    C. FSH and estrogen
    D. LH and estrogen
    E. estrogen and progesterone

85. Which of the following is a distinction between the follicle and the corpus luteum?

    A. The follicle produces large amounts of progesterone and the corpus luteum does not.
    B. The follicle contains an ovule and the corpus luteum does not.
    C. The follicle produces large amounts of GnRH and the corpus luteum does not.
    D. The follicle produces FSH and the corpus luteum produces LH.
    E. The follicle is stimulated by estrogen and the corpus luteum is stimulated by progesterone.

86. The hypothalamus produces hormone 1 in response to low levels of which two hormones?

    A. GnRH and progesterone
    B. LH and FSH
    C. FSH and estrogen
    D. LH and estrogen
    E. estrogen and progesterone

87. The box in the figure labeled "endometrium development" is a reference to

    A. the menstrual flow
    B. menopause
    C. ovulation
    D. eggs in preparation for ovulation and their release into the fallopian tubes
    E. the thickening of the endometrium in preparation for the implantation of the embryo

For Questions 86–87 refer to the following.

The following graph plots the size of the stomatal aperture as a function of time of day for a succulent and for a typical plant. For the typical plant, three environments are investigated: normal conditions, very dry soil, and an experimentally induced low CO_2 environment.

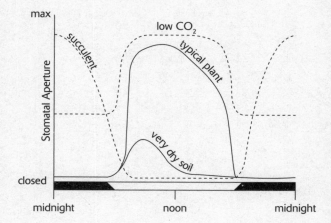

88. According to the figure, the stomata for a typical plant under normal conditions are

A. closed during the entire daytime and open during the entire nighttime
B. open during the entire daytime and closed during the entire nighttime
C. open during both daytime and nighttime
D. open for only part of the daytime
E. open for only part of the nighttime

89. Which of the following could explain the stomatal behavior of the succulent?

A. very dry soil
B. high humidity
C. CAM photosynthesis
D. C_4 photosynthesis
E. high water stress during the night

90. According to the figure, which of the following is associated with the opening of stomata in a typical plant?

A. darkness
B. high humidity
C. low humidity
D. low CO_2
E. dry soil

GO ON TO THE NEXT PAGE

Practice Exam 2

Questions 91–93 refer to the following.

The graphs that follow show the absorption spectra for individual pigments found inside a chloroplast and the action spectrum for photosynthesis.

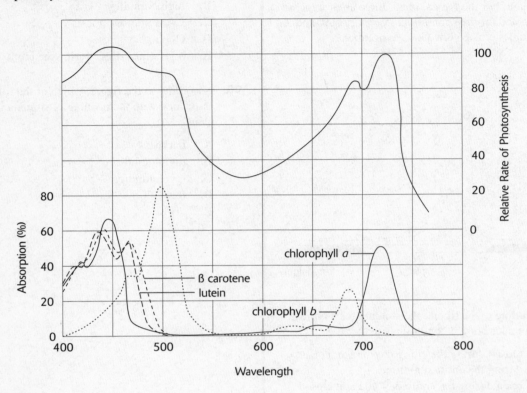

91. Which of the pigments absorbs the most light energy at the *longest* wavelength?

    A. β carotene
    B. lutein
    C. chlorophyll *a*
    D. chlorophyll *b*
    E. unable to determine from information in figure

92. At what wavelength of light is the rate of photosynthesis *greatest?*

    A. 450 nm
    B. 500 nm
    C. 550 nm
    D. 650 nm
    E. 700 nm

93. What wavelengths would most contribute to the composition of light *reflected* from a chloroplast?

    A. 400–450 nm
    B. 450–500 nm
    C. 550–600 nm
    D. 650–700 nm
    E. 700–750 nm

Questions 94–96 refer to the following cladogram.

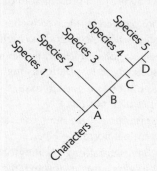

94. Which species most likely represents the outgroup for this analysis?

   A. Species 1
   B. Species 2
   C. Species 3
   D. Species 4
   E. Species 5

95. According to this analysis, which two species are most closely related?

   A. Species 1 and 3
   B. Species 1 and 5
   C. Species 2 and 5
   D. Species 3 and 5
   E. Species 4 and 5

96. Which of the following is a correct interpretation of this analysis?

   A. Species 4 is the ancestor of Species 5.
   B. Species 5 is the ancestor of Species 4.
   C. Species 3 is the ancestor of Species 4 and 5.
   D. Species 4 and 5 share a common ancestor.
   E. Species 5 is the most recent species to have evolved.

Questions 97–100 refer to the following.

The graph that follows plots the hemoglobin-oxygen dissociation curve. The curve shows the relationship between the amount of oxygen bonded to hemoglobin in red blood cells (% Hb O_2) and the amount of oxygen in the surrounding tissues (partial pressure of oxygen, P_{O_2}). The normal pH of blood is 7.4.

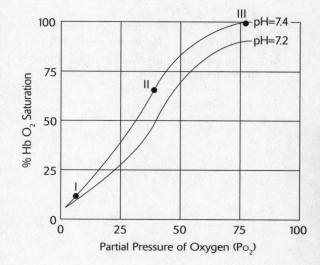

97. According to the graph, which of the following is correct?

   A. Hemoglobin saturation increases as P_{O_2} increases.
   B. Blood pH decreases as P_{O_2} increases.
   C. Hemoglobin saturation increases as blood pH decreases.
   D. Blood pH has no effect on oxygen saturation of hemoglobin.
   E. There is no relationship between P_{O_2} and oxygen saturation of hemoglobin.

98. According to the graph, which of the following correctly describes the activity of hemoglobin in a higher than normal acid environment?

   A. Hemoglobin is unable to release oxygen.
   B. Hemoglobin releases less oxygen to the tissues.
   C. Oxygen saturation of hemoglobin is higher.
   D. Oxygen saturation of hemoglobin is lower.
   E. Oxygen saturation of hemoglobin is unaffected.

GO ON TO THE NEXT PAGE

99. Points on the graph indicated by I, II, and III represent areas of a human circulatory system. In this order, I, II, III, these areas could represent

  A. capillaries in tissues at rest, capillaries in heart tissue, pulmonary arteries
  B. capillaries in tissues at rest, capillaries in tissues during exercise, pulmonary arteries
  C. pulmonary veins, capillaries in heart tissue, pulmonary arteries
  D. capillaries in tissues during exercise, capillaries in tissues at rest, pulmonary veins
  E. aorta, capillaries in tissues at rest, capillaries in tissues during exercise

100. Which of the following hypotheses is best supported by the data presented in the graph?

  A. More oxygen is released by hemoglobin in tissues where respiration is high.
  B. Less oxygen is released by hemoglobin in tissues where respiration is high.
  C. Respiration is higher in tissues where pH is higher than normal.
  D. Respiration is lower in tissues where pH is lower than normal.
  E. Oxygen saturation of hemoglobin increases as blood progresses through the systemic circuit of the circulatory system.

Section II (Free-Response Questions)

Reading Time: 10 minutes (for organizing your thoughts and outlining your answer)
Writing Time: 90 minutes

1. All cells use the following classes of molecules for structural elements and for metabolism, yet organisms can be dramatically diverse in both respects.

   - polysaccharides
   - proteins
   - nucleic acids

   A. Give one example of each molecule with a detailed description of its molecular structure.
   B. Compare the similarities of these molecules and the characteristics they possess that contribute to their use in a wide range of applications.
   C. Give one example each for a plant, a bacterium, and a virus for how each of these molecules is used in a different way.

2. Darwin proposed the mechanism of natural selection to explain evolution.

   A. Describe the process of natural selection as put forward by Darwin.
   B. Define fitness.
   C. Describe how natural selection promotes the evolution of insecticide resistance.
   D. Explain how altruistic behavior can be adaptive.

3. There are many examples of coevolution. Describe each of the following relationships and the evolution of mechanisms or behaviors that each member brings to the relationship.

   A. predator and prey
   B. flowers and flower pollinators
   C. plants and leaf-eating insects

GO ON TO THE NEXT PAGE

4. The temperature of ectothermic animals is determined mostly by the temperature of their surroundings. The heart rate of the water flea *Daphnia* was measured under different environmental temperatures. The following data were collected.

Temperature (°C)	5	10	15	20	25	30
Beats/min	50	95	125	170	230	275

- **A.** Graph this data on the grid provided.
- **B.** Explain why temperature affects heart rate in *Daphnia*.
- **C.** How would the results of this experiment differ if an endothermic organism were tested?
- **D.** Design an experiment to determine if the chirp rate of crickets varies with environmental temperature. Predict results and give a justification for your prediction.

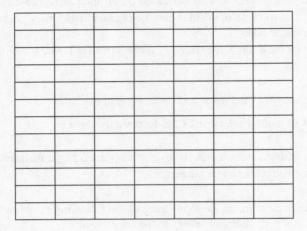

Answer Key for Practice Exam 2

Section I (Multiple-Choice Questions)

1. D	26. C	51. C	76. E
2. D	27. E	52. B	77. D
3. E	28. B	53. A	78. A
4. A	29. C	54. D	79. B
5. E	30. B	55. C	80. E
6. D	31. E	56. E	81. D
7. A	32. A	57. C	82. A
8. C	33. D	58. A	83. B
9. D	34. C	59. B	84. E
10. B	35. C	60. C	85. B
11. C	36. B	61. B	86. E
12. A	37. B	62. A	87. E
13. D	38. D	63. E	88. B
14. E	39. E	64. B	89. C
15. E	40. B	65. E	90. D
16. A	41. C	66. C	91. C
17. A	42. D	67. A	92. A
18. E	43. B	68. D	93. C
19. B	44. B	69. E	94. A
20. A	45. C	70. E	95. E
21. C	46. D	71. B	96. D
22. E	47. C	72. A	97. A
23. C	48. D	73. B	98. D
24. A	49. C	74. D	99. D
25. A	50. D	75. E	100. A

Scoring Your Practice Exam

Section I (Multiple-Choice Questions)

Number of questions you answered correctly: _____ × 1   =   _____

Number of questions you answered wrong: _____ × ¼   =   –_____ *

Number of questions you left unanswered: _____ × 0   =   ___0___

TOTAL for Section I (0–100 points):   =   _____ **

(subtract number wrong from number correct)

Round to nearest whole number.
** If less than zero, enter zero.

Section II (Free-Response Questions)

For each correct and relevant piece of information you include in your answers to the free-response questions, you earn one point. Refer to the scoring standards that follow the multiple-choice explanations.

Score for essay 1 (0–10 points):   _____

Score for essay 2 (0–10 points):   _____

Score for essay 3 (0–10 points):   _____

Score for essay 4 (0–10 points):   _____

Combined Score (Sections I + II)

Total for Section I (from above):   _____ × 0.6 =   _____

(60% of 100 points = 60 points maximum)

Total for Section II (from above):   _____ × 1.0 =   _____

(100% of 40 points = 40 points maximum)

Combined Score (Add Sections I and II)_____

(0–100 points possible)

Probable AP Grade	
61–100	5
47–60	4
39–46	3
30–38	2
0–29	1

Answers and Explanations for Practice Exam 2

1. **D.** Photosynthesis takes inorganic carbon from the atmosphere (in the form of CO_2) and converts it to an organic form ("fixes" it). The organic form is glucose or other carbohydrates.

2. **D.** Determinant growth describes the growth of an organism whose growth ends when the organism reaches maturity. Most animals, for example, stop growing when they reach reproductive maturity. In contrast, growth in plants is indeterminant—they continue to grow until they die.

3. **E.** Chromosomes replicate during interphase, specifically during the S phase of the cell cycle. Chromosome replication is the making of a second chromatid from the single chromatid that makes up a chromosome following cell division.

4. **A.** Pyruvate is a product of glycolysis. The pyruvate is then used in the Krebs cycle to generate ATP and NADH, which are used, in turn, to generate ATP during oxidative phosphorylation.

5. **E.** Speech, conscious thinking, and control of skeletal muscles occur in the cerebral cortex. The cerebral cortex is a thin outer layer of cerebrum. The cerebrum consists of two hemispheres connected by a bundle of association neurons, the corpus callosum.

6. **D.** A dehydration reaction occurs when the loss of a water molecule follows the bonding of two monomers. Such loss of water molecules follows the joining of two amino acids in the formation of a protein, two monosaccharides in the formation of a disaccharide or polysaccharide, and when a fatty acid joins a glycerol molecule in the formation of a triglyceride.

7. **A.** Some RNA-like molecules function as enzymes, so it is believed that RNA originated before DNA, which requires a much more complicated process to assemble enzymes. Respiration could not evolve until enzymes evolved, and oxygen didn't appear in the atmosphere until after photosynthesis evolved.

8. **C.** Cancer cells divide excessively and uncontrollably. The cellular mechanisms that normally control this growth do not work.

9. **D.** Central vacuoles are found in many plant cells but not in any animal cells. Plant cells lack centrioles and lysosomes, while mitochondria and nuclei are common to both plant and animal cells.

10. **B.** Meiotic divisions are visible in the anther of a flower, where haploid microspores are produced and pollen grains develop.

11. **C.** Carbon dioxide collects in the stroma, not in the thylakoids. In the stroma, the CO_2 is fixed into PGAL by the Calvin-Benson cycle.

12. **A.** Most (90%) of the energy leaving one trophic level is lost before entering the next trophic level. Much of the energy is lost in the form of heat. Other energy is lost due to inefficient mechanisms of transfer between trophic levels (much of the energy in food remains in the food after it is processed by an animal).

13. **D.** The cotyledon stores food for the developing seedlings of many kinds of plants. In other plants, this function mainly belongs to the endosperm.

14. **E.** Acquired characteristics do not get passed on to the next generation. Only information in hereditary material gets passed on. Keeping a tree closely pruned or keeping your hair short by having it cut often are traits that do not get passed on to progeny.

15. **E.** Alcohol fermentation and lactic acid fermentation convert NADH to NAD^+ to make available needed NAD^+ for glycolysis when oxygen is unavailable. If oxygen is available, then the conversion of NADH to NAD^+ occurs during oxidative phosphorylation as ATP is generated.

16. **A.** Called evaporative cooling, the water left behind cools because of the energy used (heat of vaporization) to convert the evaporating water molecules from the liquid to the gaseous state.

17. **A.** Tracheids are relatively long, narrow cells that have tapered ends that overlap with the next tracheid. Water passes through the overlapping ends through pits. Vessels are more evolutionarily advanced. They are shorter and wider than tracheids, and the ends that border the next vessel allow for the movement of water between the vessels through perforations, essentially open holes.

18. E. An individual with the genotype *RrTt* produces equal quantities of haploid sperm that are *RT, Rt, rT, rt*. For one pair of homologous chromosomes (*Rr*), one chromosome has two chromatids, both with *R,* and its homologue has two chromatids, both with *r*. For the second homologous pair (*Tt*), one chromosome has two chromatids, both with *T,* and its homologue has two chromatids, both with *t*. The resulting sperm have genotypes that represent all the possible ways that two pairs of homologous chromosomes can segregate and randomly assort during meiosis.

19. B. With one exception, prokaryotic cells lack all organelles typically found in eukaryotic cells. The organelle that does occur in prokaryotic cells is the ribosome, necessary for protein synthesis. Many prokaryotes have flagella, but they are not constructed of microtubules as they are in eukaryotes.

20. A. The two major heart sounds, "lup-dup," originate from the turbulence in the blood produced by the closing of the atrioventricular valves and the semilunar valves, respectively.

21. C. Cyanobacteria are autotrophic prokaryotes. They produce their own food by photosynthesis.

22. E. A pollen tube bears three nuclei: two sperm nuclei and a tube cell nucleus. The tube cell nucleus regulates the growth of the pollen tube. One sperm nucleus fertilizes the egg to produce a diploid embryo, and the second sperm nucleus fertilizes the two polar nuclei in the embryo sac to form a triploid endosperm.

23. C. It is important that cells have a large surface area relative to their volume in order to maximize the ability of cells to import necessary nutrients and export wastes. The greater the surface, the greater the area for carrying out these processes. A large cell may not have enough surface area to accommodate the transport needs of the cell. Another limitation to cell size is the genome to volume ratio. The genome of a cell (the cell's genetic material or chromosomes) remains fixed in size and fixed in its ability to control the activity of the cell (by producing RNA, which in turn produces proteins). The genome may not be able to accommodate the protein (and enzyme) needs of a large cell.

24. A. Reproductive isolation is the initial requirement for the evolution of two species from one species. Mutations, genetic drift, and gene flow can cause changes that result in a population evolving into a new species, but *two* species will only be created from one species if the population is divided into two groups that are reproductively isolated.

25. A. Abscisic acid slows growth in plants preparing for winter and induces dormancy in seeds.

26. C. When resources are limited and individuals must compete for survival, some individuals will not survive. The most fit individuals survive and leave offspring with traits similar to their own, traits that give them the competitive edge for survival. So advantageous traits get passed on to the next generation. Evolution occurs as these advantageous traits accumulate in the population. Natural selection is a process that "selects" individuals with traits that give them the ability to compete successfully. This is the *opposite* of random. Strength may or may not contribute to an individual's ability to compete, survive, and produce offspring. Only populations evolve, not individuals. Generally, individuals can't "change" their traits and become better competitors. In any case, the traits that are important to natural selection are the ones that are inherited and passed on to the next generation.

27. E. As enzymes, proteins are responsible for regulating nearly all metabolic processes, so you would expect them to be everywhere. But the question asks about proteins in the plasma membrane. In the plasma membrane, proteins are active in transport mechanisms and involved in reactions or signaling processes on both sides of the membrane and in the formation of junctions between cells (desmosomes). Proteins of the plasma membrane are not involved in DNA replication because that process occurs in the nucleus.

28. B. External fertilization occurs when both sperm and egg meet outside of the bodies of the individuals that produced them, and fertilization occurs in the environment.

29. C. Changes in the timing of developmental features caused by small mutations in regulatory genes can have a major impact on phenotype. A deletion of a single nucleotide is a frame shift mutation with every subsequent nucleotide displaced one position. The mRNA made from this DNA would have all codons after the mutation changed, resulting in a nonfunctioning polypeptide. Changes in genes that code for ribosomal or cytochrome proteins would likely lead to failures in ribosome function during protein synthesis or inefficient or nonfunctional electron transport in oxidative phosphorylation.

30. B. Histones in chromosomes of Archaea give these prokaryotes a trait in common with eukaryotes but different from the other prokaryotes (Bacteria).

31. E. Thick cuticles reduce water loss from the surface of leaves. Stomata that occur in leaf depressions help conserve water loss because the stomata are protected from moving air (or wind) that increases transpiration. Hairs on leaf surfaces slow the movement of air or help disperse heat. A leaf oriented in the vertical direction reduces the amount of surface area exposed to the sun. The green color of chlorophyll does not reduce water loss.

32. A. Males only get one copy of an X-linked gene. They express the trait carried by that one allele. So only one copy of a recessive allele is required to express the recessive trait. Because females get two copies of a gene, they must receive two copies of the recessive allele to express the recessive trait. It is much easier to receive one copy of a recessive allele than two copies, so males express the recessive trait more often.

33. D. The Calvin cycle fixes carbon dioxide and produces PGAL, which is then used to make glucose. In order to repeat the cycle, the energy in ATP (ATP $\rightarrow$ ADP + P_i) is used to regenerate RuBP. RuBP can then combine with carbon dioxide again.

34. C. The molecular formula gives the number of each kind of atom in a molecule. But two molecules with the same molecular formula can have different structural formulas, that is, a different arrangement of the same atoms. These are isomers. Isomers can have different chemical and physical characteristics.

35. C. The hydrogen bonds holding water together allow the water to be pulled up through the vascular system as water molecules transpire from the surface of leaves. This kind of movement is bulk flow, like water flowing through a rain gutter (but in the opposite direction).

36. B. Glycoproteins are proteins with a carbohydrate attached. After amino acids are assembled into a protein by ribosomes bound to the rough endoplasmic reticulum (rough ER), the rough ER attaches a carbohydrate to the protein. From there, the glycoprotein is shuttled by a transport vesicle to a Golgi apparatus, where it is further modified before its export from the cell. The modified glycoprotein is packaged in another vesicle, which transports it to the plasma membrane. The vesicle fuses with the membrane, releasing its contents from the cell.

37. B. Oxygen is the final electron acceptor for electrons passing through the electron transport chain in oxidative phosphorylation. It is here, in oxidative phosphorylation, that much ATP is generated. Without oxygen as the final electron acceptor, oxidative phosphorylation would stop, followed by the shutting down of the Krebs cycle. Anaerobic processes (alcohol fermentation or lactic acid fermentation) would begin in order to replenish NAD^+. NAD^+ would allow for the continuation of glycolysis and the generation of a minimal amount of ATP.

38. D. A climax community is generally a stable, long-lived community. Catastrophic events such as fires, floods, and disease can destroy a climax community and initiate ecological succession anew.

39. E. Since adenine pairs with thymine, adenine equals thymine in their numbers. Since cytosine pairs with guanine, cytosine equals guanine in their numbers. If adenine = thymine = 28%, and adenine + thymine = 56%, then cytosine + guanine must equal 44% and cytosine = guanine = 44/2 = 22% and answer E is false (and the correct answer to this question). Also uracil = 0% because there is no uracil in DNA (only in RNA).

40. B. Transferring hydrogen to oxygen atoms to form H_2O_2 is the job of the peroxisome. The toxic H_2O_2 is subsequently broken down in the peroxisome to form H_2O.

41. C. High-fructose corn syrup, as the name implies, is fructose made from corn starch. Because starch is a polymer of glucose, starch must be broken down into glucose monomers and each glucose monosaccharide must be converted into a fructose monosaccharide. (For the final HFCS product, the manufactured fructose is back blended with glucose to produce a sweetener that is about 55% fructose and 45% glucose. This turns out to be a cheaper way of making a sweetener than by extracting sucrose, a disaccharide of glucose and fructose, from sugar cane or sugar beets.)

42. D. Species with a K-selected life history strategy contribute a considerable amount of time and energy to raising their offspring. Little or no parental care is characteristic of the r-selected life history strategy.

43. B. The vascular cambium is a cylinder of cells that parallels the bark. When cells of the vascular cambium divide, they produce cells on the inside of the cylinder (toward the center of a trunk or branch) and cells on the outside of the cylinder. The cells produced on the inside become xylem cells; those on the outside become phloem cells. As xylem cells accumulate on the inside of the vascular cambium and phloem cells to the outside, the diameter of the trunk increases.

44. B. The anterior pituitary secretes hormones that regulate the activity of the adrenal cortex (with adrenocorticotropic hormone), the ovaries and testes (with FSH and LH), and the thyroid (with thyroid-stimulating hormone).

45. C. Crossing over does not result in nondisjunction.

46. D. If $r > 0$, population growth is exponential. The difference between $r = 0.001$ and $r = 1$ is the length of time it takes before the sharply rising part of the "J" shape begins.

47. C. The "words" of the genetic code are codons each consisting of three "letters" (three nucleotides).

48. D. There are 64 different "words" or codons. Because each codon consists of 3 nucleotides and there are 4 different nucleotides, the number of ways the 4 nucleotides can be arranged in groups of 3 is $4 \times 4 \times 4 = 64$.

49. C. Three of the 64 codons are "stop" codons, and the remaining 61 codons all code for amino acids.

50. D. The bands and centromere of the chromosome segment in box 2 of the orangutan are in reverse order (inverted) compared to the bands and centromere of the chromosome segment in box 2 for the human, chimpanzee, and gorilla. Similarly, the segment of the chromosome in box 3 for the orangutan is inverted compared to the other species.

51. C. Pure water, with no solutes, has a water potential of zero. The presence of solutes in water or in the water of the potato cells decreases the water potential (makes it more negative). The potato, with central vacuoles filled with water containing solutes, has a negative water potential.

52. B. Water moves across a selectively permeable membrane from a region of higher water potential to a region of lower water potential. Because pure water has a water potential of zero and the potato has a water potential of less than zero, water moves into the potato across the plasma membrane. Plasmolysis occurs when water leaves cells, causing the cells to lose turgidity and collapse.

53. A. The competitive exclusion principle (Gause's principle) argues that when two species occupy the same ecological niche (that is, they compete for the same resources under the same conditions), one of the species will out-compete the other. Changing minor conditions, however, could change the outcome of the competition. With the paramecia, changes in some of the environmental conditions could reverse which species survived.

54. D. Each species of warbler feeds in a different part of the spruce tree or feeds in a different manner. Such a division of resources among different species is called resource partitioning.

55. C. When only one species of barnacles was present, it occupied its fundamental niche. In the company of another species, both species occupied their realized niches.

56. E. Character displacement occurs to minimize competition. Finches of the two species with similar beak size competed for the same food, were less successful, and passed on fewer offspring. Eventually, only birds of each species with beaks different from those of the other species could acquire enough resources to survive.

57. C. The evolution of similar traits in unrelated animals is convergent evolution. In this case, the common traits are adaptations to a common lifestyle—living underground.

58. A. This is an example of adaptive radiation. Because the islands are isolated, the first fruit flies that arrived encountered many unoccupied niches and available lifestyles in varied habitats. Individuals with traits that gave them slight competitive advantages in these niches flourished. Specialization to habitat and physical barriers between populations promoted reproductive isolation. Among the Hawaiian fruit flies, divergence in mating behaviors was most intense.

59. B. Coevolution is the evolution of one species in response to the evolution of another species. The contest between *Optunia* cactus to avoid being eaten and the tortoises to reach higher into the vegetation produced these traits—tree-like cactus and saddleback carapaces.

60. C. Make a Punnett square to show that $Aa \times Aa \rightarrow \frac{1}{4} AA + \frac{1}{2} Aa + \frac{1}{4} aa$.

61. B. You could make another Punnett square to show that $Bb \times Bb \rightarrow \frac{1}{4} BB + \frac{1}{2} Bb + \frac{1}{4} bb$, but this is the same cross you made in question 60. Calculate the frequency of *aabb* by multiplying the frequency of *aa* by the frequency of *bb*, or $\frac{1}{4} \times \frac{1}{4} = \frac{1}{16}$.

62. A. Note that one parent (*AaBB*) has no *b*. No offspring can inherit a *b* from both parents if only one parent has a *b* to offer, so the frequency of *Aabb* progeny is zero.

63. E. $Bb \times Bb \rightarrow \frac{1}{4} BB + \frac{1}{2} Bb + \frac{1}{4} bb$. Black offspring are $\frac{1}{4} BB + \frac{1}{2} Bb = \frac{3}{4}$.

64. B. In general, bryophytes (mosses and liverworts) have no specialized transport system. This requires that they live in wet habitats and that each individual cell can absorb water from its surroundings (keeping these plants small). In addition, water is required for the flagellated sperm.

65. E. The sporophyte stage of a fern represents the dominant generation. The sporophyte produces spores which germinate to become gametophytes. The gametophytes produce eggs and flagellated sperm. Fertilization occurs after the sperm swim to the eggs. The fertilized zygote grows to become the plant typically called a fern.

66. C. Gymnosperms (including conifers) produce male cones that bear microspores that develop into pollen. Female cones bear ovules that are not enclosed in an ovary. One single haploid megaspore survives within the ovule. The megaspore produces eggs which are fertilized by sperm cells in the pollen grain. A seed consisting of the embryo, a food supply, and a seed coat develops.

67. A. Double fertilization is unique to angiosperms (flowering plants). Two sperm cells from a pollen grain enter the embryo sac within an ovule. One sperm cell fertilizes the egg to produce a diploid embryo. A second sperm cell joins two polar nuclei to form a triploid endosperm.

68. D. The first time the bear encounters humans with their food and equipment, it is essentially a learning experience. By using trial-and-error, the bear learns what smells can be associated with food and which smells can be associated with nonfood. Trial-and-error is a form of associative learning.

69. E. This experienced bear, who knows which smells are associated with human food, is displaying classical conditioning behavior. The smell of human food is the substitute stimulus for bear food, the normal stimulus.

70. E. As in question 69, this is again classical conditioning. The car is a substitute stimulus for bear food, the normal stimulus.

71. B. Habituation occurs when the bear learns to ignore a stimulus because it is no longer meaningful.

72. A. The mRNA carries the genetic instructions from DNA into the cytoplasm to be translated by ribosomes to form a polypeptide.

73. B. The function of a tRNA is to bond to a specific amino acid and transport it to the ribosome when the appropriate codon on the mRNA codes for its amino acid.

74. D. DNA polymerase is the main enzyme responsible for DNA replication.

75. E. Using the template provided by DNA in the nucleus, RNA polymerase makes mRNA, tRNA, and rRNA, which all move to the cytoplasm to assemble polypeptides.

76. E. Plasma B cells, active in the humoral immune response, target antigens such as molecules, viruses, and foreign cells with the production of antibodies.

77. D. Cytotoxic T cells, active in the cell-mediated immune response, target self cells that display aberrant (nonself) molecules on their cell surfaces.

78. A. Neutrophils are phagocytic cells that destroy pathogens by phagocytosis.

79. B. A cell infected with viruses may secrete interferons that stimulate neighboring cells to produce proteins that help them defend against viruses.

80. E. Adding protons to the nucleus of an atom changes the atom from one kind of element to another. For example, carbon has 6 protons and nitrogen has 7 protons.

81. D. Adding neutrons to the nucleus of an atom creates an isotope of that atom. Carbon with 6 neutrons and carbon with 7 neutrons are isotopes.

82. A. Adding electrons, which have a negative charge, to a neutral atom makes the total negative charge greater than the positive charge (from protons). An atom or molecule with a nonzero charge is an ion.

83. B. Hormones 2 and 3 are FSH and LH, products of the anterior pituitary that target the follicle and the corpus luteum.

84. E. The follicle and corpus luteum produce estrogen and progesterone, hormones that target the endometrium.

85. B. The follicle contains a developing ovule. When the ovule is mature, ovulation occurs (the ovule leaves the follicle) and the follicle becomes the corpus luteum.

86. E. Falling levels of both estrogen and progesterone in the blood act in negative feedback fashion to stimulate the hypothalamus to begin the menstrual cycle by secreting GnRH (hormone 1). In turn, GnRH stimulates the anterior pituitary to secrete LH and FSH.

87. E. A primary purpose of the menstrual cycle is to prepare the endometrium for the implantation of a fertilized egg. Preparation of the endometrium includes an increase in vascularization (blood vessels) and a general thickening of the tissue.

88. B. The graph shows that the stomata are open during the day and closed during the night. This makes sense because stomata must be open to allow for the diffusion of CO_2 into the leaf for photosynthesis. Because photosynthesis does not occur at night, CO_2 is not needed, and stomata close to reduce transpiration.

89. C. The behavior of the stomata in the succulent is nearly the opposite of that for the typical plant but is in agreement for what would be expected for a plant doing CAM photosynthesis. In CAM, stomata open at night to allow CO_2 to enter the leaf. The CO_2 collects in the cell vacuoles in the form of malic acid. During the day, the stomata close, but CO_2 is released from the vacuoles for photosynthesis.

90. D. Note that low levels of CO_2 cause the typical plant to partially open its stomata at night. High humidity might also cause this, but data for the effects of humidity are not reported in the graph.

91. C. Chlorophylls *a* and *b* have absorption peaks in the long wavelength area (between 600 and 700 nm). Of the two, chlorophyll *a* has the greatest absorption at the longest wavelength of light.

92. A. The action spectrum is a plot of photosynthetic rate against light wavelengths absorbed. The highest rate of photosynthetic activity occurs at about 450 nm.

93. C. Light that is not absorbed is reflected. The wavelengths of light that are not absorbed in photosynthesis occur mostly in the 550–600 nm region. Not coincidentally, the color of light in the 525–575 nm region is green, the color we see when we look at a leaf.

94. A. Species 1 is most likely the outgroup for this cladogram. As the outgroup, it is the least closely related species to the ingroup (the remaining members of the cladogram that are the subject of the analysis).

95. E. Of the answer choices provided, species 4 and 5 are the most closely related because they have the greatest number of shared characteristics.

96. D. The cladogram indicates that species 4 and 5 share a common ancestor. The cladogram does not provide information about ancestry, just information about relatedness. The cladogram does not provide information about when a new species evolves.

97. A. As P_{O_2} increases (moves to the right on the graph), hemoglobin saturation also increases (moves up on the graph). Note that the graph does not tell you anything about cause and effect—which quantity causes an effect in the other quantity. It's possible that they both increase together for unrelated reasons.

98. D. The plot representing a higher than normal acid environment (which is a *lower* than normal pH, or in this graph, pH = 7.2) is below the plot representing a normal pH (pH = 7.4). The lower curve corresponds with lower hemoglobin saturation. Be extra careful with questions that have pH or acid/base information. Make notes on the exam indicating which pH is acid and which is basic.

99. D. Point I corresponds to blood in muscle tissue during exercise, when both hemoglobin oxygen saturation and the partial pressure of oxygen in the muscle tissue is lowest (as a result of extensive cellular respiration to support muscle contractions). Point II corresponds to blood in muscle tissue at rest, when only some of the oxygen from the hemoglobin and tissue has been used. Point III corresponds to the lungs, where blood has its maximum hemoglobin oxygen saturation and where the partial pressure of oxygen in surrounding tissues (lungs) is greatest.

100. A. When respiration is high, more CO_2 is produced. As CO_2 enters the blood, it diffuses into red blood cells where the enzyme carbonic anhydrase combines the CO_2 with H_2O to form H^+ and HCO_3^-. These ions return to the blood, where the increase in H^+ lowers the pH (makes it more acidic). Thus, the lower plot, representing a more acidic (than normal) blood, corresponds with tissues where respiration is higher. The lower plot indicates a lower hemoglobin saturation. So this graph *supports* the hypothesis that more oxygen is released in tissues where respiration is high.

Section II (Free-Response Questions)

Scoring Standards for the Essay Questions

To score your answers, award your essay points using the standards given below. For each item listed below that matches the content and vocabulary of a statement or explanation in your essay, add the indicated number of points to your essay score (to the maximum allowed for each section). Scores for each essay question range from 0 to 10 points.

Words appearing in parentheses in answers represent alternative wording.

Question 1 (10 points maximum)

A. molecule example and description (*6 points maximum*)

Polysaccharides (*2 points maximum*):

1 pt: Starch (glycogen, cellulose, chitin, or peptidoglycan) is an example of a polysaccharide.

1 pt: Starch (or glycogen) is a polymer of α-glucose monomers, linked together with 1–4 glycosidic covalent bonds, consisting of thousands of individual α-glucose monomers, which may branch to form additional chains.

1 pt: *or* Cellulose is a polymer of β-glucose monomer, linked together with 1–4 glycosidic covalent bonds, consisting of thousands of individual β-glucose monomers.

1 pt: *or* Chitin is a polymer of β-glucosamine monomer (a β-glucose with a nitrogen-containing group attached), unbranched and similar to cellulose.

1 pt: *or* Peptidoglycan is a lattice of interlinked chains of polymers. The monomer of each chain consists of two modified glucose molecules, one with a nitrogen-containing group, the other similar, but with an additional short polypeptide chain of four or five amino acids attached.

Proteins (*3 points maximum*):

1 pt: Any example of a protein such as insulin, antidiuretic hormone (ADH), myoglobin, hemoglobin, cytochrome *c,* an antibody, actin, tubulin, keratin, maltase, rubisco, etc.

1 pt: Proteins are polymers of amino acids formed from peptide linkages between 20 different amino acids.

1 pt: The primary structure of a protein is the order and number of amino acids in the polymer.

1 pt: The secondary structure of a protein contributes to its 3-dimensional shape and results from hydrogen bonding between amino acids to form either an α-helix or a β-pleated sheet.

1 pt: The tertiary structure of a protein adds to its three-dimensional shape and results from hydrogen and ionic bonding between R groups of amino acids, clumping of hydrophobic and hydrophilic portions of the polypeptide, and cross links of disulfide bonds between two cysteine amino acids.

1 pt: The quaternary structure of a protein is the assemblage of two or more individual polypeptides.

Nucleic acids (*3 points maximum*):

1 pt: An example of a nucleic acid is DNA or RNA.

1 pt: Nucleic acids are polymers of nucleotides. A nucleotide consist of a nitrogen base, a sugar, and a phosphate group.

1 pt: DNA is a double helix formed from two strands that are each a polymer of four different DNA nucleotides: adenine, thymine, cytosine, and guanine. DNA nucleotides contain the sugar deoxyribose.

1 pt: The two strands of DNA are linked together by hydrogen bonds between the bases of the nucleotides, always adenine to thymine, guanine to cytosine.

1 pt: RNA is a polymer of four RNA nucleotides: adenine, uracil, cytosine, and guanine. RNA nucleotides contain the sugar ribose.

1 pt: RNA may be single stranded, as in messenger RNA (mRNA), globular, as in ribosomal RNA (rRNA), or partially double stranded, as in transfer RNA (tRNA).

B. similarities of these molecules (*3 points maximum*)

1 pt: All three molecules are polymers.

1 pt: Proteins have 20 different monomers, and nucleic acids have 4 different monomers, allowing a vast number of combinations and potential functions.

1 pt: Although proteins and nucleic acids are simple linear sequences of monomers, the interactions among the individual monomers (especially for proteins) are able to create a vast variety of three-dimensional-shaped molecules that can perform many different functions.

C. plant, bacterium, and virus examples of a polysaccharide, a protein, and a nucleic acid (*3 points maximum*)

1 pt: Plants use cellulose for cell walls, rubisco for fixing carbon in photosynthesis, and DNA for hereditary information.

1 pt: Bacteria use peptidoglycans for cell walls, restriction enzymes for attacking invading viruses, and DNA for plasmids.

1 pt: Some viruses use carbohydrates attached to proteins (glycoproteins) in their envelopes and RNA for hereditary material.

1 pt: Any other examples.

Question 2 (10 points maximum)

A. process of natural selection (*5 points maximum*)

1 pt: Populations have great reproductive potential.

1 pt: Natural population sizes remain constant.

1 pt: Resources are limited.

1 pt: Individuals compete for survival.

1 pt: There is variation among individuals in a population.

1 pt: Much variation is inherited.

1 pt: Individuals with the best (most adaptive, most fit) variations are more successful at survival and reproduction.

1 pt: Evolution proceeds as adaptive traits accumulate in a population.

B. definition of fitness (*1 point maximum*)

1 pt: number of offspring contributed to the next generation

1 pt: relative ability to survive and leave offspring

1 pt: relative adaptive value of a trait

C. evolution of insecticide resistance (*3 points maximum*)

1 pt: Insecticide resistance is an example of directional selection.

1 pt: Directional selection occurs when an uncommon trait (one with low frequency in the population) becomes favored.

1 pt: Insecticide-resistant trait becomes favorable when environmental pressures change.

1 pt: Any one example: mosquitoes and DDT resistance, tuberculosis bacteria and antibiotic resistance.

D. adaptive value of altruism (*3 points maximum*)

1 pt: Definition of altruism: unselfish behavior that appears to reduce the fitness of the individual while increasing the fitness of another.

1 pt: Altruism increases inclusive fitness.

1 pt: Inclusive fitness is the relative ability of an individual to leave to the next generation its own offspring plus offspring of relatives with whom it shares some genes.

1 pt: Selection for behaviors that increase inclusive fitness is kin selection.

1 pt: Any one example: Belding's ground squirrels or bees and haplodiploidy.

1 pt: Reciprocal altruism occurs between unrelated animals with the expectation by the altruist that he will receive a favorable behavior in return.

Question 3 (10 points maximum)

A. predator and prey (*4 points maximum*)

1 pt: A true predator kills and eats another animal.

1 pt: Both predator and prey may evolve camouflage to help them to avoid detection.

1 pt: Fur of predator or prey may be white in winter, brown or another color in summer.

1 pt: Fur of predator or prey may be spotted or striped to provide camouflage in forested backgrounds.

1 pt: Predators may hunt in packs for more effective capture of prey.

1 pt: Prey may form herds or flocks for more efficient vigilance or for a more effective defense.

B. flowers and flower pollinators (*4 points maximum*)

1 pt: Flowers and their pollinators form a mutualistic relationship.

1 pt: Flowers provide rewards, such as nectar and pollen, to attract pollinators.

1 pt: Pollinators, such as bees, moths, butterflies, and beetles, transfer pollen between flowers.

1 pt: Flower color is an evolved mechanism to attract specific pollinators, such as birds (attracted to red and yellow), or bees (yellow, blue, purple).

1 pt: Flower odor is an evolved mechanism to attract night pollinators such as moths and bats.

1 pt: Flowers often have nectar guides, ultraviolet patterns on petals that help direct the flight of pollinators.

1 pt: Pollinators, such as butterflies, moths, and bats, have evolved long tongues to help them obtain nectar and pollen.

1 pt: Any additional flower or pollinator structures or behaviors that are examples of coevolution.

C. plants and leaf-eating insects (*4 points maximum*)

1 pt: Leaf-eating insects are herbivores, animals with a predatory lifestyle.

1 pt: Plants have evolved chemicals that are toxic to herbivores.

1 pt: Any one chemical of a plant used to deter insects: tannins, nicotine, caffeine, cocaine, opium, oils of mustard, cinnamon, cloves, or mint.

1 pt: Insects have evolved physiological mechanisms to break down plant toxins.

1 pt: The monarch butterfly uses the toxins it ingests from the milkweed plant for its own defense.

1 pt: Plants have evolved sticky or prickly hairs to thwart the movement of insects over their surfaces.

1 pt: Some moth caterpillars bite off prickly plant hairs before feeding.

1 pt: Any additional plant defense against leaf-eating insects or leaf-eating insect mechanism for avoiding plant defenses.

Question 4 (10 points maximum)

A. graph of data (*3 points maximum*)

1 pt: Axes oriented correctly: *x*-axis—temperature; *y*-axis—beats/min.

1 pt: Data plotted correctly (one error in data point entry allowed).

1 pt: Graph has title, correct linear scaling, labels, and units.

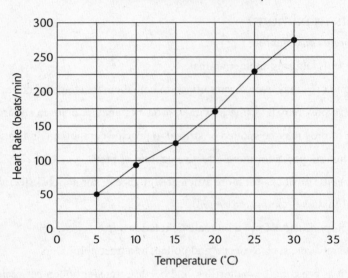

Heart Rate of the Water Flea *Daphnia*

B. why temperature affects heart rate (*3 points maximum*)

1 pt: For an ectothermic organism such as *Daphnia,* its internal temperature increases as the temperature of its surroundings increases.

1 pt: A higher body temperature increases the rate of chemical reactions and as a result increases the rate of physiological processes.

1 pt: An increase in temperature lowers the required activation energy for chemical reactions.

1 pt: As body temperature rises and the rate of physiological processes increases, the need for oxygen for respiration increases.

C. different results for endothermic organism (*2 points maximum*)

1 pt: For an endothermic organism, body temperature is internally controlled and normally does not increase significantly with environmental temperature.

1 pt: The graph results would show a horizontal line, indicating no change in heart rate with changes in environmental temperature.

D. chirp rate of crickets vs. environmental temperature (*4 points maximum*)

1 pt: Identify variables: temperature is independent, chirp rate is dependent.

1 pt: Describe experimental procedure: use a single species of cricket.

1 pt: Describe experimental procedure: test subjects must be as similar as possible to avoid introducing uncontrolled variables: all about the same age, same size, all male (only males chirp).

1 pt: Provide a graph showing temperature (*x*-axis) versus chirps/min (*y*-axis).

1 pt: Justification for prediction: an increase in environmental temperature increases body temperature of ectothermic organisms, which, in turn, increases physiological processes.

Answer Sheet for Practice Exam 3

1 Ⓐ Ⓑ Ⓒ Ⓓ Ⓔ	26 Ⓐ Ⓑ Ⓒ Ⓓ Ⓔ	51 Ⓐ Ⓑ Ⓒ Ⓓ Ⓔ	76 Ⓐ Ⓑ Ⓒ Ⓓ Ⓔ
2 Ⓐ Ⓑ Ⓒ Ⓓ Ⓔ	27 Ⓐ Ⓑ Ⓒ Ⓓ Ⓔ	52 Ⓐ Ⓑ Ⓒ Ⓓ Ⓔ	77 Ⓐ Ⓑ Ⓒ Ⓓ Ⓔ
3 Ⓐ Ⓑ Ⓒ Ⓓ Ⓔ	28 Ⓐ Ⓑ Ⓒ Ⓓ Ⓔ	53 Ⓐ Ⓑ Ⓒ Ⓓ Ⓔ	78 Ⓐ Ⓑ Ⓒ Ⓓ Ⓔ
4 Ⓐ Ⓑ Ⓒ Ⓓ Ⓔ	29 Ⓐ Ⓑ Ⓒ Ⓓ Ⓔ	54 Ⓐ Ⓑ Ⓒ Ⓓ Ⓔ	79 Ⓐ Ⓑ Ⓒ Ⓓ Ⓔ
5 Ⓐ Ⓑ Ⓒ Ⓓ Ⓔ	30 Ⓐ Ⓑ Ⓒ Ⓓ Ⓔ	55 Ⓐ Ⓑ Ⓒ Ⓓ Ⓔ	80 Ⓐ Ⓑ Ⓒ Ⓓ Ⓔ
6 Ⓐ Ⓑ Ⓒ Ⓓ Ⓔ	31 Ⓐ Ⓑ Ⓒ Ⓓ Ⓔ	56 Ⓐ Ⓑ Ⓒ Ⓓ Ⓔ	81 Ⓐ Ⓑ Ⓒ Ⓓ Ⓔ
7 Ⓐ Ⓑ Ⓒ Ⓓ Ⓔ	32 Ⓐ Ⓑ Ⓒ Ⓓ Ⓔ	57 Ⓐ Ⓑ Ⓒ Ⓓ Ⓔ	82 Ⓐ Ⓑ Ⓒ Ⓓ Ⓔ
8 Ⓐ Ⓑ Ⓒ Ⓓ Ⓔ	33 Ⓐ Ⓑ Ⓒ Ⓓ Ⓔ	58 Ⓐ Ⓑ Ⓒ Ⓓ Ⓔ	83 Ⓐ Ⓑ Ⓒ Ⓓ Ⓔ
9 Ⓐ Ⓑ Ⓒ Ⓓ Ⓔ	34 Ⓐ Ⓑ Ⓒ Ⓓ Ⓔ	59 Ⓐ Ⓑ Ⓒ Ⓓ Ⓔ	84 Ⓐ Ⓑ Ⓒ Ⓓ Ⓔ
10 Ⓐ Ⓑ Ⓒ Ⓓ Ⓔ	35 Ⓐ Ⓑ Ⓒ Ⓓ Ⓔ	60 Ⓐ Ⓑ Ⓒ Ⓓ Ⓔ	85 Ⓐ Ⓑ Ⓒ Ⓓ Ⓔ
11 Ⓐ Ⓑ Ⓒ Ⓓ Ⓔ	36 Ⓐ Ⓑ Ⓒ Ⓓ Ⓔ	61 Ⓐ Ⓑ Ⓒ Ⓓ Ⓔ	86 Ⓐ Ⓑ Ⓒ Ⓓ Ⓔ
12 Ⓐ Ⓑ Ⓒ Ⓓ Ⓔ	37 Ⓐ Ⓑ Ⓒ Ⓓ Ⓔ	62 Ⓐ Ⓑ Ⓒ Ⓓ Ⓔ	87 Ⓐ Ⓑ Ⓒ Ⓓ Ⓔ
13 Ⓐ Ⓑ Ⓒ Ⓓ Ⓔ	38 Ⓐ Ⓑ Ⓒ Ⓓ Ⓔ	63 Ⓐ Ⓑ Ⓒ Ⓓ Ⓔ	88 Ⓐ Ⓑ Ⓒ Ⓓ Ⓔ
14 Ⓐ Ⓑ Ⓒ Ⓓ Ⓔ	39 Ⓐ Ⓑ Ⓒ Ⓓ Ⓔ	64 Ⓐ Ⓑ Ⓒ Ⓓ Ⓔ	89 Ⓐ Ⓑ Ⓒ Ⓓ Ⓔ
15 Ⓐ Ⓑ Ⓒ Ⓓ Ⓔ	40 Ⓐ Ⓑ Ⓒ Ⓓ Ⓔ	65 Ⓐ Ⓑ Ⓒ Ⓓ Ⓔ	90 Ⓐ Ⓑ Ⓒ Ⓓ Ⓔ
16 Ⓐ Ⓑ Ⓒ Ⓓ Ⓔ	41 Ⓐ Ⓑ Ⓒ Ⓓ Ⓔ	66 Ⓐ Ⓑ Ⓒ Ⓓ Ⓔ	91 Ⓐ Ⓑ Ⓒ Ⓓ Ⓔ
17 Ⓐ Ⓑ Ⓒ Ⓓ Ⓔ	42 Ⓐ Ⓑ Ⓒ Ⓓ Ⓔ	67 Ⓐ Ⓑ Ⓒ Ⓓ Ⓔ	92 Ⓐ Ⓑ Ⓒ Ⓓ Ⓔ
18 Ⓐ Ⓑ Ⓒ Ⓓ Ⓔ	43 Ⓐ Ⓑ Ⓒ Ⓓ Ⓔ	68 Ⓐ Ⓑ Ⓒ Ⓓ Ⓔ	93 Ⓐ Ⓑ Ⓒ Ⓓ Ⓔ
19 Ⓐ Ⓑ Ⓒ Ⓓ Ⓔ	44 Ⓐ Ⓑ Ⓒ Ⓓ Ⓔ	69 Ⓐ Ⓑ Ⓒ Ⓓ Ⓔ	94 Ⓐ Ⓑ Ⓒ Ⓓ Ⓔ
20 Ⓐ Ⓑ Ⓒ Ⓓ Ⓔ	45 Ⓐ Ⓑ Ⓒ Ⓓ Ⓔ	70 Ⓐ Ⓑ Ⓒ Ⓓ Ⓔ	95 Ⓐ Ⓑ Ⓒ Ⓓ Ⓔ
21 Ⓐ Ⓑ Ⓒ Ⓓ Ⓔ	46 Ⓐ Ⓑ Ⓒ Ⓓ Ⓔ	71 Ⓐ Ⓑ Ⓒ Ⓓ Ⓔ	96 Ⓐ Ⓑ Ⓒ Ⓓ Ⓔ
22 Ⓐ Ⓑ Ⓒ Ⓓ Ⓔ	47 Ⓐ Ⓑ Ⓒ Ⓓ Ⓔ	72 Ⓐ Ⓑ Ⓒ Ⓓ Ⓔ	97 Ⓐ Ⓑ Ⓒ Ⓓ Ⓔ
23 Ⓐ Ⓑ Ⓒ Ⓓ Ⓔ	48 Ⓐ Ⓑ Ⓒ Ⓓ Ⓔ	73 Ⓐ Ⓑ Ⓒ Ⓓ Ⓔ	98 Ⓐ Ⓑ Ⓒ Ⓓ Ⓔ
24 Ⓐ Ⓑ Ⓒ Ⓓ Ⓔ	49 Ⓐ Ⓑ Ⓒ Ⓓ Ⓔ	74 Ⓐ Ⓑ Ⓒ Ⓓ Ⓔ	99 Ⓐ Ⓑ Ⓒ Ⓓ Ⓔ
25 Ⓐ Ⓑ Ⓒ Ⓓ Ⓔ	50 Ⓐ Ⓑ Ⓒ Ⓓ Ⓔ	75 Ⓐ Ⓑ Ⓒ Ⓓ Ⓔ	100 Ⓐ Ⓑ Ⓒ Ⓓ Ⓔ

CUT HERE

Section I (Multiple-Choice Questions)

Time: 80 minutes

100 questions

Directions: Each of the following questions or statements is followed by five possible answers or sentence completions. Choose the one best answer or sentence completion.

1. If ATP is being produced in the cytosol, it is generated by which of the following processes?

   A. glycolysis
   B. Krebs cycle (citric acid cycle)
   C. alcoholic fermentation
   D. lactate fermentation
   E. oxidative phosphorylation

2. All of the following are proteins EXCEPT:

   A. hemoglobin
   B. actin
   C. immunoglobulin
   D. chitin
   E. myosin

3. Which of the following has a dominant haploid generation in its life cycle?

   A. ferns
   B. mosses
   C. club mosses
   D. conifers
   E. angiosperms

4. Assuming there is no crossing over and that A and B are linked genes, which of the following could be true for sperm of the individual with the genotype *AaBb*?

   A. all *AaBb*
   B. ¼ *AABB* + ½ *AaBb* + ¼ *aabb*
   C. ½ *Aa* + ½ *Bb*
   D. ½ *AB* + ½ *ab*
   E. ¼ *AB* + ¼ *Ab* + ¼ *aB* + ¼ *ab*

5. Which of the following best explains why oogenesis in humans produces only one viable ovum and three polar bodies rather than four viable ova?

   A. It is a mechanism for reducing the genetic material to one-half of that contained in the primary oocyte.
   B. It is a mechanism for reducing the genetic material to one-fourth of that contained in the primary oocyte.
   C. The polar bodies help nourish the one viable ovum.
   D. The polar bodies form the yolk.
   E. One viable ovum contains most of the cytoplasm, organelles, and resources that would otherwise be divided among four ova.

6. Which of the following best describes the flow of information within the cell?

   A. RNA → DNA → protein → trait
   B. RNA → DNA → glycoprotein → trait
   C. DNA → trait
   D. DNA → protein → trait
   E. DNA → RNA → polypeptide → trait

GO ON TO THE NEXT PAGE

7. All of the following correctly describe characteristics of an enzyme EXCEPT:

    A. Enzymes are catalysts.

    B. Enzymes are proteins.

    C. An enzyme is highly selective to its substrate.

    D. An enzyme is specific in the direction of activity, only converting reactants into products and not products back into reactants.

    E. Following an enzymatic reaction, an enzyme can be reused to catalyze additional reactions.

8. In which of the following does O_2 interfere with the production of glucose?

    A. Calvin cycle

    B. cyclic photophosphorylation

    C. noncyclic photophosphorylation

    D. photolysis

    E. chemiosmosis

9. The placenta consists of tissue derived from

    A. the fetus only

    B. the mother only

    C. the trophoblast only

    D. the umbilical cord

    E. both the fetus and mother

10. In tropical regions where temperature, precipitation, and light are uniform throughout the year, growth rings that reveal the age of a tree

    A. occur because wood growth in the spring produces larger cells than in the fall

    B. occur because wood growth in the fall produces larger cells than in the spring

    C. occur because cytoplasmic pigmentation is more abundant in spring wood than in winter wood

    D. occur because pigmentation resulting from nutrient storage in vacuoles is greater in winter than in spring

    E. do not occur

11. Which of the following is the correct sequence of developmental events in animal embryos?

    A. morula → blastopore → blastula → gastrulation → blastocoel

    B. morula → blastocoel →blastula → gastrulation → blastopore

    C. morula → blastula → blastopore → blastocoel → gastrulation

    D. blastula → blastocoel → blastopore → morula → gastrulation

    E. blastula → blastocoel → blastopore → morula → gastrulation

12. If mangos, cashews, and poison ivy belong to the plant family Anacadiaceae, all three plants must also belong to the

    A. genus *Rhus*

    B. order Sapindales

    C. genus Toxicodendron

    D. family Solanaceae

    E. domain Archaea

13. All of the following are found in animal cells EXCEPT:

    A. gap junctions

    B. cholesterol in plasma membrane

    C. extracellular matrix

    D. peroxisomes

    E. central vacuole

14. When a plant is put into a chamber that lacks oxygen, the rate of glycolysis is found to increase. This occurs because

    A. as glycolysis increases, ATP production during the Krebs cycle will increase

    B. as glycolysis increases, ATP production during photorespiration will increase

    C. as glycolysis increases, ATP production during oxidative phosphorylation will increase

    D. glycolysis stimulates an increase in photosynthesis

    E. glycolysis generates 2 ATP from the breakdown of glucose

15. Ethylene and cell apoptosis in plants is associated with which of the following?

   A. cytokinesis
   B. bolting
   C. leaf abscission
   D. photosynthesis
   E. germination

16. The chemical colchicine prevents the assembly of microtubules by binding to tubulin protein subunits. Which of the following processes would be most impaired by the application of colchicine?

   A. mitosis
   B. protein synthesis
   C. DNA replication
   D. active transport
   E. chemiosmosis

17. Oligomycin is an antibiotic that blocks proton channels in the cristae of mitochondria by binding to ATP synthase. Which of the following would be the first expected response after the application of oligomycin to cells?

   A. Water production would increase.
   B. ATP production would increase.
   C. H^+ would increase inside the mitochondrial outer compartment (intermembrane space between inner and outer membranes).
   D. H^+ would increase in the matrix (inside mitochondrial inner membrane).
   E. H^+ would increase outside mitochondria.

18. A high surface-to-volume ratio is advantageous in all of the following EXCEPT:

   A. absorption of nutrients through the intestinal wall
   B. water absorption through root hairs
   C. gas exchange through alveoli of lungs
   D. thermoregulation in cold climates
   E. distribution of nutrients across blood vessels

19. In angiosperms, which of the following develops into an embryo after it is fertilized?

   A. the polar nuclei
   B. the embryo sac
   C. the ovule
   D. the egg
   E. the micropyle

20. During a knee-jerk reflex, nerve impulses that originate with a sensory neuron are transmitted

   A. to the brain, which relays the impulses to a motor neuron
   B. to the brain, which relays the impulses through several interneurons before the impulses are transmitted to a motor neuron
   C. to an interneuron, which transmits the impulses to a motor neuron
   D. directly to a motor neuron
   E. directly to a neuromuscular junction

21. The antibiotic penicillin is an enzyme inhibitor that prevents the cross-linking of peptides in peptidoglycan. Why does penicillin stop the growth of certain bacteria but has no effect on the growth of plant or animal cells?

   A. Peptide links are not formed in plant and animal cells.
   B. Only bacteria require peptidoglycan for cell growth.
   C. Plant and animal cells are resistant to penicillin.
   D. Penicillin comes from a fungus that does not cause disease in plants and animals.
   E. Plant and animal cells use a different metabolic pathway to manufacture peptidoglycan than that used by bacteria.

22. Duchenne muscular dystrophy is an X-linked recessive trait that results in muscle deterioration. Death usually occurs before puberty. Assuming that no individual with the disease reaches puberty and passes the gene to the next generation, how can the appearance of the disease be explained in females?

   A. Affected females are homozygous recessive for the Duchenne allele.
   B. Affected females are homozygous dominant for the Duchenne allele.
   C. In females heterozygous for Duchenne muscular dystrophy, both alleles are expressed in muscle cells.
   D. In females heterozygous for Duchenne muscular dystrophy, X-inactivation in muscle cells of the chromosome with the normal allele allows expression of the disease.
   E. The disease cannot occur in females.

GO ON TO THE NEXT PAGE

23. What is the significance of the gray crescent in amphibians?

- **A.** It is the line formed by cells as they invaginate during gastrulation.
- **B.** It must appear in a blastomere if the individual blastomere can successfully be used to produced a normal individual.
- **C.** It forms the notochord.
- **D.** It is the beginning of mesoderm formation.
- **E.** It is the beginning of endosperm formation.

24. To manufacture the components of the plasma membrane, activity from all of the following are required EXCEPT:

- **A.** lysosomes
- **B.** rough ER
- **C.** mRNA
- **D.** Golgi apparatus
- **E.** vesicles

25. The human immunodeficiency virus (HIV) is an RNA virus that generates DNA that becomes integrated into the genome of the host cell. When integrated into the genome of the host cell, HIV is called a(n)

- **A.** nucleovirion
- **B.** episome
- **C.** vector
- **D.** provirus
- **E.** prophage

26. Which of the following describes a product common to oogenesis and spermatogenesis?

- **A.** haploid cells
- **B.** polar bodies
- **C.** flagellated cells
- **D.** four viable daughter cells from one primary oocyte or spermatocyte
- **E.** one daughter cell approximately every 28 days in humans

27. *Nymphaea odorata,* a water lily, is an aquatic plant whose leaves and flowers float on the surface of the water. Which of the following characteristics would be expected for leaves of this plant?

- **A.** stomata on the top surface and relatively few xylem cells
- **C.** stomata on the top surface and relatively many xylem cells
- **B.** stomata on the bottom surface and relatively few xylem cells
- **D.** stomata on the bottom surface and relatively many xylem cells
- **E.** stomata on both top and bottom surfaces and many xylem cells

28. The movement of water across a plasma membrane

- **A.** is facilitated by Na^+/K^+ pumps
- **B.** is facilitated by aquaporin proteins
- **C.** is facilitated by exocytosis
- **D.** is facilitated by pinocytosis
- **E.** occurs passively and never requires assistance

29. All of the following correctly describe sites of antigen recognition EXCEPT:

- **A.** variable regions of antibodies
- **B.** plasma membranes of B cells
- **C.** plasma membranes of T cells
- **D.** plasma membranes of memory cells
- **E.** plasma membranes of erythrocytes

30. Which of the following best describes mitosis?

- **A.** cell division
- **B.** nuclear division
- **C.** cell replication
- **D.** nuclear replication
- **E.** binary fission

31. An individual with which of the following complements of human sex chromosomes is most likely to show the most male features? (Note: A "0" represents the absence of one of the sex chromosomes.)

- **A.** XX
- **B.** XXY
- **C.** XXX
- **D.** 0Y
- **E.** X0

32. Which of the following statements about the nitrogen cycle is TRUE?

    A. The largest reservoir of nitrogen is in the root nodules of legumes.

    B. The abundance of nitrogen is such that it is generally not a limiting factor upon the growth of an ecosystem.

    C. Nitrification is the production by bacteria of NO_3^- from ammonia.

    D. Denitrification is the removal and fixation by bacteria of nitrogen from the atmosphere.

    E. Ammonification is the decomposition by bacteria of ammonia into nitrogen and hydrogen gases.

33. Which of the following tissue types does NOT occur in plants?

    A. parenchyma tissue

    B. ground tissue

    C. adipose tissue

    D. dermal tissue

    E. vascular tissue

34. During alcoholic fermentation, which of the following molecules is the last to accept electrons originally removed from glucose?

    A. oxygen

    B. pyruvate

    C. acetaldehyde

    D. lactate

    E. NAD^+

35. A human tapeworm lives in the small intestines of its hosts. The digestive system of the tapeworm most likely consists of which of the following?

    A. stomach, small intestine, large intestine

    B. stomach, small intestine

    C. stomach, large intestine

    D. small intestine, large intestine

    E. no digestive system

36. The genome of a virus can have any of the following forms EXCEPT:

    A. single-stranded DNA

    B. double-stranded DNA

    C. triple-stranded DNA

    D. single-stranded RNA

    E. double-stranded RNA

37. Which of the following is an energy source for chemoautotrophs?

    A. inorganic molecules

    B. organic molecules

    C. water

    D. carbon dioxide

    E. sunlight

38. In humans, carbohydrate digestion begins in the

    A. mouth

    B. stomach

    C. large intestine

    D. duodenum

    E. small intestine, after the duodenum

39. Which of the following can be described as a disease of the cell cycle?

    A. apoptosis

    B. meiosis

    C. cancer

    D. cell dormancy

    E. inability of a cell to regenerate

40. Water in plant roots that follow the symplastic route

    A. enters the root without passing through a root hair

    B. enters the xylem without passing through the endodermis

    C. passes between cells without entering any cell

    D. passes through the cell walls of cells without passing through the cell membrane of any cell

    E. passes through the plasmodesmata of adjacent cells

41. The reaction $A + B \rightarrow C$ is catalyzed by enzyme K. If the reaction is in equilibrium, which of the following would allow more product C to be produced?

    A. Remove some of reactant A.

    B. Remove some of reactant B.

    C. Remove some of reactant C.

    D. Add more enzyme K.

    E. Increase the temperature of the system.

GO ON TO THE NEXT PAGE

42. Worker honeybees communicate to other workers the location of food sources using all of the following EXCEPT:

    A. the position of the sun

    B. the scent of the flower providing the food source

    C. tactile signals transmitted through dances

    D. visual signals transmitted through dances

    E. audible signals produced from vibrating wings

43. In a C_4 photosynthesis plant, what happens to CO_2 when it enters mesophyll cells in the leaf?

    A. It is fixed by rubisco, and the product is used to make glucose.

    B. It is fixed by rubisco, and the product is transported to bundle sheath cells.

    C. It is fixed by rubisco, and the product is stored in the cytosol.

    D. It is fixed by PEP carboxylase, and the product is stored in the vacuole.

    E. It is fixed by PEP carboxylase, and the product is transported to bundle sheath cells.

44. A common vector used to insert foreign DNA into bacteria is a

    A. plasmid

    B. capsid

    C. mitochondrion

    D. chloroplast

    E. yeast cell

45. As cleavage divisions occur during development from zygote to morula the

    A. individual blastomeres increase in size

    B. individual blastomeres decrease in size

    C. individual blastomeres remain the same size

    D. the entire morula increases in size

    E. the entire morula decreases in size

46. Which of the following has an open circulatory system?

    A. sponge

    B. jellyfish

    C. grasshopper

    D. earthworm

    E. hummingbird

47. All of the following may play a role in determining whether or not a gene is transcribed EXCEPT:

    A. promoter regions in the DNA

    B. TATA box

    C. microtubules

    D. histone acetylation

    E. DNA methylation

48. Which of the following is the *first* event that occurs during fertilization in humans after a sperm cell penetrates an egg?

    A. Meiosis I of the oocyte

    B. Meiosis II of the oocyte

    C. production of a polar body

    D. fusion of sperm nucleus and nucleus of the secondary oocyte

    E. cleavage of the zygote

49. Which of the following is always TRUE when two alleles at the same locus, one dominant and one recessive, occur in a population?

    A. The dominant allele is the more common allele.

    B. The dominant allele is the least common allele.

    C. A gamete bearing the dominant allele is more likely to become fertilized.

    D. The trait encoded by the dominant allele is expressed when it occurs in the heterozygote condition.

    E. The trait encoded by the dominant allele produces the superior trait.

50. More than a dozen species of Darwin's finches with various specialized adaptations inhabit the Galápagos Islands. Each species possesses a specialized adaptation for obtaining food. Why is it that similar adaptations do not exist among the finches of the South American mainland, the presumed origin of the Galápagos finch ancestor?

    A. The various foods available on the mainland are different from those on the Galápagos Islands.

    B. South American predators limited evolution of the mainland finch.

    C. Reproductive isolation is not possible on the mainland.

    D. The available niches that the Darwin's finches exploited on the Galápagos Islands were already occupied by other species of birds on the mainland.

    E. The Galápagos Islands provide a more varied habitat than the mainland.

51. All of the following help prevent the temperature of an animal from getting too cold EXCEPT:

    A. sweating

    B. shivering

    C. constriction of blood vessels

    D. countercurrent exchange

    E. fat or blubber

52. A eukaryotic organism uses sunlight to produce carbohydrates. Which of the following describes the kinds of structures most likely to be found in its light-absorbing cells?

    A. chloroplasts, mitochondria, and peroxisomes

    B. chloroplasts and mitochondria, but no peroxisomes

    C. chloroplasts and peroxisomes, but no mitochondria

    D. chloroplasts, but no mitochondria and no peroxisomes

    E. various membranes, including those for absorbing light, but none is bound within organelle-like bodies

53. Which of the following is true for both erythrocytes and leukocytes in humans?

    A. When mature, both have nuclei.

    B. When mature, both have DNA.

    C. When mature, both have mitochondria.

    D. Both are made in the red bone marrow.

    E. When mature, both are restricted to movement in the bloodstream.

Questions 54–56 refer to the following.

Two genes control hair color in Labrador retrievers. A dominant allele *B* produces black hair pigment, and the recessive allele *b* produces brown pigment. The dominant allele, *E,* of a second gene allows expression of hair pigment, while *e* prevents pigmentation. When pigmentation is prevented, hair color is yellow.

54. All of the following genotypes produce black hair EXCEPT:

    A. *BBEE*

    B. *BBEe*

    C. *BBee*

    D. *BbEE*

    E. *BbEe*

55. What is the probability that a dog with yellow hair will be produced by the cross *BBEE* × *Bbee?*

    A. 0

    B. $\frac{1}{16}$

    C. ¼

    D. ½

    E. ¾

56. The inheritance of hair color in Labrador retrievers by these two genes occurs as result of

    A. incomplete dominance

    B. codominance

    C. pleiotropy

    D. epistasis

    E. linked genes

GO ON TO THE NEXT PAGE

Questions 57–58 refer to the following cladograms.   *Question 59 refers to the following ecological pyramid.*

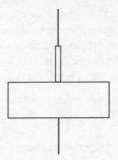

57. The ancestry among taxa A, B, C, and D

   A.   is the same in I and II but is different in III
   B.   is the same in I and III but is different in II
   C.   is the same in II and III but is different in I
   D.   is different in each tree
   E.   is the same in all three trees

58. In Figure II, which of the following two taxa have the most shared characteristics?

   A.   A and B
   B.   A and C
   C.   B and C
   D.   A and D
   E.   C and D

59. If the figure illustrates a pyramid of *numbers,* which of the following would best explain the relative sizes of the trophic levels?

   A.   The lowest trophic level represents decomposers.
   B.   The lowest trophic level represents carnivorous plants.
   C.   The lowest trophic level represents a single tree in a forest.
   D.   The pyramid represents the ecological state of an early successional stage.
   E.   The pyramid construction is in error because the bottom trophic level in a pyramid of numbers must always have more individuals than the level above it.

Directions: Questions that follow consist of a phrase or sentence. Each question is preceded by five lettered choices. Select the one lettered choice that best matches the phrase or sentence. Each lettered choice may be used once, more than once, or not at all.

Questions 60–63 refer to the following.

- **A.** habitat isolation
- **B.** behavioral isolation
- **C.** mechanical isolation
- **D.** hybrid infertility
- **E.** temporal isolation

60. One species of columbine, an herbaceous plant, grows below 3,000 m and is pollinated by hummingbirds, while another columbine species grows above 3,000 m and is pollinated by moths. Hybrids between the two species where their ranges meet are uncommon.

61. A mule produced by a mating between a horse and donkey is sterile.

62. In the Galápagos Islands, the mating ritual of two species of seabirds, the blue-footed booby and the red-footed booby, involves alternately lifting their webbed-feet into the air. The blue-footed booby performs the ritual while on the ground and the red-footed booby performs the ritual in trees.

63. A light-colored form of the green lacewing insect breeds twice a year, in the winter and the summer. A closely related dark form of the insect breeds only during the spring.

Questions 64–66 refer to the following.

- **A.** myosin
- **B.** acetylcholinesterase
- **C.** actin
- **D.** tropomyosin
- **E.** troponin

64. the protein attached to the Z-lines of a sarcomere that pulls both ends of a sarcomere together during muscle contraction

65. the protein to which ATP binds to supply the energy for muscle contraction

66. the protein to which Ca^{2+} must attach in order to initiate muscle contraction

Questions 67–70 refer to the following.

- **A.** ascomycetes
- **B.** basidiomycetes
- **C.** chytridiomycetes
- **D.** oomycetes
- **E.** zygomycetes

67. Spores are not flagellated and most hyphae lack septa.

68. Spores are flagellated and cell walls contain chitin.

69. Sexual reproduction typically bears eight spores enclosed in a sac.

70. Sexual reproduction typically bears four spores at the tip of a stalk.

Questions 71–73 refer to the following figures of DNA fragments.

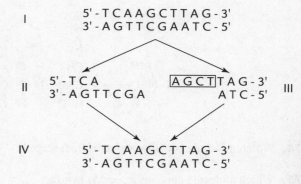

- **A.** DNA polymerase
- **B.** polymerase chain reaction
- **C.** DNA ligase
- **D.** sticky end
- **E.** restriction enzyme

71. The agent that causes the conversion of molecule I to molecules II and III.

72. The sequence AGCT in molecule III

73. The agent that causes the conversion of molecules II and III to molecule IV.

GO ON TO THE NEXT PAGE

Questions 74–77 refer to the following structural formulas.

A.

B.

C.

D.

E.

74. Which molecule contains a glycosidic linkage?

75. Which molecule contains a peptide bond?

76. Which molecule is drawn to show only its primary structure?

77. Which molecule forms a hydrophilic head and a hydrophobic tail?

Questions 78–81 refer to the following map showing the position of islands off the coast of a mainland. Assume that all islands appeared simultaneously in the indicated positions relative to the mainland.

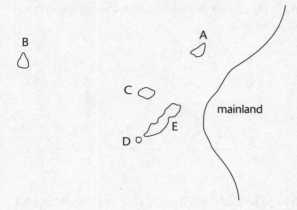

78. Which island would be expected to have the greatest number of species?

79. Which island would be expected to have the fewest number of species?

80. Which island would be expected to have the highest extinction rates?

81. Which island would be expected to have the most endemic species?

GO ON TO THE NEXT PAGE

Directions: Questions that follow involve data from experiments or laboratory analyses. In each case, study the information provided. Then choose the one best answer for each question.

Questions 82–84 refer to the following figure that plots blood pressure changes with time as recorded with a sphygmomanometer. The blood pressure of the patient was determined to be 120/80.

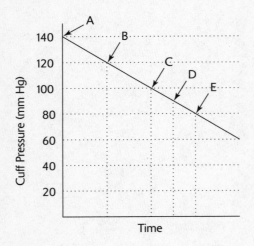

Question 85 refers to the following diagram which shows the change in biomass with time during ecological succession.

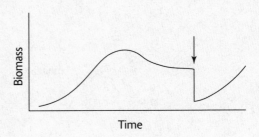

85. Which of the following could be responsible for the biomass crash indicated by the arrow?

    A. fire
    B. storm
    C. earthquake
    D. climate change
    E. disease

82. At what point in the graph are tapping or snapping sounds *first* heard?

83. At what point in the graph do all sounds fade away?

84. Sounds heard during the blood pressure measurements are cause by

    A. heart muscle contracting
    B. heart muscle relaxing
    C. heart valves closing
    D. heart valves being forced open
    E. turbulent blood flow through a constricted blood vessel

Questions 86–89 refer to the following equation:

$$\frac{\Delta N}{\Delta t} = rN \frac{(K-N)}{K}$$

where

    N = population size

    r = intrinsic rate of growth

    t = time

    K = carrying capacity

86. If $r > 0$ and $K > 0$, a plot of population size against time produces which of the following graphs?

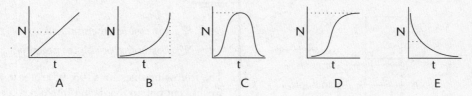

87. When the carrying capacity is equal to the population size, the net rate of increase in the population equals

    A.   less than 0
    B.   0
    C.   1
    D.   the intrinsic rate of growth
    E.   the carrying capacity

88. For which of the following is the net rate of increase in the population greatest?

    A.   when $N = 0$
    B.   when $N = 1$
    C.   when N is small compared to K
    D.   when $N = K$
    E.   when $N > K$

89. The preceding equation is called the

    A.   survivorship equation
    B.   exponential growth equation
    C.   Lotka-Volterra equation
    D.   logistic equation
    E.   Gause's equation

GO ON TO THE NEXT PAGE

Questions 90–92 refer to the following.

A biologist uses paper chromatography to separate pigments obtained from chloroplasts. In this procedure, leaf extracts containing a mixture of pigments are streaked near the bottom edge of a strip of chromatography paper. Chromatography paper is made of cellulose, an organic, polar molecule. The paper is mounted so that its bottom edge makes contact with a relatively nonpolar, organic solvent.

After the paper touches the solvent, the solvent and the pigments in the leaf extract move up the chromatography paper. The figure that follows shows the leading edges of four pigments relative to the point of pigment application.

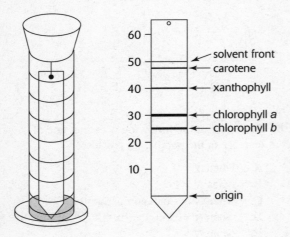

90. The R_f value of a pigment is the ratio of the distance traveled by a pigment to the distance traveled by the solvent. Which pigment has the greatest R_f value?

   A.   carotene
   C.   chlorophyll *a*
   D.   chlorophyll *b*
   B.   xanthophyll
   E.   unable to determine from data provided

91. Which of the following is most responsible for the separation of pigments on the chromatography paper?

   A.   the attraction of the pigment to the chromatography paper
   B.   the speed at which the solvent moves up the chromatography paper
   C.   the time allowed for the solvent to move up the chromatography paper
   D.   the length of the chromatography paper
   E.   the temperature of the solvent

92. Molecules of which of the following are most likely the most polar or contain the most polar groups?

   A.   carotene
   B.   xanthophyll
   C.   chlorophyll *a*
   D.   chlorophyll *b*
   E.   solvent

Questions 93–96 refer to water potential, Ψ, as expressed by the formula

$$\Psi = \Psi_P + \Psi_s$$

where

   Ψ_P = pressure potential and
   Ψ_s = osmotic (or solute) potential.

The following questions (93–95) refer to a section of a freshly cut potato that is put into a beaker of distilled water.

   A.   is greater than 0
   B.   is equal to 0
   C.   is less than 0
   D.   is the same in the distilled water as it is in the potato cell
   E.   cannot be determined from the information given

93. the value of Ψ for the distilled water before the potato is added

94. the value of Ψ_s inside a potato cell before it is added to the water

95. the value of Ψ_P inside a potato cell before it is added to the water

96. Soon after the potato section is added to the water

   A.   the value of Ψ for a potato cell will decrease because water moves into the potato cell
   B.   the value of Ψ_s for a potato cell will decrease because water moves into the potato cell
   C.   the value of Ψ for a potato cell will increase because water moves into the potato cell
   D.   the value of Ψ for a potato cell will increase because water moves out of the potato cell
   E.   the value of Ψ for a potato cell will remain unchanged

Question 97 refers to the following.

Phases of mitosis in a randomly dividing section of a root tip were observed through a microscope in the following numbers.

Phase	Number of Cells
anaphase	15
interphase	40
metaphase	10
prophase	20
telophase	15

97. Which of the following can be correctly concluded from this data

   A. DNA replication occurs during interphase.
   B. Interphase takes longer than all other phases combined.
   C. Metaphase consumes the least amount of time during the cell cycle.
   D. Prophase is the fourth phase in the cell cycle.
   E. Prophase consumes 10 percent of the time required to complete a cell cycle.

Questions 98–100 refer to the following.

   A. conditioning
   B. kinesis
   C. imprinting
   D. taxis
   E. habituation

Pillbugs (or sowbugs) are terrestrial isopods that use modified gills for respiration. A scientist prepares a "choice chamber" that consists of a dry area separated from but connected to a damp area. Ten pillbugs are put into each area. During the next 30 minutes, the scientist observes that the pillbugs put into the dry chamber migrate to the damp chamber. The pillbugs that were put into the damp chamber randomly move within the damp chamber, slowing as time progresses.

98. What kind of behavior was demonstrated by the pillbugs that were put into the dry chamber and who migrated to the damp chamber?

99. What kind of behavior was demonstrated by the pillbugs that were put in the damp chamber and remained in the damp chamber?

100. If the scientist were to count the number of pillbugs in the dry chamber every minute and record the results in graph form, what would be the independent variable?

   A. number of pillbugs
   B. humidity in the dry chamber
   C. humidity in the moist chamber
   D. temperature in the dry chamber
   E. time

GO ON TO THE NEXT PAGE

Section II (Free-Response Questions)

Reading Time: 10 minutes (for organizing your thoughts and outlining your answer)

Writing Time: 90 minutes

1. Establishing a concentration gradient is a critical step to many metabolic processes.

    A. Describe the relationship of a concentration gradient to osmosis.

    B. Describe how a proton gradient is established in chloroplasts and how the gradient is responsible for the generation of ATP.

    C. Describe how a concentration gradient is established around the loop of Henle in human kidneys and how that gradient is responsible for the production of concentrated urine.

2. The plasmid in the following drawing has a length of 12,000 base pairs (12 kilobase pairs). The arrows indicate the site of digestion for enzymes A and B. Assume that digestion of the plasmid by the enzymes is complete.

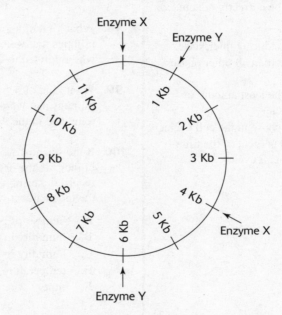

    A. If enzyme X were acting alone, how many fragments would be produced?

    B. If enzyme Y were acting alone, how many base pairs would each fragment produced have?

    C. If both enzymes X and Y are applied to the plasmid, how many base pairs would each fragment produced have?

A diagram of an electrophoresis gel follows. The digested or undigested DNA samples are loaded into the wells (shown as rectangles) at the top of the gel. Use the following plot of migration distances for fragments of known sizes for reference.

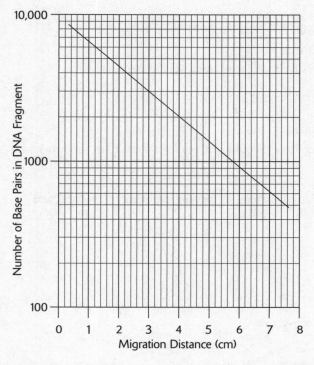

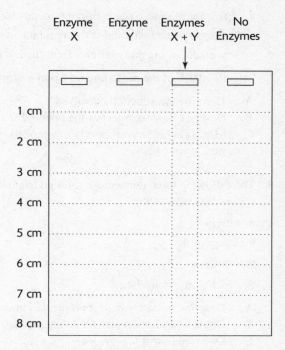

D. Draw a horizontal line (band or bar) on the electrophoresisgel at the correct migration distance to represent each fragment produced by enzymes X and Y. Use the lane (column) marked "Enzyme X + Y."

E. Label each band with the weight (in Kb) of the fragment it represents.

F. Explain why DNA fragments move from the top to the bottom of the figure.

G. Explain why the DNA fragments separate.

GO ON TO THE NEXT PAGE

3. Multicellular organisms must be able to transport materials from one area of the organism to another. Following are examples of five transport systems.

   - Translocation of sugar in angiosperms
   - Transport of water in angiosperms
   - Transport of *most* oxygen through human blood vessels
   - Transport of carbon dioxide through human blood vessels
   - Movement of organic nutrients from the human digestive tract to the circulatory system

   Select THREE of the preceding transport systems. For each system

   A. Describe the structures involved.
   B. Describe how transport of the material is accomplished.
   C. Identify whether transport is accomplished by bulk flow, osmosis, diffusion, or some other process, and justify your answer.

4. The following three items move through trophic levels in ecosystems as they are captured, assimilated, and released by organisms.

   - nitrogen
   - phosphorus
   - energy

   For each of the items listed

   A. Describe its pathway as it progresses through an ecosystem.
   B. Describe its importance for living organisms.
   C. Describe how it is recycled.

Answer Key for Practice Exam 3

Section I (Multiple-Choice Questions)

1. A	26. A	51. A	76. E
2. D	27. A	52. A	77. D
3. B	28. B	53. D	78. E
4. D	29. E	54. C	79. B
5. E	30. B	55. A	80. B
6. E	31. B	56. D	81. B
7. D	32. C	57. A	82. B
8. A	33. C	58. A	83. E
9. E	34. C	59. C	84. E
10. E	35. E	60. B	85. A
11. B	36. C	61. D	86. D
12. B	37. A	62. B	87. B
13. E	38. A	63. E	88. C
14. E	39. C	64. C	89. D
15. C	40. E	65. A	90. A
16. A	41. C	66. E	91. A
17. C	42. D	67. E	92. D
18. D	43. E	68. C	93. B
19. D	44. A	69. A	94. C
20. D	45. B	70. B	95. A
21. B	46. C	71. E	96. C
22. D	47. C	72. D	97. C
23. B	48. B	73. C	98. D
24. A	49. D	74. C	99. B
25. D	50. D	75. E	100. E

Scoring Your Practice Exam

Section I (Multiple-Choice Questions)

Number of questions you answered correctly: _____ × 1   =   _____

Number of questions you answered wrong: _____ × ¼   = $\underline{\hspace{1cm}}$*

Number of questions you left unanswered: _____ × 0   = $\underline{\quad 0 \quad}$

TOTAL for Section I (0–100 points):   =   _____**

(subtract number wrong from number correct)

Round to nearest whole number.

*** If less than zero, enter zero.*

Section II (Free-Response Questions)

For each correct and relevant piece of information you include in your answers to the free-response questions, you earn 1 point. Refer to the scoring standards that follow the multiple-choice explanations.

Score for essay 1 (0–10 points):   _____

Score for essay 2 (0–10 points):   _____

Score for essay 3 (0–10 points):   _____

Score for essay 4 (0–10 points):   _____

Combined Score (Sections I + II)

Total for Section I (from above):   _____ × 0.6 =   _____

(60% of 100 points = 60 points maximum)

Total for Section II (from above):   _____ × 1.0 =   _____

(100% of 40 points = 40 points maximum)

Combined Score (Add Sections I and II) _____

(0–100 points possible)

Probable AP Grade	
61–100	5
47–60	4
39–46	3
30–38	2
0–29	1

Answers and Explanations for Practice Exam 3

1. **A.** Glycolysis occurs in the cytoplasm and generates a net of 2 ATP for each glucose broken down to 2 pyruvates. The Krebs cycle and oxidative phosphorylation generate ATP in the mitochondria. Alcoholic fermentation and lactate fermentation occur in the cytosol, but they don't generate ATP. Instead, fermentation oxidizes NADH to produce NAD^+, which is used to continue glycolysis.

2. **D.** Chitin is a polysaccharide similar to cellulose, except the monomer is a glucose with a nitrogen-containing group (glucosamine). Chitin is found in the cell walls of many fungi, exoskeletons of arthropods (insects, spiders), and shells of crustaceans (crabs, lobsters). Hemoglobin is the oxygen-carrying protein in red blood cells, actin and myosin are the contracting proteins in muscles, and immunoglobulins are a group of proteins that function as antibodies.

3. **B.** The leaf-like stage of mosses is the dominant haploid generation. Within specialized structures of the haploid generation, flagellated sperm and eggs are produced by mitosis. The diploid generation begins with the fertilization of an egg by a sperm. The diploid zygote that results from fertilization grows out of the leafy haploid, producing a stalk with a capsule. Inside the capsule, meiosis produces haploid spores, which, following dispersal and germination, begin the dominant haploid generation again.

4. **D.** If the two genes are linked (on the same chromosome), then one possible arrangement for the two genes in the genotype *AaBb* is that alleles *AB* are together on one chromosome and *ab* are together on its homologous chromosome. If that's the case, then the possible gametes are ½ *AB* and ½ *ab*, because, following meiosis, each chromosome (and ultimately each chromatid of each chromosome) will end up in a separate sperm. Although the answer choice is not provided, another possibility is that the alleles are arranged so that *Ab* and *aB* are on each homologue, producing gametes that are ½ *Ab* and ½ *aB*.

5. **E.** In order to maximize the resources available to a fertilized ovum, the maximum amount of cytoplasm, containing as many of the organelles as possible, is concentrated in one surviving cell.

6. **E.** DNA carries the hereditary information of the cell. In order for that information to be used to build or control a cell, the DNA information is used to make RNA (the process called transcription), which, in turn, is used to make polypeptides, or proteins (the process called translation). Proteins that act as catalysts (enzymes) regulate chemical reactions that give the cell its traits and maintain the cell in working order.

7. **D.** Enzymes catalyze a reaction in the forwards or backwards direction depending on the concentrations of reactants and products and the equilibrium constant for the reaction.

8. **A.** Rubisco (ribulose bisphosphate carboxylase oxygenase) is the enzyme that fixes CO_2 (incorporates CO_2 into an organic molecule). Unfortunately, rubisco fixes O_2 as well. (Note that the last two words of rubisco indicate that it is a carboxylase and an oxygenase, acting upon both carbon and oxygen.) As a result, the efficiency of CO_2 fixation is decreased. The effect of damaging products from O_2 fixation is partially remediated by peroxisome activity.

9. **E.** Both the outer layer of the blastocyst (the trophoblast) and the lining of the uterus (the endometrium) commingle to become the placenta. Wastes and CO_2 from the embryo (and later, the fetus) travel through the umbilical cord to the placenta where they diffuse from the blood vessels of the embryo into blood vessels of the mother. Oxygen and nutrients follow the opposite pathway.

10. **E.** Growth rings appear because of the variations in precipitation, temperature, and light that occur with changing seasons. At the beginning of the growing season when water availability and light are increasing, xylem cells are large. At the end of the growing season, xylem cells are small. Large cells appear as light-colored rings, while small cells, consisting of mostly cell walls with little interior, appear dark colored. One light-colored ring together with one dark colored ring represent one year of growth. Because many tropical regions lack seasonal variation, growth rings are not distinct.

11. **B.** Early cleavage divisions form the morula, a solid ball of 16–64 cells. During subsequent divisions fluid forms in the center, creating a cavity (the blastocoel). Following formation of the blastocoel, the embryo is called a blastula. Gastrulation begins as a group of cells invaginate (move inward), producing a two-layered embryo. The opening formed by the invagination is the blastopore.

12. B. If the three plants belong to the same family, they must all be in the same order (the taxon above, or more inclusive than family).

13. E. A central vacuole is unique to plant cells. Peroxisomes are found in both plants and animals. Gap junctions and cholesterol-containing plasma membranes surrounded by an extracellular matrix of glycolipids and glycoproteins occur only in animals.

14. E. In the absence of O_2, a plant can still do photosynthesis to obtain ATP. In fact, in the absence of O_2, it can do photosynthesis even better than if O_2 were present (because photorespiration would be avoided). But in this case, a continuation of glycolysis in the absence of O_2 must signal that photosynthesis cannot occur (perhaps because of darkness). The next best available option when O_2 and photosynthesis are not available is glycolysis. Glycolysis produces a net of 2 ATP. Eventually, however, glycolysis would stop because as glycolysis proceeds, NAD^+ is used up as it is all converted to NADH. This occurs because in the absence of oxygen, oxidative phosphorylation is not available to convert the NADH back to NAD^+. However, alcoholic fermentation (an anaerobic pathway) is available to plants for exactly this purpose—to convert NADH back to NAD^+.

15. C. Leaf abscission is the dropping of leaves from deciduous trees when the weather turns colder and the daylight hours shorten as winter approaches. Increasing amounts of ethylene (relative to decreasing amounts of auxin) promote cell apoptosis, or programmed cell death. Abscission begins with the removal from the leaf of recyclable nutrients followed by the development of an abscission zone consisting of a layer of fragile cells and a protective layer of cork over the remaining stem.

16. A. Microtubules are the components of the spindle apparatus used in mitosis (and meiosis). The microtubules organize the chromosomes, separate the chromosomes into chromatids, and tow the chromatids to opposite poles that eventually become nuclei of the daughter cells. Because colchicine prevents microtubule assembly, mitosis cannot advance beyond prophase.

17. C. If the proton channels associated with ATP synthase are blocked, H^+ cannot move from the mitochondrial outer compartment across the cristae membranes into the matrix. The expectation, then, is that H^+ concentration increases in the mitochondrial outer compartment (becomes more acidic).

18. D. As surface-to-volume ratio increases, the amount of materials that are able to move in and out of a structure increases. Thermoregulation in cold climates favors a low surface-to-volume ratio to minimize the loss of heat from inside a body.

19. D. After the egg is fertilized by a sperm nucleus, it becomes the embryo. The ovules are the bodies in the ovary of the flower that contain the megaspore mother cells. A megaspore mother cell divides by meiosis to produce four haploid daughter cells. One of those haploid cells survives and divides by mitosis three times to produce eight daughter nuclei, all enclosed within the cell membrane of the original daughter cell (and forming the embryo sac). All of this is still enclosed within the original ovule, which is still attached to the ovary of the flower. In summary and in descending order of size, the ovary of the flower contains ovules which contain the megaspore mother cell which divides to form 8 nuclei, one of which is the egg, which, after fertilization by a pollen nucleus, becomes the embryo (ovary $\rightarrow$ ovule $\rightarrow$ megaspore mother cell $\rightarrow$ egg $\rightarrow$ embryo). The ovary develops into the fruit.

20. D. The knee-jerk reflex is the simplest reflex and involves only a sensory and a motor neuron. Other reflexes may be more involved, with a reflex arc (pathway) that passes through an interneuron in the spinal cord or brain stem. Generally, it is the spinal cord that is responsible for sensory integration and motor response during a reflex. Keep in mind that as a reflex occurs, other neurons are also stimulated that may inhibit the reflex or that may send other signals to the brain.

21. B. Peptidoglycan is a sugar-protein polymer unique to the cell walls of bacteria. Because animals do not have cell walls and the cell walls of plants are made from cellulose, penicillin does not interfere with animal or plant metabolism.

22. D. Because Duchenne muscular dystrophy is an X-linked recessive trait, adult males are only $X^N Y$ (letting $N =$ normal and $n =$ muscular dystrophy). Males who are $X^n Y$ do not reach reproductive age. Adult females are $X^N X^N$ or $X^N X^n$; there are no $X^n X^n$ females because no adult males have an X^n chromosome to pass to offspring. Since Duchenne muscular dystrophy is recessive, females who are $X^N X^N$ or $X^N X^n$ should not express the trait. However, one of the female X chromosomes will be inactivated in each cell early in embryonic development. Which of the two X chromosomes in each cell that is inactivated is random, but all cells descended from each of these original embryonic cells will have the same X chromosome inactivated. Those $X^N X^n$ females whose muscle cells have X^n expressed (X^N inactivated) will express the muscular dystrophy trait. The purpose of X-inactivation is to allow an equal dosage of X-chromosome genes for females (who have two X chromosomes) and males (who have only one X chromosome). This is called dosage compensation.

23. **B.** In a famous experiment, Hans Spemann manipulated the early development of a frog egg so that only some of the descendent cells contained remnants of the gray crescent material, a gray region that appears in blastomeres (daughter cells) during early cleavage divisions of the embryo. Spemann then separated the blastomeres and allowed each to grow into a new individual. Only those blastomeres with gray crescent material developed into a normal frog.

24. **A.** As bodies that specialize in the breakdown of materials, lysosomes are unnecessary for construction of the plasma membrane. In contrast, the mRNA is necessary for assembling amino acids into proteins, the rough endoplasmic reticulum adds polysaccharides to proteins to form glycoproteins, Golgi bodies modify glycoproteins, and vesicles shuttle materials from one place to another and finally to the plasma membrane.

25. **D.** A provirus is a virus whose genetic material has become incorporated into the genome of its host cell. If the virus is one that attacks bacteria, the virus is called a bacteriophage, or phage, and the bacteriophage is called a prophage when its DNA has become incorporated into the bacterial chromosome.

26. **A.** Oogenesis is the production of haploid eggs and spermatogenesis is the production of haploid sperm. Only oogenesis produces polar bodies, and only spermatogenesis produces flagellated sperm. Following puberty, oogenesis in humans occurs about every 28 days, and spermatogenesis occurs continuously.

27. **A.** Because only the top surface of the leaf is exposed to air, stomata occur only on that surface. Xylem, the tissue that transports water, is not necessary because all leaf cells interface directly or nearly directly with the surrounding water. Also, the spongy mesophyll has many large air spaces that help provide buoyancy for the floating leaves.

28. **B.** The function of aquaporin proteins in the plasma membranes of cells is to speed up the transfer of water (and other small molecules) across the membranes. Although these proteins are the subject of advanced research and have not yet found their way into many undergraduate textbooks, researchers who described the structure of aquaporins received a Nobel prize in chemistry in 2003, and, as a result, questions about aquaporins could appear on an AP exam.

29. **E.** The major function of erythrocytes, or red blood cells, is to transport oxygen attached to hemoglobin. Erythrocytes do not have an immune system function. B cells and T cells and memory cells of B cells and T cells have antigen recognition sites on their plasma membranes. Antibodies are proteins with constant regions (where polypeptide sequence is constant among antibody proteins) and variable regions (where polypeptide sequence varies among antibodies). The variable region of antibodies provides the antigen-binding site.

30. **B.** Mitosis is the division of the chromosomal material in the nucleus of a cell into two sets of chromosomal material in two nuclei. In contrast, cytokinesis is the process that describes the division of the cytoplasm to form two separate daughter cells. Replication of the DNA (making copies of the existing DNA) takes place when the nuclei and cell are not dividing (interphase, or the S phase of the cell cycle). In prokaryotes (bacteria), binary fission is a process that *does* include replication of DNA and division of the cell into two daughter cells. But a prokaryote does not have a nucleus, and so mitosis (or a process like mitosis) is not necessary.

31. **B.** The *presence* of a Y chromosome determines maleness, not its absence. The 0Y complement cannot produce a viable embryo because the missing X chromosome provides essential genes.

32. **C.** Nitrification by bacteria increases the nitrogen in the soil that is available to plants by these processes: $NH_4^+ \rightarrow NO_2^-$ (nitrite) and $NO_2^- \rightarrow NO_3^-$ (nitrate). Denitrification is the conversion by denitrifying bacteria of NO_3^- back to NO_2^- and N_2. Denitrification contributes to a loss of nitrogen from the soil to the atmosphere. Ammonification also contributes to the loss of available nitrogen in the soil by converting the nitrogen in nitrogen-containing compounds back to ammonia (NH_4^+ or NH_3). Even though the atmosphere is a reservoir for a huge amount of nitrogen (as nitrogen gas, N_2), nitrogen in gaseous form cannot be used by plants. In general, nitrogen is the greatest limiting factor to plant growth.

33. **C.** Adipose tissue is found in animals and consists of adipose cells that store fat. All of the remaining answers are tissues that occur in plants: dermal tissue (epidermis and periderm), ground tissue (parenchyma, collenchyma, sclerenchyma), and vascular tissue (xylem and phloem).

34. C. During glycolysis, the energized electrons from glucose are passed to NAD$^+$ to form NADH. During fermentation, the electrons from NADH are transferred to acetaldehyde to form ethanol. The purpose of fermentation is to replenish the NAD$^+$ needed to allow glycolysis to continue (in the absence of oxygen).

35. E. A tapeworm does not need a digestive system because the materials it absorbs from the digestive track of its hosts are already (conveniently) broken down (digested).

36. C. There are no forms of DNA that are triple-stranded, in viruses or any other living thing.

37. A. Chemoautotrophs obtain energy from inorganic molecules, such as NH_3, H_2S, Fe^{2+}, NO^{2-}, or SO^{3-}, for the reduction of CO_2 to form carbohydrates.

38. A. Carbohydrate digestion begins in the mouth with the digestion of starches into maltose molecules or into oligosaccharides by salivary amylase, an enzyme secreted by the salivary glands.

39. C. The cell cycle is controlled by cellular mechanisms that instruct the cell to prepare for subsequent phases (ultimately leading to mitosis) or to maintain a holding pattern. During the G_1 phase of the cell cycle, for example, the overall status of the cell is evaluated, and a signal to continue would advance the cycle to the S phase (where DNA replication occurs) and then on to preparations for mitosis. Alternatively, the cell may not go forward and instead remain a nondividing cell in the G_0 phase. A cancerous cell appears to lose the mechanisms that regulate the cell cycle and divides repeatedly without regard for its effects on other cells. Because cancerous cells divide uncontrollably, it is considered a disease of the cell cycle. In contrast, apoptosis is programmed cell death. This is a normal, scheduled event in the life of a cell, as all cells die (and are usually replaced with new cells). Similarly, when normal cells remain in a nondividing state (like most neurons), it is because that is the programmed fate for that cell.

40. E. The symplast is the route that consists entirely of cytoplasm, passing from cell to cell through plasmodesmata. The apoplastic route is the pathway confined within cell walls or extracellular spaces. In order to enter the vascular cylinder, water must enter the symplast of the endodermis, because the apoplastic route through the cell walls of the endodermal cells is blocked by the Casparian strip (a band of waxy, water-impenetrable material called suberin).

41. C. The reaction is in equilibrium because the concentrations of reactants and product are such that the rate of the forward reaction (formation of product C) equals that of the reverse reaction (formation of A and B from C), and the *net* production of C (or A and B) is zero. By decreasing C, the forward reaction will again exceed that of the reverse reaction, producing more C, until equilibrium is reached again. Adding more enzyme would only help if the reaction were not in equilibrium and there were a considerable excess of reactants (essentially, not enough enzyme to go around). Increasing the temperature could increase the rate of reactions (in *both* directions), but if the reaction is in equilibrium, the net production of product will still be zero.

42. D. Visual signals would not be a very effective means of communication inside a *dark* beehive. Visual signals that are often perceived through sight, such as those provided with the round and waggle bee dances, however, can be communicated through touch (tactile sense). The bee dances are often performed on vertical surfaces of the hive with an angle adjustment relative to the position of the sun. This imparts information about the location of and distance to a food source. Wing vibrations of the dancers and food scents on their bodies provide additional information about the food source.

43. E. In C_4 plants, PEP carboxylase fixes carbon dioxide, forming malate. The malate is transported to bundle sheath cells (specialized cells surrounding small leaf veins). Within the bundle sheath cells, the CO_2 in malate is released, and the Calvin cycle carries out the processes associated with C_3 photosynthesis to produce glucose. The purpose of all this extra activity is to transport the CO_2 to an area of the plant where there is less free oxygen (away from the spongy mesophyll). Within the bundle sheath cells, fixation of CO_2 by the enzyme rubisco can occur without competition from oxygen, which rubisco will also fix if it is available. As a result, carbon fixation is increased and photorespiration is minimized for C_4 plants.

44. A. Bacterial plasmids (as well as viruses) are useful vectors for recombinant DNA research. Foreign DNA can easily be added to plasmids, and plasmids can easily be transferred back to the bacteria (by transformation).

45. B. As the cells divide, the blastomeres (daughter cells) get smaller because no cell growth occurs between divisions.

46. **C.** Grasshoppers and other arthropods have an open circulatory system where a heart pumps blood into a single cavity (hemocoel) or into multiple cavities (sinuses). In a closed circulatory system, such as those found in earthworms and hummingbirds, blood always remains within blood vessels. In simple architectures, like sponges and jellyfish, a formal circulatory system is unnecessary because all cells are near enough to the external environment to absorb food as it passes by. In sponges, for example, flagellated choanocytes (collar cells) move water through chambers bordered by cells. In jellyfish and other cnidarians, water and food pass into an internal gastrovascular cavity where both digestion and absorption occurs.

47. **C.** Microtubules are not known to be involved in the regulation of gene transcription. Regulatory genes, operator regions, and promoter regions (and the TATA box), on the other hand, are all involved in controlling which regions of DNA will be transcribed. Various feedback mechanisms (such as those in the *lac* operon or the *trp* operon) may influence whether transcription will be turned on or off. Nucleosome packing also influences whether a section of DNA will be transcribed. Packing includes acetylation (addition of acetyl groups) of histones and methylation (addition of methyl groups) of histones and DNA. These mechanisms serve to retain DNA in a tightly coiled state or to allow uncoiling of a specific DNA region that would permit its transcription.

48. **B.** Meiosis I and prophase of meiosis II occur before ovulation (during embryonic development and during the follicular phase of the menstrual cycle). After a sperm enters the egg, meiosis II in the egg resumes, producing a polar body (which is discharged from the cell) and an ovum. Finally, the chromosomes from both the ovum and sperm nuclei are pulled together by a mitotic spindle, which begins a mitosis that results in the first cleavage division.

49. **D.** The trait encoded by the dominant allele is expressed when an individual inherits the homozygote dominant or heterozygote genotypes. It is a common misconception that dominant alleles are necessarily more common than or more adaptive than the recessive alleles. For example, an allele that causes a form of dwarfism is both dominant and rare. In fact, any allele that is dominant and codes for a deleterious or severely debilitating disease is very likely to be rare because an individual need inherit only one copy of the allele to express the trait. If the trait is expressed, death occurs before puberty or, if the individual survives, the trait may prevent the onset of puberty. Thus, the allele cannot be passed on to the next generation. Its recurrence in the population must originate from mutation.

50. **D.** All available niches on the mainland were long ago filled by species who, over millions of years, became highly specialized for their niches. Whereas the woodpecker finch is well adapted for seeking insects on the Galápagos Islands, various species of woodpeckers are even more specialized for the same purpose on the mainland. Had an actual woodpecker found its way to the Galápagos Islands before the adaptive radiation of finches, evolution of the woodpecker finch would have been unlikely.

51. **A.** The purpose for sweating is to keep an animal from getting too hot. As sweat evaporates from skin, the energy required to change the state of water (the sweat) from a liquid to a vapor is carried away with the vapor, thus cooling the body. In contrast, shivering generates heat as energy is transferred from ATP to the motion of contracting muscle protein. Constriction of blood vessels in extremities of the body (fingers and toes) prevents heat loss in areas with a high surface-to-volume ratio. In countercurrent exchange, heat from "outgoing" blood (in vessels going to a cold extremity) diffuses into "incoming" blood (vessels returning to internal body areas).

52. **A.** In eukaryotes, chloroplasts carry out photosynthesis to produce glucose. Glucose is broken down by mitochondria to supply energy when photosynthesis cannot occur (at night, for example). Peroxisomes break down damaging products of photorespiration.

53. **D.** Both erythrocytes (red blood cells) and leukocytes (white blood cells) are made in the red bone marrow, although many leukocytes mature in the thymus, spleen, or lymph nodes. Erythrocytes lack DNA, nuclei, mitochondria, and most other organelles. The absence of these organelles allows the erythrocytes to carry more hemoglobin (and the oxygen that attaches to the hemoglobin).

54. **C.** The genotype *BBee* is yellow because *ee* prevents pigmentation. All other genotypes are either *BB* or *Bb* with at least one *E* allele to allow pigmentation.

55. **A.** In order to have yellow hair, the genotype must contain two recessive copies of the *E* gene. This cross, *EE* × *ee* → *Ee*, cannot produce an offspring that is yellow (*ee*). In order to produce an offspring with a genotype containing *ee*, both parents must have at least one *e* allele.

56. D. Epistasis describes inheritance when one gene (like *E*) influences or masks the expression of another gene (like *B*).

57. A. Cladograms I and II are the same. This can be seen by rotating the branches in II, as shown here.

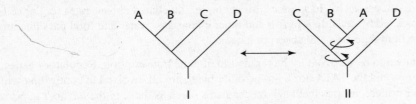

58. A. The taxa in cladogram II (or I, because I and II are the same) that have the most shared characteristics are A and B. The number of branch points between A and B are fewer than between any other taxa in the tree.

59. C. A single tree can support large numbers of insects (represented by the second tier of the pyramid) which can, in turn, support many birds (or other insects) who eat the insects. One or two large predators, such as hawks, may occupy the fourth tier.

60. B. The difference in their pollination mechanisms is a form of behavioral isolation.

61. D. The sterile mule is an example of hybrid infertility. Because mules cannot provide gene flow between donkeys and horses, these two animals remain reproductively isolated.

62. B. Because the mating rituals of the two booby species are different, they are reproductively isolated. This is behavioral isolation. It is not habitat isolation because the actual habitats of the birds overlap (although they choose slightly different areas of the habitat in which to mate).

63. E. Temporal isolation occurs when breeding periods do not overlap.

64. C. The contracting protein that is attached to the Z-lines of a muscle sarcomere is the thin filament actin. The thick filament myosin is not attached to the Z-lines but rather forms cross bridges with actin during contraction.

65. A. ATP binds to the myosin heads and remains attached until the sliding action of contraction begins (when Ca^{2+} allows the myosin cross bridges to attach).

66. E. When Ca^{2+} is released from the sarcoplasmic reticulum, it binds to troponin, which, in turn, causes tropomyosin to change shape, exposing the sites on the actin filament for the myosin heads to attach. Once the myosin heads attach, energy from ATP is released and contraction ensues.

67. E. The hyphae of zygomycetes lack cross walls that would divide the hyphae into separate cells. That makes the hyphae coenocytic, or multinucleate.

68. C. Flagellated spores (zoospores) occur among the chytrids. The spores of the other fungal groups listed are nonmotile. Oomycetes (water molds), which superficially resemble fungi (but are classified with algae), have flagellated spores, but their cell walls do not contain chitin. Instead, their cell walls contain celluose and other β-glucans.

69. A. The asci of ascomycetes are unique in that a single ascus sac contains 8 spores. Meiosis of a 2*n* nucleus produces four haploid (*n*) nuclei. This is followed by mitosis, bringing the total number of nuclei to eight. These nuclei develop into ascospores in a terminal hypha, the nuclei and hypha together forming an ascus. In many ascomycetes, the asci are grouped together in a fruiting body (ascocarp).

70. B. The basidia of basidiomycetes bear four haploid spores that are produced by meiosis. Meiosis is not followed by mitosis (as in ascomycetes), and the spores are not enclosed in a sac (like those of ascomycetes) but are attached to the external surface of hyphae within the fruiting body (basidiocarp).

71. E. Restriction enzymes cut DNA molecules. Like all enzymes, restriction enzymes have active sites that are specific to their substrates, so the sequence of nucleotides on the DNA molecule where the cut occurs is different for different restriction enzymes.

72. **D.** Many restriction enzymes do not make a straight cut across a DNA double helix but instead leave single-stranded DNA tails on the DNA segments produced. These single-stranded DNA tails are called sticky ends.

73. **C.** Catalyzing the union of two DNA segments with complementary sticky ends occurs with the enzyme DNA ligase, the same enzyme that joins Okazaki segments together on the lagging strands of DNA during replication.

74. **C.** This is a drawing of starch. A glycosidic linkage is the bond between two monosaccharides. Numerous αh-glycosidic linkages form when αh-glucose monomers join to form starch, and β-glycosidic linkages form when β-glucose monomers join to form cellulose. Thus, starch and cellulose are polymers of glucose bonded together by glycosidic linkages. When a glycosidic bond forms, a H_2O molecule is released (a dehydration reaction).

75. **E.** This is a drawing of a polypeptide. A peptide bond links two amino acids together. A polypeptide is a polymer of amino acids linked by peptide bonds. When a peptide bond forms, an H_2O molecule is released (a dehydration reaction).

76. **E.** This polypeptide is drawn to show only its primary structure, that is, a linear display of its amino acids. Most functioning polypeptides (proteins) have complex three-dimensional shapes that are essential for their proper functioning.

77. **D.** This is a drawing of a phospholipid. The phosphate group on the left forms a hydrophilic head. The two long hydrocarbon chains extending to the right are hydrophobic tails. Hydrophilic ("water loving") means that a molecule (or group of atoms) has a strong affinity for, or is capable of mixing with or dissolving in, water. Hydrophobic ("water fearing") means the molecule resists mixing with water.

78. **E.** The number of species that colonize an island is proportional to the distance between the island and the mainland and proportional to the size of the island (bigger target for colonization). Island E is the largest island and closest to the mainland. Also, a large island is far more likely to have a greater variety of resources and habitats than one that is smaller and thus can provide niches for a greater number of different species.

79. **B.** In contrast to question 77, the more distance the island is from the mainland, the more difficult it will be for colonizers to successfully reach the island, and the smaller the island, the smaller the target for colonizers. Also, small islands are likely to have fewer and less varied habitats than larger islands, and thus smaller islands are able to support fewer kinds of species.

80. **B.** Small islands are only able to maintain small populations, and small populations have a greater likelihood for extinction. Island B is relatively small. It is also farther away than any other island, making recolonization after extinction more difficult.

81. **B.** Endemic species are maintained by isolation. Island B is the most isolated. Island E, the largest island, is too close to the mainland to maintain the isolation necessary to promote speciation. Note that Island B is about the same size or larger than all the other islands (except, of course, E, which is eliminated for the answer to this question because of its closeness to the mainland), so habitat variation, although generally important to sustain populations, is not a variable for this question.

82. **B.** As the cuff is allowed to depressurize and constriction of the blood vessels decreases, a point is reached where blood begins to flow again through the blood vessels. When this occurs, the blood moving through the still constricted blood vessels experiences turbulence, which in turn generates the tapping or snapping sounds. The pressure reading on the sphygmomanometer at this point is the systolic pressure. In this question, the blood pressure is given as 120/80, so the tapping sounds should begin at 120 mm Hg, the systolic pressure.

83. **E.** When all sounds have disappeared, the pressure reading on the sphygmomanometer is the diastolic pressure. In this question, the blood pressure is given as 120/80, so that all sounds should disappear at 80 mm Hg, the diastolic pressure.

84. **E.** The tapping, snapping, and muffled sounds heard from the stethoscope come from the turbulence of the blood flow created as blood is released into an empty blood vessel.

85. **A.** A sudden and large biomass collapse as shown in this figure is most likely due to fire. Disease, storms, or earthquakes will lead to gradual or selective damage, not the sudden disappearance of almost all the biomass. A devastating fire is capable of incinerating everything but the seeds stored in the ground, although some vegetation usually escapes the fire if the fire is not too hot.

86. **D.** For this, the logistic equation, early stages of growth are depicted by a rapid (logarithmic) rise in the population size, followed by a gradual tapering off of the growth rate as the carrying capacity is approached. When the population size reaches the carrying capacity, the net rate of growth is zero, as expressed by the horizontal line (slope of the line is zero) of the plotted equation.

87. **B.** As the population size approaches the carrying capacity, the growth rate decreases and becomes zero when $N = K$

88. **C.** The net rate of growth is greatest early in the plotted equation, when N is still small compared to K. To see this mathematically, rearrange the equation like this:

$$\frac{\Delta N}{\Delta t} = rN \frac{(K - N)}{K} = rN\left(1 - \frac{N}{K}\right)$$

When N is small compared to K, the fraction N/K is small compared to 1. Thus, $1 - N/K$ is approximately equal to 1 and the value of the equation is maximum and equal to rN.

89. **D.** The equation is called the logistic equation.

90. **A.** The R_f value for carotene is $^{48}/_{50} = 0.96$. All the remaining pigments have a lower R_f.

91. **A.** The reason why one pigment moves faster than another is because it has a lower affinity for the hydrophilic, polar molecules of the chromatography paper. Conversely, the stronger the affinity between pigment and paper, the slower the pigment movement relative to other pigments. The remaining answer choices are not so much responsible for the primary separation of pigments as they are for increasing (or decreasing) the separation that results from the affinity between pigment and paper. There are also some interactions between the pigments and the solvent, but none of the answer choices addresses this.

92. **D.** The more polar the molecule, the greater its attraction to the hydrophilic, polar molecules of cellulose. The greater the attraction, the slower the movement relative to other pigments.

93. **B.** Because there is no pressure applied to the distilled water in the beaker ($\Psi_P = 0$) and because there are no solutes in the distilled water ($\Psi_s = 0$), the value of Ψ for the distilled water is $\Psi = \Psi_P + \Psi_s = 0 + 0 = 0$.

94. **C.** There are solutes in the cytoplasm of cells, so $\Psi_s < 0$.

95. **A.** Pressure is applied to the contents of the cell by the cell wall, so $\Psi_P > 0$.

96. **C.** The value of Ψ for the potato cell is negative before the potato is put into the water. This is because Ψ for any normally hydrated plant cell is negative (that is, Ψ_s is more negative than Ψ_P is positive). Because Ψ for the distilled water is 0 and Ψ for the potato is negative, water, which moves from areas of higher water potential to lower water potential, will move into the potato. As the water concentration increases in the potato cell, Ψ_s will increase (it will become less negative), and the value of Ψ in the potato will increase (it will become less negative).

97. **C.** The more often a phase appears, the longer it takes for that phase to occur. According to the data, metaphase appeared the fewest number of times, so that compared to the other phases, metaphase took the least amount of time to occur. Interphase took the most time but not longer than all other phases combined (according to the data presented).

98. **D.** Upon their release, the pillbugs display directed motion away from the dry chamber and toward the damp chamber. Directed motion in response to a stimulus is called taxis.

99. **B.** The pillbugs remained in the chamber into which they were introduced. Therefore, their activity was not taxis (directed toward or away from a stimulus) but undirected motion, with a change in speed, from fast to slow (kinesis).

100. **E.** The independent variable is time (in minutes). The dependent variable is the number of pillbugs counted.

Section II (Free-Response Questions)

Scoring Standards for the Essay Questions

To score your answers, award your essay points using the standards given. For each item listed that matches the content and vocabulary of a statement or explanation in your essay, add the indicated number of points to your essay score (to the maximum allowed for each section). Scores for each essay question range from 0 to 10 points.

Words appearing in parentheses in answers represent alternative wording.

Question 1 (10 points maximum)

A. concentration gradient and osmosis (*3 points maximum*)

1 pt: A concentration gradient is a change in concentration of a substance from one area to another.

1 pt: The concentration gradient in osmosis is a difference in the relative concentrations of solvent (water) and solute (dissolved) molecules between two sides of a selectively permeable (semipermeable) membrane.

1 pt: Osmosis is the diffusion of water across a semipermeable membrane.

OR

The semipermeable membrane allows water to diffuse (to pass through) but not one (or more) of the solutes.

1 pt: Water moves randomly across the membrane in both directions.

1 pt: The *net* movement of water is from the region of higher concentration of water (higher water potential) to the region of lower concentration of water (lower water potential).

B. proton gradient in chloroplast (*4 points maximum*)

1 pt: In each chloroplast, thylakoids create compartments that isolate their contents from the surrounding material (stroma).

1 pt: Photolysis (the splitting of water, $H_2O \rightarrow H^+ + \frac{1}{2}O_2$) occurs inside the thylakoids increasing the concentration of H^+ (protons) inside the thylakoids.

1 pt: The light reactions (electron transport chains) occur in the thylakoid membranes (not inside the thylakoid) ($NADP + H^+ \rightarrow NAPH$).

1 pt: When NADP and H^+ enter the thylakoid membrane from the stroma for the light reactions, the concentration of H^+ (protons) decreases in the stroma.

1 pt: The increase in H^+ (protons) concentration inside the thylakoid and the decrease in H^+ concentration in the stroma establishes a proton gradient.

1 pt: ATP synthase, an enzyme attached to the thylakoid membrane, synthesizes ATP (from $ADP + P_i$) using energy generated by the diffusion of H^+ across the thylakoid membrane from inside the thylakoid to the stroma.

C. concentration gradient and loop of Henle (*4 points maximum*)

1 pt: The nephron of a kidney consists of the glomerulus, proximal tubule, descending limb of the loop of Henle, ascending limb of the loop of Henle, distal tubule, and collecting duct. (Description of a nephron can be supported by a drawing, but a drawing without description receives no points.)

1 pt: In the descending limb, H_2O diffuses out because the descending limb is permeable to water and the surrounding environment is hyperosmotic (contains more solutes that inside the descending limb). This concentrates urine.

1 pt: In the ascending limb, sodium ions (Na^+) are actively (by active transport) pumped out. This makes the surrounding environment hyperosmotic and creates a solute gradient (that allows diffusion of H_2O out of the descending limb).

1 pt: In the ascending limb, water cannot diffuse out because the ascending limb is not permeable to water. This maintains the solute gradient.

1 pt: In the ascending limb, chloride ions (Cl^-) passively follow Na^+ out due to the attraction of oppositely charged ions. This also increases the solute gradient outside the ascending limb.

1 pt: The ion gradient between the inside and outside of the loop of Henle is greatest at the bottom of the loop.

1 pt: As the collecting duct descends into the area at the bottom of the loop of Henle, water passively moves out of the collecting duct, concentrating the urine.

No points: There are considerably more details about how the urine is concentrated (filtration from the glomerulus, role of ADH, and so on), but the answer should focus on the creation and effect of concentration gradients.

Question 2 (10 points maximum)

A. (*1 point maximum*)

1 pt: There would be two fragments.

B. (*1 point maximum*)

1 pt: 5 Kb (5000 bp) and 7 Kb (7000 bp)

C. (*1 point maximum*)

1 pt: 1 Kb, 2 Kb, 3 Kb, and 6 Kb

D. (*4 points maximum*)

1 pt: For each correctly positioned fragment (see figure)

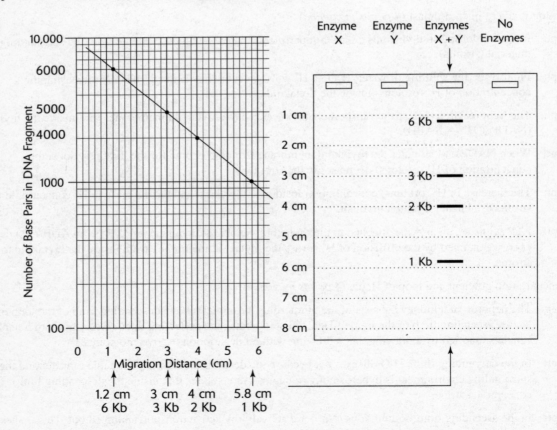

E. (*1 point maximum*)

    1 pt: All fragments are correctly labeled.

F. (*1 point maximum*)

    1 pt: Because DNA has an overall negative charged from the phosphate groups, the fragments migrate toward the positive electrode of the electrical current applied.

G. (*1 point maximum*)

    1 pt: The migration of the fragment varies with its length, weight, and charge.

    1 pt: The longer, heavier fragments meet more resistance and therefore move more slowly as they migrate through the gel.

Question 3 (10 points maximum). Only three of the five parts to be scored.

Translocation of sugar in angiosperms (*4 points maximum*)

A. structures involved (*1 point maximum*)

    1 pt: The transport of sugars in angiosperms occurs through phloem cells (or sieve-tube members).

B. transport process (*3 points maximum*)

    1 pt: Sugars (fructose, sucrose, soluble carbohydrates) are transported into sieve-tube members by active transport.

    1 pt: Water passively follows the concentration gradient of sugars, diffusing into sieve-tube members.

    1 pt: Hydrostatic pressure builds in the sieve-tube members as water enters.

    1 pt: Hydrostatic pressure in sieve-tube members forces movement of water and sugars to adjacent sieve-tube members where hydrostatic pressure is lower.

C. transport mechanism (*2 points maximum*)

    1 pt: Movement of sugars through phloem is by bulk flow.

    1 pt: Movement of sugars is cause by the force of hydrostatic pressure of water in adjacent sieve-tube members.

Transport of water in angiosperms (*4 points maximum*)

A. structures involved (*1 point maximum*)

    1 pt: Movement of water in angiosperms occurs through xylem cells (or tracheids, or vessel elements).

B. transport process (*3 points maximum*)

    1 pt: Water forms a continuous column of molecules as a result of hydrogen bonding.

        OR

        Water forms one long polymer of water as a result of hydrogen bonding.

        OR

        Water is held together by cohesion produced by hydrogen bonding.

    1 pt: Transpiration of water molecules from leaves pulls the water column up from the roots.

    1 pt: Energy for the movement of water molecules comes from the sun.

C. transport mechanism (*2 points maximum*)

    1 pt: Movement of water through the xylem is by bulk flow.

    1 pt: The energy supplied by the sun causes transpiration, which creates a force that pulls columns of water molecules up the xylem.

Transport of oxygen through human blood vessels (*4 points maximum*)

A. structures involved (*2 points maximum*)

1 pt: Most oxygen is transported by red blood cells (erythrocytes).

1 pt: Oxygen attaches to the protein hemoglobin inside red blood cells.

1 pt: Oxygen attaches to the heme portion of the hemoglobin molecule inside red blood cells.

B. transport process (*2 points maximum*)

1 pt: A large area for oxygen exchange is provided by sacs in the lung (alveoli).

1 pt: When red blood cells arrive at the lungs, the lungs are oxygenated and the hemoglobin is deoxygenated. When red blood cells leave the lungs, hemoglobin is oxygenated.

1 pt: Oxygen is picked up when it diffuses from the lungs (area of high O_2 concentration) across the moist membrane of an alveolus, across a capillary wall, into the blood stream, and into the red blood cells (area of low O_2 concentration).

1 pt: Oxygen is delivered when it diffuses out of a red blood cell, across a capillary wall, and into the fluids surrounding cells.

C. transport mechanism (*2 points maximum*)

1 pt: The transport of oxygen (inside red blood cells) from lungs to target cells is by bulk flow.

1 pt: The force for bulk flow is supplied by the pumping action of the heart.

Transport of carbon dioxide through human blood vessels (*4 points maximum*)

A. structures involved (*2 points maximum*)

1 pt: Most carbon dioxide is transported as bicarbonate (HCO_3^-) in the blood plasma.

1 pt: Some carbon dioxide is transported attached to (the globin part of) hemoglobin (carbaminohemoglobin, $HbCO_2$).

B. transport process (*2 points maximum*)

1 pt: Carbonic anhydrase, an enzyme in red blood cells, converts CO_2 into $HCO_3^- + H^+$.

1 pt: When blood arrives at the lungs, the lungs contain low concentrations of CO_2, and the plasma contains high concentrations of CO_2 and HCO_3^-. When blood leaves the lungs, the plasma contains low concentrations of CO_2 and HCO_3^-.

1 pt: CO_2 diffuses from the plasma (area of high concentration) across the alveolar wall and into the lungs (area of low concentration).

C. transport mechanism (*2 points maximum*)

1 pt: The transport of CO_2 (as HCO_3^-) from body cells to lungs is by bulk flow.

1 pt: The force for bulk flow is supplied by the contraction of skeletal muscles surrounding the veins. Veins have valves that prevent backflow.

OR

1 pt: The force for bulk flow is supplied by the expansion and contraction of lungs during breathing, which acts on nearby veins. Veins have valves that prevent backflow.

Movement of organic nutrients from the human digestive tract to the circulatory system (*4 points maximum*)

A. structures involved (*2 points maximum*)

1 pt: Absorption (transport from digestive tract to circulatory system) of most nutrients occurs across the wall of the small intestine and into *blood* capillaries.

1 pt: Absorption of fatty acids (fats, lipids) occurs across the wall of the small intestine and into *lymphatic* capillaries.

1 pt: Absorption of certain vitamins (vitamins B, K) occurs across the wall of the *large* intestine and into blood capillaries.

B. transport process (*2 points maximum*)

1 pt: A large area for absorption is provided by villi and microvilli (minute projections into the intestinal cavity).

1 pt: A blood capillary and a lymph capillary lie inside each microvillus, beneath the absorptive cells on the surface.

1 pt: Transport occurs through the absorptive cell and into the adjacent capillary under the surface of the microvillus.

1 pt: Bile salts bind to the fatty acids to form micelles. Fatty acids pass from the micelles to the intestinal absorptive cells. Within the absorptive cells, the fatty acids are coated with lipoproteins, forming chylomicrons. Chylomicrons pass from the absorptive cells to the lymphatic capillaries.

C. transport mechanism (*2 points maximum*)

1 pt: Absorption occurs by active transport (for amino acids, glucose).

1 pt: The concentration of nutrients is higher in the blood, so active transport, requiring energy (ATP), is required for transport up the concentration gradient from intestine to blood.

OR (instead of the preceding two):

1 pt: Absorption occurs by diffusion (facilitated diffusion) (for fructose).

1 pt: The concentration of nutrients is lower in the blood than in the small intestine, so they move passively down the concentration gradient from intestine to blood.

OR (instead of the preceding two):

1 pt: Absorption occurs by diffusion (for fatty acids).

1 pt: The concentration of fatty acids (attached to micelles) is lower in the lymph than in the small intestine, so they move passively down the concentration gradient from intestine to lymph.

Question 4 (10 points maximum)

Nitrogen (*4 points maximum*)

A. pathway (*2 points maximum*)

1 pt: The major source (reservoir) for nitrogen is (as N_2) the atmosphere and the soil (as NH_4^+ or ammonium, NH_3 or ammonia, NO_2^- or nitrite, NO_3^- or nitrate).

1 pt: Nitrogen fixation, the conversion of N_2 to NH_4^+ or NO_3^-, occurs by prokaryotes (bacteria) in soil (or root nodules).

1 pt: Plants (and other producers) acquire nitrogen from soil (or from the water in aquatic habitats) as NO_2^- (or nitrite) or NO_3^- (or nitrate).

1 pt: Animals acquire nitrogen by eating plants or other animals.

B. importance (*1 point maximum*)

    1 pt: All organisms require nitrogen for amino acids (proteins) and nucleic acids (nucleotides, DNA, RNA).

C. recycle (*2 points maximum*)

    1 pt: Denitrification occurs when denitrifying bacteria convert NO_3^- back to N_2.

    1 pt: Ammonification occurs when detritivorous bacteria convert fixed nitrogen back to NH_4^+.

    1 pt: Conversion of fixed nitrogen back to NH_4^+ or NH_3 occurs during metabolism and excretion in certain animals.

Phosphorus (*4 points maximum*)

A. pathway (*2 points maximum*)

    1 pt: The major source (reservoir) for phosphorus is terrestrial rocks (or ocean sediments).

    1 pt: Phosphorus becomes available to organisms after it erodes from rocks and is distributed by streams.

    1 pt: Phosphorous is absorbed by plants (and other producers) from the soil (or from the water in aquatic habitats) and is transferred to other trophic levels when a heterotroph eats an autotroph or another heterotroph.

B. importance (*1 point maximum*)

    1 pt: All organisms require phosphorus for the manufacture of ATP and all nucleic acids (nucleotides, DNA, RNA) (or phospholipids, bones, teeth).

C. recycle (*1 point maximum*)

    1 pt: Phosphorus is recycled when organisms excrete phosphorous in their waste products and when dead organisms decompose.

    1 pt: Waste phosphorus from organisms accumulates on ocean floors and becomes a terrestrial source of phosphorus when ocean floors are uplifted.

Energy (*4 points maximum*)

A. pathway (*2 points maximum*)

    1 pt: Source of (nearly) all energy is the sun.

    1 pt: Energy is captured by photosynthesis.

    1 pt: Some energy is transferred to other trophic levels when a heterotroph eats an autotroph or another heterotroph.

    1 pt: Most energy is lost when food molecules are captured and assimilated by organisms. Heat and unused energy in waste products contribute to energy loss.

B. importance (*1 point maximum*)

    1 pt: All living organisms require energy to carry out metabolic (chemical) processes that allow them to perform work (for growth, reproduction, cell maintenance, or homeostasis).

C. recycle (*1 point maximum*)

    1 pt: Energy is not recycled.

Answer Sheet for Practice Exam 4

1	Ⓐ Ⓑ Ⓒ Ⓓ Ⓔ	26	Ⓐ Ⓑ Ⓒ Ⓓ Ⓔ	51	Ⓐ Ⓑ Ⓒ Ⓓ Ⓔ	76	Ⓐ Ⓑ Ⓒ Ⓓ Ⓔ
2	Ⓐ Ⓑ Ⓒ Ⓓ Ⓔ	27	Ⓐ Ⓑ Ⓒ Ⓓ Ⓔ	52	Ⓐ Ⓑ Ⓒ Ⓓ Ⓔ	77	Ⓐ Ⓑ Ⓒ Ⓓ Ⓔ
3	Ⓐ Ⓑ Ⓒ Ⓓ Ⓔ	28	Ⓐ Ⓑ Ⓒ Ⓓ Ⓔ	53	Ⓐ Ⓑ Ⓒ Ⓓ Ⓔ	78	Ⓐ Ⓑ Ⓒ Ⓓ Ⓔ
4	Ⓐ Ⓑ Ⓒ Ⓓ Ⓔ	29	Ⓐ Ⓑ Ⓒ Ⓓ Ⓔ	54	Ⓐ Ⓑ Ⓒ Ⓓ Ⓔ	79	Ⓐ Ⓑ Ⓒ Ⓓ Ⓔ
5	Ⓐ Ⓑ Ⓒ Ⓓ Ⓔ	30	Ⓐ Ⓑ Ⓒ Ⓓ Ⓔ	55	Ⓐ Ⓑ Ⓒ Ⓓ Ⓔ	80	Ⓐ Ⓑ Ⓒ Ⓓ Ⓔ
6	Ⓐ Ⓑ Ⓒ Ⓓ Ⓔ	31	Ⓐ Ⓑ Ⓒ Ⓓ Ⓔ	56	Ⓐ Ⓑ Ⓒ Ⓓ Ⓔ	81	Ⓐ Ⓑ Ⓒ Ⓓ Ⓔ
7	Ⓐ Ⓑ Ⓒ Ⓓ Ⓔ	32	Ⓐ Ⓑ Ⓒ Ⓓ Ⓔ	57	Ⓐ Ⓑ Ⓒ Ⓓ Ⓔ	82	Ⓐ Ⓑ Ⓒ Ⓓ Ⓔ
8	Ⓐ Ⓑ Ⓒ Ⓓ Ⓔ	33	Ⓐ Ⓑ Ⓒ Ⓓ Ⓔ	58	Ⓐ Ⓑ Ⓒ Ⓓ Ⓔ	83	Ⓐ Ⓑ Ⓒ Ⓓ Ⓔ
9	Ⓐ Ⓑ Ⓒ Ⓓ Ⓔ	34	Ⓐ Ⓑ Ⓒ Ⓓ Ⓔ	59	Ⓐ Ⓑ Ⓒ Ⓓ Ⓔ	84	Ⓐ Ⓑ Ⓒ Ⓓ Ⓔ
10	Ⓐ Ⓑ Ⓒ Ⓓ Ⓔ	35	Ⓐ Ⓑ Ⓒ Ⓓ Ⓔ	60	Ⓐ Ⓑ Ⓒ Ⓓ Ⓔ	85	Ⓐ Ⓑ Ⓒ Ⓓ Ⓔ
11	Ⓐ Ⓑ Ⓒ Ⓓ Ⓔ	36	Ⓐ Ⓑ Ⓒ Ⓓ Ⓔ	61	Ⓐ Ⓑ Ⓒ Ⓓ Ⓔ	86	Ⓐ Ⓑ Ⓒ Ⓓ Ⓔ
12	Ⓐ Ⓑ Ⓒ Ⓓ Ⓔ	37	Ⓐ Ⓑ Ⓒ Ⓓ Ⓔ	62	Ⓐ Ⓑ Ⓒ Ⓓ Ⓔ	87	Ⓐ Ⓑ Ⓒ Ⓓ Ⓔ
13	Ⓐ Ⓑ Ⓒ Ⓓ Ⓔ	38	Ⓐ Ⓑ Ⓒ Ⓓ Ⓔ	63	Ⓐ Ⓑ Ⓒ Ⓓ Ⓔ	88	Ⓐ Ⓑ Ⓒ Ⓓ Ⓔ
14	Ⓐ Ⓑ Ⓒ Ⓓ Ⓔ	39	Ⓐ Ⓑ Ⓒ Ⓓ Ⓔ	64	Ⓐ Ⓑ Ⓒ Ⓓ Ⓔ	89	Ⓐ Ⓑ Ⓒ Ⓓ Ⓔ
15	Ⓐ Ⓑ Ⓒ Ⓓ Ⓔ	40	Ⓐ Ⓑ Ⓒ Ⓓ Ⓔ	65	Ⓐ Ⓑ Ⓒ Ⓓ Ⓔ	90	Ⓐ Ⓑ Ⓒ Ⓓ Ⓔ
16	Ⓐ Ⓑ Ⓒ Ⓓ Ⓔ	41	Ⓐ Ⓑ Ⓒ Ⓓ Ⓔ	66	Ⓐ Ⓑ Ⓒ Ⓓ Ⓔ	91	Ⓐ Ⓑ Ⓒ Ⓓ Ⓔ
17	Ⓐ Ⓑ Ⓒ Ⓓ Ⓔ	42	Ⓐ Ⓑ Ⓒ Ⓓ Ⓔ	67	Ⓐ Ⓑ Ⓒ Ⓓ Ⓔ	92	Ⓐ Ⓑ Ⓒ Ⓓ Ⓔ
18	Ⓐ Ⓑ Ⓒ Ⓓ Ⓔ	43	Ⓐ Ⓑ Ⓒ Ⓓ Ⓔ	68	Ⓐ Ⓑ Ⓒ Ⓓ Ⓔ	93	Ⓐ Ⓑ Ⓒ Ⓓ Ⓔ
19	Ⓐ Ⓑ Ⓒ Ⓓ Ⓔ	44	Ⓐ Ⓑ Ⓒ Ⓓ Ⓔ	69	Ⓐ Ⓑ Ⓒ Ⓓ Ⓔ	94	Ⓐ Ⓑ Ⓒ Ⓓ Ⓔ
20	Ⓐ Ⓑ Ⓒ Ⓓ Ⓔ	45	Ⓐ Ⓑ Ⓒ Ⓓ Ⓔ	70	Ⓐ Ⓑ Ⓒ Ⓓ Ⓔ	95	Ⓐ Ⓑ Ⓒ Ⓓ Ⓔ
21	Ⓐ Ⓑ Ⓒ Ⓓ Ⓔ	46	Ⓐ Ⓑ Ⓒ Ⓓ Ⓔ	71	Ⓐ Ⓑ Ⓒ Ⓓ Ⓔ	96	Ⓐ Ⓑ Ⓒ Ⓓ Ⓔ
22	Ⓐ Ⓑ Ⓒ Ⓓ Ⓔ	47	Ⓐ Ⓑ Ⓒ Ⓓ Ⓔ	72	Ⓐ Ⓑ Ⓒ Ⓓ Ⓔ	97	Ⓐ Ⓑ Ⓒ Ⓓ Ⓔ
23	Ⓐ Ⓑ Ⓒ Ⓓ Ⓔ	48	Ⓐ Ⓑ Ⓒ Ⓓ Ⓔ	73	Ⓐ Ⓑ Ⓒ Ⓓ Ⓔ	98	Ⓐ Ⓑ Ⓒ Ⓓ Ⓔ
24	Ⓐ Ⓑ Ⓒ Ⓓ Ⓔ	49	Ⓐ Ⓑ Ⓒ Ⓓ Ⓔ	74	Ⓐ Ⓑ Ⓒ Ⓓ Ⓔ	99	Ⓐ Ⓑ Ⓒ Ⓓ Ⓔ
25	Ⓐ Ⓑ Ⓒ Ⓓ Ⓔ	50	Ⓐ Ⓑ Ⓒ Ⓓ Ⓔ	75	Ⓐ Ⓑ Ⓒ Ⓓ Ⓔ	100	Ⓐ Ⓑ Ⓒ Ⓓ Ⓔ

CUT HERE

Practice Exam 4

Section I (Multiple-Choice Questions)

Time: 80 minutes

100 questions

Directions: Each of the following questions or statements is followed by five possible answers or sentence completions. Choose the one best answer or sentence completion.

1. Which of the following describes a prokaryote but not a eukaryote?

   A.   photoautotroph
   B.   chemoautotroph
   C.   obligate aerobe
   D.   facultative anaerobe
   E.   decomposer

2. Many species of *Arctostaphylos,* or manzanita, have stomata and palisades mesophyll along both surfaces of their leaves. This would most likely suggest that

   A.   the plants grow in a wet habitat
   B.   the plants carry out C_4 photosynthesis
   C.   the plants carry out CAM photosynthesis
   D.   the leaves are oriented in a vertical, rather than horizontal, direction
   E.   most leaves grow near the surface of the soil

3. In the inherited disorder called Pompe's disease, glycogen breakdown in the cytosol occurs normally and blood glucose levels are normal, yet glycogen accumulates in lysosomes. This suggests a malfunction with

   A.   catabolic enzymes in the mitochondria
   B.   anabolic enzymes in the lysosomes
   C.   catabolic enzymes in the lysosomes
   D.   membrane transport during exocytosis
   E.   membrane transport during endocytosis

4. If genes *A, B, C,* and *D* are unlinked and autosomal, what is the probability of producing an individual with the genotype *AaBbCcDd* from the cross *AABBccdd × aabbCCDD?*

   A.   0
   B. $\frac{1}{16}$
   C. $\frac{1}{8}$
   D. $\frac{1}{4}$
   E.   1

5. All of the following are fruits EXCEPT:

   A.   tomatoes
   B.   potatoes
   C.   watermelons
   D.   strawberries
   E.   apples

6. During early stages of infection, a typical DNA virus generates copies of its DNA. Where does this process occur within a eukaryotic host cell?

   A.   in the lysosomes of the host cell
   B.   in the cytoplasm of the host cell
   C.   in the nucleolus of the host cell
   D.   in the nucleus of the host cell, but not in the nucleolus
   E.   outside of the host cell, before infection

GO ON TO THE NEXT PAGE

7. During glycolysis and the Krebs cycle, energy-rich electrons are removed from organic molecules and transferred to

   A. ATP
   B. ADP
   C. NAD⁺ and FAD
   D. water
   E. oxygen

8. Which of the following describes how binary fission and mitosis are the *same?*

   A. Two genetically identical daughter cells are produced.
   B. Replication of DNA occurs.
   C. Only one chromosome is involved.
   D. Division of the nucleus occurs.
   E. Chromosomes are separated.

☐ Male
○ Female

9. In the pedigree shown, circles indicate females, and squares indicate males. A horizontal line connecting a male and female indicate that these two individuals produced offspring. Offspring are indicated by a descending vertical line that branches to the offspring. A filled circle or filled square indicates that the individual has a particular trait.

   The pedigree can be explained by all of the following inheritance patterns EXCEPT:

   A. autosomal dominant allele
   B. autosomal recessive allele
   C. X-linked dominant allele
   D. X-linked recessive allele
   E. Y-linked trait

10. The penetration of an animal sperm cell into the plasma membrane of an egg is facilitated by

   A. the length of the flagellum of the sperm cell
   B. the speed at which the sperm cell impacts with the plasma membrane of the egg
   C. enzymes secreted by the acrosome
   D. the amount of ATP available to the egg cell
   E. the amount of ATP available to the sperm cell

11. All of the following are true about viruses EXCEPT:

   A. The genomes of some viruses contain both DNA and RNA.
   B. The envelopes of viruses are derived from the plasma membranes of their hosts.
   C. Viral envelopes contain phospholipids.
   D. Viral proteins are present on the surface of viral envelopes.
   E. The capsids of viruses are an assembly of one or more proteins of viral origin.

12. A chemical that is used for communication between individuals of the same animal species is

   A. a hormone
   B. a neurotransmitter
   C. a pheromone
   D. an allergen
   E. an operon

13. A mutation of an X-linked, recessive allele is lethal. Male fetuses that inherit the allele and female fetuses that are homozygous recessive abort before birth. What is the probability that a child born to a female who is heterozygous for the mutation will have one copy of the allele?

   A. ¼
   B. ⅓
   C. ½
   D. ⅔
   E. ¾

14. Homeostasis of Ca²⁺ is maintain by which of the following two hormones?

   A. norepinephrine and epinephrine (adrenaline)
   B. insulin and glucagon
   C. thyroxin and thyroid stimulating hormone (TSH)
   D. calcitonin and parathyroid hormone (PTH)
   E. aldosterone and antidiuretic hormone (ADH)

15. All of the following are examples of density-dependent regulators of population growth EXCEPT:

   A. Ground-nesting birds build nests that are just beyond pecking distance from nests of other birds.

   B. In the absence of oxygen, yeasts acquire energy by alcoholic fermentation but die after the alcohol concentration exceeds 12 percent.

   C. Red squirrels defend territories that possess good food supplies.

   D. Bees huddle together to help survive cold temperatures.

   E. Many orange trees in orchards die when temperatures drop below freezing.

16. Water entering a root can pass through intercellular spaces of the cortex. In contrast, water cannot penetrate the spaces between the epithelial cells that line many of the surfaces of animal bodies and organs because of the presence of

   A. cholesterol
   B. tight junctions
   C. plasmodesmata
   D. phospholipids
   E. suberin

17. Which of the following best summarizes the process of allopatric speciation?

   A. differential changes in allele frequencies → reproductive isolation → reproductive barriers → new species

   B. catastrophic event → reproductive isolation → reproductive barriers → new species

   C. biological isolation → reproductive isolation → differential changes in allele frequencies → reproductive barriers → new species

   D. reproduction isolation → differential changes in allele frequencies → reproductive barriers → new species

   E. geographic isolation → reproductive isolation → differential changes in allele frequencies → reproductive barriers → new species

18. A major function of the skin in frogs and other amphibians most closely supplements the function of which of the following organs?

   A. gall bladder
   B. intestines
   C. kidneys
   D. lungs
   E. liver

19. All of the following promote cell growth in plants EXCEPT:

   A. auxin
   B. gibberellin
   C. cytokinin
   D. abscisic acid (ABA)
   E. indoleacetic acid (IAA)

20. On average, social behavior

   A. increases the number of deaths
   B. increases agonistic behavior
   C. increases individual fitness
   D. decreases the amount of available food
   E. decreases group survival

21. A spindle apparatus and cytoplasmic streaming can both be observed in plant cells, but the cells of most plants lack flagella and cilia. Consistent with these observations for these plants, plant cells would also lack

   A. actin
   B. basal bodies
   C. a cytoskeleton
   D. microfilaments
   E. microtubules

22. In general, as ecological succession progresses from early to middle stages,

   A. biomass increases and species diversity increases

   B. biomass increases and species diversity decreases

   C. biomass remains constant and species diversity increases

   D. biomass decreases and species diversity decreases

   E. biomass decreases and species diversity increases

GO ON TO THE NEXT PAGE

23. All of the following are true for the translocation of sugars in angiosperms EXCEPT:

   A. Movement of sugars through transporting cells is driven by columns of water molecules held together by hydrogen bonding.

   B. Movement of sugars through transporting cells occurs by bulk flow.

   C. The transporting cells are sieve-tube members.

   D. A single translocation pathway may, at different times, transport sugars in either direction.

   E. Pressure builds in transporting cells at the source end when water enters by osmosis.

24. Botulin toxins are produced by *Clostridium botulinum* bacteria growing in improperly canned fruits and vegetables. Which of the following symptoms from botulism poisoning is most likely if the toxin inhibits the release of acetylcholine?

   A. kidney failure
   B. liver failure
   C. muscle paralysis
   D. skin bruises
   E. shivering

25. One kind of pigmentation in corn seeds (kernels) occurs when anthocyanin is deposited in the aleurone, or outer layers of the endosperm. If the dominant allele of any one of three genes, *A, C,* or *R,* is present, pigmentation occurs. Another gene, *C′,* inhibits pigmentation if the dominant allele is present no matter what *A, C,* or *R* alleles are present. Which of the following genotypes will have a pigmented aleurone?

   A. *Aa Cc Rr C′c′*
   B. *aa cc rr c′c′*
   C. *Aa cc rr C′C′*
   D. *aa cc Rr c′c′*
   E. *AA CC RR C′C′*

26. Which of the following mutations is *most* likely to produce a polypeptide identical to the polypeptide produced without the mutation?

   A. a frameshift mutation
   B. a missense mutation
   C. a nonsense (or stop) mutation
   D. a silent mutation
   E. None of these mutations will produce a polypeptide identical to the polypeptide produced without the mutation.

27. All of the following contribute to the differentiation of cells in a developing embryo EXCEPT:

   A. variation in cytoplasmic content among cells
   B. asymmetrical cleavage divisions
   C. cell-to-surface interactions between adjacent cells
   D. differences in mitotic and meiotic daughter cells
   E. inductive signals from organizer cells

28. During courtship a male *Drosophila melanogaster* fruit fly will vibrate his wings, tap the female with his forelegs, and extend one wing out at 90 degrees from his body. These behaviors are

   A. the result of operant conditioning
   B. the result of classical conditioning
   C. the result of imprinting
   D. the result of insight
   E. innate

29. Which of the following varies in function from one cell to another to perform various processes including the synthesis of steroid hormones, the detoxification of organic materials, and the storage and regulated release of Ca^{2+} ions?

   A. smooth endoplasmic reticulum
   B. rough endoplasmic reticulum
   C. peroxisomes
   D. the nucleus
   E. Golgi complexes

30. Within an infected or cancerous cell, the MHC produces proteins that

A. transfer antigens to lysosomes where the antigens are destroyed

B. destroy antigens by phagocytosis

C. are secreted from the cell to stimulate nearby cells to prepare for infection

D. are secreted from the cell into the blood stream to form the complement system of circulating antimicrobial proteins

E. bind to antigens and display a "nonself" signature on the plasma membrane

31. All of the following may be found in secondary tissues of plants EXCEPT:

A. cork cambium

B. heartwood

C. root hairs

D. xylem

E. phloem

32. If C and D are linked genes with a crossover frequency of 50 percent, which of the following is true for sperm of the individual with the genotype *CcDd?*

A. all *CcDd*

B. ¼ *CCDD* + ½ *CcDd* + ¼ *ccdd*

C. ½ *Cc* + ½ *Dd*

D. ½ *CD* + ½ *cd*

E. ¼ *CD* + ¼ *Cd* + ¼ *cD* + ¼ *cd*

33. Sea otters eat bottom-dwelling organisms, abalone, and sea urchins. Sea urchins eat kelp. Kelp forests provide habitat for fish and reduce shore erosion. In the early 1900s, sea otter populations declined in response to overhunting by humans (for otter furs), followed by an increase in the sea urchin population, followed by the disappearance of many kelp forests. Which is the keystone species in this community?

A. sea otters

B. abalone

C. sea urchins

D. kelp

E. humans

34. All of the following are membrane-bound bodies in eukaryotic cells EXCEPT:

A. lysosome

B. mitochondrion

C. endoplasmic reticulum

D. nucleolus

E. Golgi body

35. All of the following are heterotrophs EXCEPT:

A. herbivores

B. omnivores

C. decomposers

D. fungi

E. algae

36. If cows, dogs, and whales are classified in different orders, they must also be in different

A. classes

B. phyla

C. kingdoms

D. families

E. domains

37. Female spotted hyenas are very aggressive, are larger than males, are dominant over males in most social interactions, and have genitals that resemble those of males. Which of the following would most likely explain this phenomenon?

A. Females have relatively high levels of testosterone.

B. Females have relatively high levels of estrogen.

C. Males have relatively low levels of testosterone.

D. Males have relatively high levels of testosterone.

E. Males have relatively high levels of estrogen.

GO ON TO THE NEXT PAGE

38. All of the following are examples of a negative feedback system EXCEPT:

   A. decreases in blood glucose brought about by increases in insulin secretion by the pancreas

   B. increases in blood glucose brought about by increases in glucagon secretion by the pancreas

   C. increases in milk production by mammary glands brought about by increasingly more nursing by a baby

   D. increases in sweat production brought about by the hypothalamus in response to increasing body temperatures

   E. increases in shivering brought about by the hypothalamus in response to decreasing body temperatures

39. Animal behaviors acquired through imprinting require

   A. habituation

   B. a sensitive or critical period

   C. insight

   D. conditioning

   E. spatial learning

40. Which of the following is the source of organelles for the evolution of eukaryotes according to the endosymbiosis theory?

   A. bacteria-like prokaryotes

   B. charophyceans

   C. mutant eukaryotes

   D. plasmids

   E. viruses

41. What is the significance of the primitive streak in birds?

   A. It is the line formed by cells as they invaginate during gastrulation.

   B. It must appear in a blastomere if the individual blastomere can successfully be used to produced a normal individual.

   C. It forms the notochord.

   D. It forms the neural plate.

   E. It represents the lineage of ancestral traits traced back to reptiles.

42. Which of the following statements about the carbon cycle is FALSE?

   A. Some carbon is removed from the atmosphere by way of respiration.

   B. Some carbon is stored in organic compounds as a result of photosynthesis.

   C. Most carbon exists in the atmosphere in the form of carbon dioxide.

   D. Some carbon is stored for millions of years in the form of oceanic sediments from marine organisms.

   E. Carbon is released into the atmosphere by the combustion of fossil fuels.

43. The A + T nucleotide content of DNA extracted from an unknown species is 46 percent. For the same DNA sample, which of the following is correct?

   A. Thymine = 21%.

   B. Adenine = 25%.

   C. Cytosine = 25%.

   D. Uracil = 27%.

   E. Guanine = 27%.

44. Which of the following correctly describes mycorrhizae?

   A. fungi that aid plant roots with the absorption of water and minerals

   B. nitrogen-fixing bacteria that supply plant roots with fixed nitrogen

   C. plants that live on other plants without harming them

   D. plants without chlorophyll that parasitize other plants

   E. filamentous algae that live in root nodules

45. All of the following are characteristic of a typical fern EXCEPT:

   A. vascular tissue

   B. dominant generation represented by the gametophyte

   C. flagellated sperm

   D. true leaves

   E. seedless

46. In the following figure, which of the following correctly describes the pathway of blood?

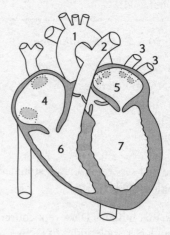

   A. $4 \to 6 \to 2 \to$ lungs $\to 1 \to 7 \to 5 \to 3$

   B. $4 \to 6 \to 2 \to$ lungs $\to 3 \to 5 \to 7 \to 1$

   C. $2 \to 6 \to 4 \to$ lungs $\to 3 \to 5 \to 7 \to 1$

   D. $1 \to 7 \to 5 \to$ lungs $\to 3 \to 2 \to 6 \to 4$

   E. $3 \to 5 \to 7 \to 1 \to$ systemic system $\to 4 \to 6 \to 2$

GO ON TO THE NEXT PAGE

Directions: Questions that follow consist of a phrase or sentence. Each question is preceded by five lettered choices. Select the one lettered choice that best matches the phrase or sentence. Each lettered choice may be used once, more than once, or not at all.

Questions 47–50 refer to the following.

- A. DNA ligase
- B. DNA polymerase
- C. primase
- D. helicase
- E. telomerase

47. Enzyme that separates double-stranded DNA into two single strands D

48. Enzyme that initiates DNA replication by attaching RNA nucleotides to DNA C

49. Enzyme that joins Okazaki fragments A

50. Enzyme that replaces lost nucleotides at ends of DNA molecules in germ cells E

Questions 51–53 refer to the following processes

- A. gastrulation
- B. osmoregulation
- C. neurulation
- D. ovulation
- E. vasodilation

51. Associated with thermoregulation E

52. Associated with the regulation of water balance B

53. Associated with the development of an embryo with two layers of cells A

Questions 54–57 refer to the following.

- A. convergent evolution
- B. divergent evolution
- C. adaptive radiation
- D. kin selection
- E. character displacement

54. Fifteen species of the plant genus *Scalesia* are native to the Galápagos Islands and exist nowhere else. The species vary in size from shrubs less than 1 m high to 20 m tall trees. Leaves, flowers, and other characteristics also vary widely. C

55. Five species of plants native to the Galápagos Islands each belong to a different plant family. All five species have branches with spines. Other members of each family that occur in other parts of the world lack spines.

56. Seven species of seed-eating ants populate California and Arizona deserts. In general, larger ants have larger mandibles and are able to harvest large and small seeds, while smaller ants are able to harvest only the smaller seeds. When two or more populations of ant species coexist, each population shows less variation in ant size (and mandible size), and the overlap of sizes between populations is smaller than when the species do not coexist.

57. In the Galápagos Islands, all three species of booby, a seabird, feed on fish. The blue-footed booby feeds close to shore, the masked booby feeds in open waters between the islands, and the red-footed booby fishes far out at sea. All three species nest in other parts of the world, and their feeding behaviors are the same whether the other species are present or not.

Questions 58–60 refer to the following properties of water.

- A. strong adhesion
- B. strong cohesion
- C. high surface tension
- D. hydrophobic property
- E. high heat capacity

58. Which property of water is responsible for holding together a vertical column of water in the xylem vessels of plants?

59. Which property of water is responsible for its movement through filter paper?

60. Which property of water is responsible for the effectiveness of sweating as a thermoregulatory mechanism in humans?

Questions 61–63 refer to the following.

    A. large intestine
    B. pancreas
    C. small intestine
    D. liver
    E. stomach

61. Secretes the inactive form of trypsin

62. Produces a substance that causes the separation of fats into smaller fat droplets

63. Location of most nutrient absorption

Questions 64–66 refer to the following.

A cleft chin (or chin dimple) is inherited as an autosomal dominant allele. A man and a woman, both with cleft chins, marry. The man's father did not have a cleft chin, and the woman has a child without a cleft chin from a previous marriage.

    A. ⅛
    B. ¼
    C. ⅜
    D. ⁹⁄₁₆
    E. ¾

64. The probability that their first child will have a cleft chin

65. The probability that their first child will be a male with a cleft chin

66. The probability that their first two children will both have cleft chins

Questions 67–68 refer to the following diagrams of the cross sections of plant roots and shoots. Black areas represent xylem and gray areas represent phloem.

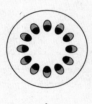    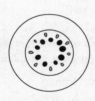

    A   B   C   D   E

67. A cross section representative of the primary *root* structure for a typical eudicot (dicot)

68. A cross section representative of the primary *stem* structure for a typical monocot

GO ON TO THE NEXT PAGE

Directions: Questions that follow involve data from experiments or laboratory analyses. In each case, study the information provided. Then choose the one best answer for each question.

Questions 69–73 refer to the following figure of a chloroplast.

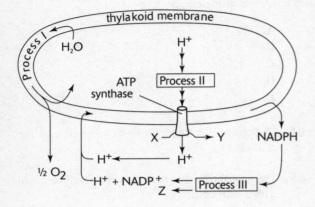

69. Process I generates O_2 and which of the following molecules?

   A. ADP
   B. ATP
   C. H_2O
   D. H^+
   E. $NADP^+$

70. In which of the following is the environment of the chloroplast most acidic?

   A. the stroma
   B. the thylakoid
   C. the thylakoid membrane
   D. the matrix
   E. the outer compartment

71. The driving force for Process II is

   A. energy obtained from ATP
   B. energy obtained from NADPH
   C. energy obtained from glucose
   D. a pH gradient across the thylakoid membrane
   E. a salt gradient across the thylakoid membrane

72. The molecule generated by Process II indicated by the letter Y is

   A. ADP
   B. ATP
   C. H_2O
   D. H^+
   E. glucose

73. The molecule generated by Process III indicated by the letter Z is

   A. ADP
   B. ATP
   C. H_2O
   D. G3P (or PGAL), a sugar
   E. H^+

Questions 74–76 refer to the following graph that plots the concentration of ions in the body of an aquatic animal against the concentration of ions in its surrounding medium.

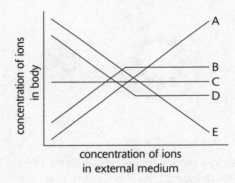

74. Which plot describes marine bony fish, animals that secrete salts, constantly drink, and rarely urinate?

75. Which plot describes jellyfish, animals that are isosmotic with their marine environment?

76. Which plot describes salmon, fish that are hypoosmotic with their marine environment but become hyperosmotic when they return to their freshwater origins to spawn?

Questions 77–79 refer to the following dichotomous key.
Each group may represent one or more phyla.

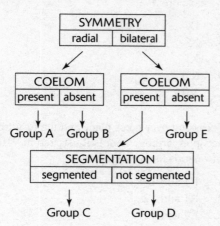

77. Platyhelminthes would be found in which group?

A. Group A
B. Group B
C. Group C
D. Group D
E. Group E

78. Which of the groups possesses an open circulatory system?

A. Group A, only
B. Groups B and C
C. Groups C and D
D. Groups B and D
E. Groups C, D, and E

79. Which of the groups possesses nephridia as part of its excretory system?

A. Group A, only
B. Groups B and C
C. Groups C and D
D. Groups B and D
E. Groups C, D, and E

80. An iodine solution (IKI or Lugol's solution) turns blue-black when it reacts with starch but not when it reacts with glucose. A bag made from a selectively permeable material and containing iodine solution is place into a beaker containing a solution of glucose and starch. Using only this information, which of the following can be correctly concluded if the solution in the beaker turns blue-black but the contents of the bag remain unchanged in color?

A. Glucose moved from the beaker into the bag.
B. The bag is permeable to IKI but not to starch.
C. The bag is permeable to IKI and glucose but not to starch.
D. The bag is permeable to IKI but not to starch and glucose.
E. The bag is permeable to IKI, glucose, and starch.

GO ON TO THE NEXT PAGE

Questions 81–84 refer to the following.

The following figures show two strains of the ascomyce-tous fungus *Sordaria* ($n = 7$) sexually reproducing and forming spores within asci. Only one chromosome (or one pair of homologous chromosomes) for each strain is shown, and that chromosome carries a gene for spore color. Black-colored chromosomes carry the black (wild type) spore color, and the gray chromosomes carry a tan-colored mutant spore color. In some figures, the spore colors are omitted. Chromatids of the chromosome for the black strain are labeled B1 and B2, and chromatids for its homologue from the tan strain are labeled T1 and T2.

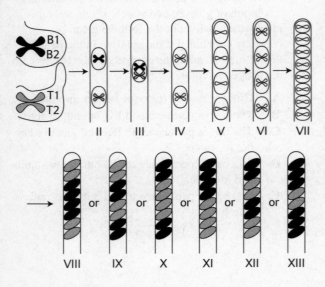

81. Where does mitosis take place in the sequence illustrated?

   A.   between I and II
   B.   between II and III
   C.   between III and IV
   D.   between IV and V
   E.   between VI and VII

82. If crossing over occurs, where would it take place?

   A.   between I and II
   B.   between II and III
   C.   between III and IV
   D.   between IV and V
   E.   between V and VI

83. If crossing over does *not* take place, which of the following figures shows the correct arrangement of ascospores?

   A.   IX
   B.   X
   C.   XI
   D.   XII
   E.   XIII

84. If crossing over takes place and the resulting ascospore arrangement is illustrated in VIII, which chromatids have crossed over?

   A.   B1 and T1
   B.   B1 and T2
   C.   B2 and T1
   D.   B2 and T2
   E.   T1 and T2

Questions 85–86 refer to the following.

The following graph shows changes in species abundance with time from early to late successional stages of a temperate forest community typical of the eastern United States.

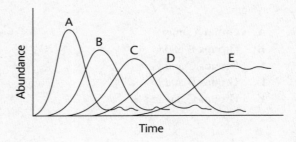

85. Which successional stage would contain the greatest abundance of plants with an *r*-selected life history?

86. Which successional stage would contain the greatest abundance of hardwood trees?

Questions 87–88 refer to the following figure, which shows carbon dioxide production from fully hydrated, germinating seeds.

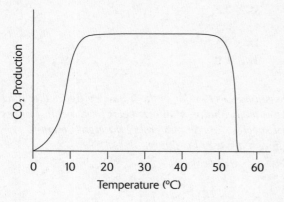

87. The production of CO_2 in the germinating seeds is most likely the result of which of the following processes?

    A. photophosphorylation
    B. Calvin cycle
    C. photorespiration
    D. glycolysis
    E. Krebs cycle

88. The rapid decrease in CO_2 production above 50°C is most likely the result of which of the following?

    A. Germination was completed and the CO_2 generating process was no longer necessary.
    B. Because of the high temperatures, CO_2 was consumed rather than produced.
    C. High temperatures inactivated the chlorophyll.
    D. Temperatures above 50°C caused glucose to decompose.
    E. The enzymes responsible for respiration were denatured.

Questions 89–90 refer to the following.

A clear plastic chamber containing a cylindrical cage was used as an animal chamber. An opening at one end of the chamber was sealed with a stopper. Passing through the stopper was a graduated buret. Gas production or consumption inside the chamber could be measured by movements of a solution rising or falling inside the buret. Potassium hydroxide (KOH) was added to the chamber to absorb any CO_2 produced.

Twenty hamsters were weighed and put into one of 20 chambers. Half of the chambers were maintained at 10°C and half were maintained at 25°C. Oxygen consumption in ml was recorded for each hamster every 30 seconds and plotted as ml per gram of hamster weight. The data are shown in the graph that follows.

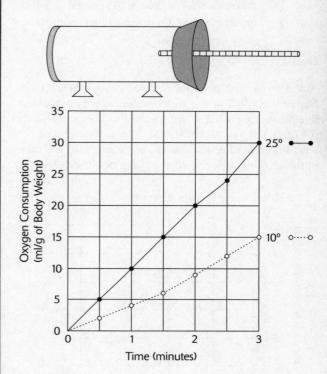

89. The data in the preceding graph are consistent with which of the following conclusions?

    A. As time progresses, respiration rate increases in hamsters.
    B. The rate of respiration increases with increases in environmental temperature for hamsters.
    C. Temperature increases with increases in the weights of hamsters.
    D. The larger the hamster, the greater its rate of respiration.
    E. The larger the hamster, the greater the breakdown of fats in hamsters.

GO ON TO THE NEXT PAGE

90. All of the following must remain unchanged during data collection EXCEPT:

    A. atmospheric pressure

    B. the volume of the animal chamber

    C. the weight of the hamster

    D. the amount of oxygen in the animal chamber

    E. the amount of CO_2 in the animal chamber

Questions 91–92 refer to the following.

A section of fresh potato was added to six beakers. One beaker was filled with distilled water, and the remaining five beakers were filled with sucrose solutions of 0.2 M, 0.4 M, 0.6 M, 0.8 M, and 1.0 M. The potato sections were removed after 15 minutes, and changes in weights of the sections were recorded in the graph that follows.

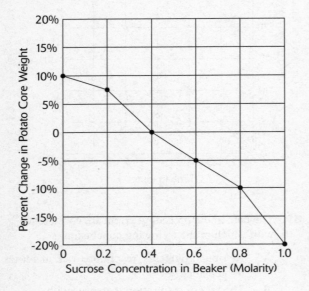

91. Which of the following is true for the potato sections in the beakers with 0.6 M, 0.8 M, and 1.0 M solutions?

    A. The potato core was hypotonic compared to the solutions in the beakers.

    B. The potato core was isotonic compared to the solutions in the beakers.

    C. The value of Ψ for the potato section was greater than 0.

    D. The value of Ψ for the solution was greater than 0.

    E. The value of Ψ for the solution was equal to 0.

92. What is the concentration of solutes inside the potato sections?

    A. 0

    B. 0.2

    C. 0.3

    D. 0.4

    E. 1.0

Questions 93–96 refer to the following figure that illustrates the evolution of nine species from a single ancestral species. Roman numerals I through V identify different areas of the figure.

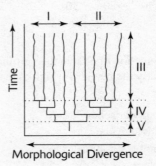

Morphological Divergence

93. During which of the indicated periods is the rate of evolution most rapid?

    A. I

    B. II

    C. III

    D. IV

    E. V

94. The evolution illustrated in this figure can best be described as

    A. coevolution

    B. molecular evolution

    C. neutral evolution

    D. phyletic gradualism

    E. punctuated equilibrium

95. Which of the following could be responsible for the evolutionary pattern indicated by area III?

- **A.** directional selection
- **B.** stabilizing selection
- **C.** disruptive selection
- **D.** sexual selection
- **E.** frequency-dependent selection

96. If the diagram describes the pattern of evolution after a single species is introduced to a remote island, the pattern in the diagram best suggests

- **A.** allopatric speciation
- **B.** hybridization
- **C.** adaptive radiation
- **D.** coevolution
- **E.** multiple occurrences of gene flow

Questions 97–100 refer to the following.

An experiment employed the light and dark bottle method to determine net primary productivity. In particular, dissolved oxygen was measured in three bottles containing pond water, and the amount of fixed carbon was calculated. The results follow.

Bottle #	Treatment	Dissolved Oxygen (ppm)	Fixed Carbon (mg/L)
1	Initial measurement	7.49	2.80
2	Light for 24 hours	7.59	2.84
3	Dark for 24 hours	7.43	2.78

- **A.** 0.02
- **B.** 0.04
- **C.** 0.06
- **D.** 0.08
- **E.** 0.10

97. What is the observed net productivity?

98. What is the observed carbon utilization due to respiration?

99. What is the gross productivity?

100. This experiment determines gross productivity by measuring changes in dissolved oxygen. An alternative procedure would be to measure changes in

- **A.** salinity
- **B.** CO_2
- **C.** temperature
- **D.** incident light
- **E.** nitrogen (as dissolved nitrates)

GO ON TO THE NEXT PAGE

Section II (Free-Response Questions)

Reading Time: 10 minutes (for organizing your thoughts and outlining your answers)
Writing Time: 90 minutes

1. Most plants obtain energy for metabolism and growth from photosynthesis. Design a controlled experiment to investigate the source of energy for germinating seeds when light is not available.

   A. Propose a hypothesis for how energy is obtained by a germinating seed and provide an explanation.
   B. Describe a controlled experiment to test your hypothesis. Include an identification of independent, dependent, and control variables.
   C. Describe the results you would expect to obtain if the experiment were performed.
   D. Graph your expected results on the axes provided.
   E. Provide an alternative hypothesis or another explanation that would explain the results you obtained.

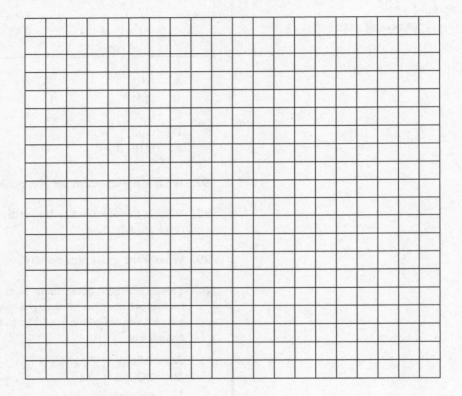

2. The human immunodeficiency virus (HIV) is a single-stranded RNA retrovirus that infects humans. Following entry into a cell, the virus genome goes through several steps and ultimately becomes embedded into the host cell's DNA as a provirus.

   A. Describe the structure of the HIV.
   B. Describe how the HIV gains entry into a cell.
   C. Describe each stage of the HIV infection from single-stranded RNA to provirus.
   D. Describe how, as a provirus, the HIV replicates.
   E. Explain why the disease caused by the HIV is called AIDS (acquired immunodeficiency syndrome).

3. All living organisms possess the ability to maintain constant internal conditions, or homeostasis. Choose THREE of the following and discuss how each contributes to homeostasis.

    A.   thermoregulation in mammals
    B.   regulation of blood glucose concentrations in humans
    C.   osmoregulation in marine and freshwater fish
    D.   water-deficit response in plant leaves

4. Each of the following describes a relationship between two species or how one species attempts to influence another species.

- mycorrhiza
- parasitoid
- mimicry
- camouflage

Select THREE of the preceding and

    A.   describe the species, the relationship of the species, or the interaction of the species involved.
    B.   describe the advantage (or disadvantage) for each organism in the relationship.

Answer Key for Practice Exam 4

Section I (Multiple-Choice Questions)

1. B	26. D	51. E	76. C
2. D	27. D	52. B	77. E
3. C	28. E	53. A	78. C
4. E	29. A	54. C	79. C
5. B	30. E	55. A	80. B
6. D	31. C	56. E	81. E
7. C	32. E	57. B	82. C
8. E	33. A	58. B	83. C
9. C	34. D	59. A	84. A
10. C	35. E	60. E	85. A
11. A	36. D	61. B	86. E
12. C	37. A	62. D	87. E
13. B	38. C	63. C	88. E
14. D	39. B	64. E	89. B
15. E	40. A	65. C	90. D
16. B	41. A	66. D	91. A
17. E	42. A	67. B	92. D
18. D	43. E	68. C	93. D
19. D	44. A	69. D	94. E
20. C	45. B	70. B	95. B
21. B	46. B	71. D	96. C
22. A	47. D	72. B	97. B
23. A	48. C	73. D	98. A
24. C	49. A	74. C	99. C
25. D	50. E	75. A	100. B

Scoring Your Practice Exam

Section I (Multiple-Choice Questions)

Number of questions you answered correctly: _____ × 1 = _____

Number of questions you answered wrong: _____ × ¼ = –_____ *

Number of questions you left unanswered: _____ × 0 = ____0____

TOTAL for Section I (0–100 points): = _____ **

(subtract number wrong from number correct)

Round to nearest whole number.

** If less than zero, enter zero.

Section II (Free-Response Questions)

For each correct and relevant piece of information you include in your answers to the free-response questions, you earn one point. Refer to the scoring standards that follow the multiple-choice explanations.

Score for essay 1 (0–10 points): _____

Score for essay 2 (0–10 points): _____

Score for essay 3 (0–10 points): _____

Score for essay 4 (0–10 points): _____

Combined Score (Sections I + II)

Total for Section I (from above): _____ × 0.6 = _____

(60% of 100 points = 60 points maximum)

Total for Section II (from above): _____ × 1.0 = _____

(100% of 40 points = 40 points maximum)

Combined Score (Add Sections I and II)_____

(0–100 points possible)

Probable AP Grade	
61–100	5
47–60	4
39–46	3
30–38	2
0–29	1

Answers and Explanations for Practice Exam 4

1. **B.** Chemoautotrophs occur only among prokaryotes. They use energy in inorganic molecules such as NH_3, H_2S, and NO_2^- to synthesize carbohydrates from CO_2. For each of the remaining answer choices, representatives can be found in both prokaryotes and eukaryotes. For example, cyanobacteria and plants are photoautotrophs (organisms that use light as a source of energy to generate carbohydrates from CO_2). Certain bacteria and all animals are obligate aerobes (organisms that require oxygen for their metabolism). Certain bacteria and yeasts are facultative anaerobes (organisms that are able to carry out metabolism both in the presence and the absence of oxygen). Various bacteria and fungi are decomposers (organisms that obtain their energy through the breakdown of dead organisms).

2. **D.** Vertical leaf orientation is an adaptation to minimize surface area to sunlight. Because many species of manzanita grow in the chaparral biome, vertical leaf orientation is one strategy to manage heat and conserve water. For such a leaf orientation, light-absorbing palisades mesophyll on both sides of the leaf allow the light incident on both surfaces to be absorbed.

3. **C.** Because lysosomes are sites of chemical breakdown (catabolic processes), the abnormal accumulation of substances within them results from the absence or malfunction of a lysosomal enzyme. These are generally called lysosomal storage diseases, and include diseases where various undigested materials, including carbohydrates and lipids, accumulate due to the absence of a correctly functioning lysosomal enzyme. Because cytosol glycogen and blood glucose levels are normal, plasma membrane transport is not the source of the problems associated with the disease.

4. **E.** To solve this problem, look at each gene separately. For the first gene, the cross $AA \times aa$ produces offspring that are all Aa, so the probability for Aa among offspring is 1. Repeating this for B, C, and D gives probabilities for Bb, Cc, and Dd among offspring each equal to 1. Multiplying the probability for each gene, $1 \times 1 \times 1 \times 1$ gives a probability of 1 for the $AaBbCcDd$ genotype. You could have also just looked at the genotypes of the parents and recognized that there could only be one possible genotype for offspring, but in cases where the parental genotypes are more varied, you'll have to do the math. For any multiple-choice question that, at first reading, appears extremely difficult, take a moment to consider easy solutions.

5. **B.** The female reproductive structure of a flower is the carpel (often called the pistil). The carpel consists of a stigma, style, and ovary. Within the ovary are the ovules, which produce seeds after pollination and fertilization. A fruit develops from the ovary, although other flower parts may contribute to the structure of the mature fruit. If the plant structure contains seeds, then the structure is a fruit. Potatoes don't contain seeds. Potatoes are starch-storing tubers that develop at the ends of underground stems (rhizomes).

6. **D.** The DNA-copying mechanism of a host eukaryotic cell is inside the nucleus, where DNA replication normally occurs for the cell. Because all the necessary enzymes and materials needed for replication are found in the nucleus, the DNA of the DNA virus is replicated there.

7. **C.** Glycolysis and the Krebs cycle generate energy-rich ATP, NADH, and $FADH_2$. During glycolysis and the Krebs cycle, NADH and $FADH_2$ are produced when electrons are removed from various intermediate organic molecules (they are said to be oxidized) and transferred (with H^+) to NAD^+ and FAD (they are said to be reduced). In contrast, ATP is produced by *substrate-level* phosphorylation when a phosphate group is transferred from one of the intermediate organic molecules (*substrate* molecules) to ADP. Additional ATP is generated during *oxidative* phosphorylation when inorganic phosphate groups (not attached to organic molecules) attach to ADP using the energy from the electrons in NADH and $FADH_2$ (forming NAD^+, FAD, and energy-poor electrons). The energy-depleted electrons combine with *oxygen* and hydrogen ions to form water.

8. **E.** In both binary fission and mitosis, chromosomes end up in two bodies (daughter cells for binary fission, nuclei for mitosis). Although both binary fission and mitosis are involved in the production of daughter cells from a parent cell, the processes are remarkably different in nearly all other respects. In prokaryotes, where binary fission occurs, there is a single chromosome that is not enclosed in a nucleus. Replication of the chromosome occurs, followed by invagination of the plasma membrane and cell wall formation that divide the cell into two

genetically identical cells (clones). In contrast, mitosis occurs in eukaryotes that have a nucleus enclosing multiple chromosomes. Mitosis is a complex process that is separate from cell division (cytokinesis) and replication. It organizes chromatin to form chromosomes, aligns chromosomes so that they can be divided into chromatids, divides the chromosomes into chromatids, segregates the chromatids to opposite poles, and forms two new nuclear membranes. These nuclei are genetically identical to that of the parent nucleus. But the production of daughter *cells* is not the result of mitosis. Rather, the division of the cell to produce two daughter cells occurs in a second process called cytokinesis. Then, replication of the chromatids occurs as a third process after cytokinesis, after the daughter cells are produced (during the S phase of the cell cycle). The reason why replication can occur after mitosis is because eukaryotic chromosomes have two identical chromatids (excepting mutations) that end up in separate daughter cells, so each daughter cell gets a copy of all the genes. In binary fission, replication must occur first, before the cell divides, if both daughter cells are to receive a complete chromosome with all of the genes.

9. **C.** If only the father expresses the trait of an X-linked dominant allele, all daughters and no sons will receive the X-chromosome and the trait. His sons receive his Y chromosome and cannot inherit the X-linked trait from him. All the remaining inheritance patterns are possible, as illustrated in the labeled pedigrees. In each of the following pedigrees, all possible genotypes, based on sex and inheritance pattern, are shown; those genotypes that do not fit the pedigree are crossed out. You should work out Punnett squares to confirm each pedigree.

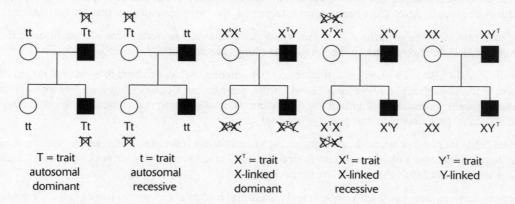

10. **C.** A specialized lysosome (produced by the Golgi body), the acrosome, is positioned at the head of a sperm. The acrosome releases enzymes that help the sperm cell penetrate the outer glycoprotein layer surrounding the egg.

11. **A.** Viruses are either DNA viruses (containing only DNA) or RNA viruses (containing only RNA). Components of the envelope of an enveloped virus are obtained from the plasma membrane of its host cell as the virus exits. Viral proteins ("spikes") are added to the envelope by the virus. The capsid, or protein coat, of a virus is generated by transcription of viral genetic material followed by its translation into proteins. Assembly of the protein and the viral genome occurs inside the host cell.

12. **C.** A pheromone is a substance that is produced by one individual to communicate with or influence the behavior of another individual of the same species. To announce their readiness to mate, female moths release pheromones into the air and female elephants release pheromones into their urine. Ants deposit pheromones on the ground to mark trails to food or to announce an alarm in response to danger. In contrast to a pheromone, a hormone is a substance that is produced in one part of the body to elicit a response in another part of the body of the same individual. A neurotransmitter transmits a nerve impulse across the gap between neurons or between neurons and muscle cells.

13. **B.** Using N and n to represent the normal and mutant alleles, the only living individual who can possess the allele is a female who is $X^N X^n$. A fetus who is $X^n X^n$ or $X^n Y$ does not survive to birth. The genotype of the father must be $X^N Y$. Thus, the cross is $X^N X^n \times X^N Y$ and the offspring are $\frac{1}{3} X^N X^N + \frac{1}{3} X^N X^n + \frac{1}{3} X^N Y$.

14. **D.** Calcitonin, secreted by the thyroid gland, increases the absorption of Ca^{2+} from the blood into bone. PTH, secreted by the parathyroid glands, stimulates the release of Ca^{2+} from bone back into the blood and also stimulates the reabsorption of Ca^{2+} by the kidneys.

15. E. The strength of a density-dependent limiting factor varies with the density of the population. As population density increases, so does the influences of the limiting factor. For example, space (for ground-nesting birds), wastes and pollution (such as alcohol production by anaerobically growing yeasts), food availability, and disease may all influence population growth. Animal behavior, such as huddling bees, can influence population growth if the behavior is only effective when the number of individuals reaches a critical number. For density-*in*dependent factors, the density of the population does not influence the strength of the factor. Natural disasters and weather extremes are usually density independent.

16. B. Tight junctions are seams that completely encircle cells, preventing the movement of water and other material from passing between adjacent cells. In addition, the adjacent cells may be held together tightly by desmosomes (protein anchors). Suberin provides the same function in plant cells when it encircles endodermal cells to form the Casparian strip.

17. E. Allopatric speciation occurs when a geographic barrier creates reproductive isolation between two parts of what was once originally a single population without reproductive barriers. After gene flow stops between the two new populations (reproductive isolation), changes in the gene pools of each population can occur independently (by mutation, genetic drift, natural selection, nonrandom mating, or gene flow from a third population). Changes in the gene pool (evolution) of the populations may lead to behavioral, physiological, or structural differences that prevent individuals of the two populations from mating or producing fertile offspring (reproductive barriers). After these barriers are established, the two populations represent two species.

18. D. The skin provides a large surface area over which gas exchange can occur. This is in addition to the gas-exchange function that takes place in the lungs (when lungs are present).

19. D. Abscisic acid (ABA) is a plant growth inhibitor. In particular, ABA is responsible for prolonging dormancy in seeds and buds. The other plant hormones listed for the question are all associated with promoting growth. Auxin (indoleacetic acid) promotes plant growth by increasing water absorption and elongation in cells, often in response to light (phototropism) and gravity (geotropism).

20. C. Social behaviors evolve because, on average, individual fitness increases. For example, among many animals, fighting between members of a group is minimized by dominance hierarchies (or pecking orders), agonistic behaviors (that do not result in injuries), or territoriality.

21. B. Because they are associated with flagella and cilia, basal bodies are absent in most plants. Centrioles, which are structurally the same as basal bodies (consisting of nine groups of three microtubules arranged in a circle) are also absent in plants. Microtubules, however, are still present as they form the spindle apparatus and contribute to the cytoskeleton. Microfilaments (actin) are responsible for cytoplasmic streaming. The exception to these observations occurs in the flagellated sperm cells of mosses, liverworts, ferns, cycads, and *Ginkgo*. The loss of flagellated sperm (and their basal bodies) in more advanced plants is attributed to the evolution of adaptations for living on land and the loss of ancestral adaptations to living in an aquatic environment.

22. A. As ecological succession progresses from early to middle stages, biomass, diversity, and the amount of organic matter generally increase.

23. A. Translocation of sugars occurs through phloem sieve-tube members by bulk flow. After sugars are actively loaded into sieve-tube members at the sugar source, water follows into the sieve-tube members by osmosis. As pressure builds in the sieve-tube members from the inflowing water, the contents of the sieve-tube members, sugar-loaded sap, are forced through sieve plates along the sieve tube until the sap reaches a destination (sink) where the sugar are unloaded (by either utilization or conversion to an insoluble molecule such as starch). A sink, such as a tuber that stores starch, and a source, such as photosynthesizing leaves, can reverse roles and, as a result, the direction of translocation is reversed. Such reversal occurs in the spring before leaves appear on deciduous trees. Although water molecules are always forming hydrogen bonds with other water molecules, cohesion of these molecules is not the mechanism responsible for the movement of sugars through phloem sieve-tube members. (But cohesion of H_2O molecules is essential for the ascent of H_2O up trees.)

24. **C.** Acetylcholine is the neurotransmitter released by motor neurons to simulate contraction in muscles. Because botulin toxins block the release of acetylcholine, muscle paralysis results. Death is usually by respiratory failure resulting from the failure of diaphragm and rib muscles to contract.

25. **D.** In the genotype *aaccRrc´c´*, the R allele promotes pigmentation and *C´* is absent, so pigmentation is not inhibited. In answers A, C, and E, at least one *C´* is present, so pigmentation is inhibited. In answer B, no pigmentation occurs because no dominant allele of *A*, *C*, or *R* is present to promote pigmentation. By the way, when one gene (like *C´*) influences or masks the expression of another gene (like *A*, *C*, or *R*), it is called epistasis.

26. **D.** A silent mutation occurs when a nucleotide is replaced with a different nucleotide but the codon on the mRNA transcript still codes for the same amino acid. This occurs because of the redundancy in the genetic code—more than one codon often specifies the same amino acid. The polypeptide that results from translation of the new mRNA is the same polypeptide produced from the mRNA transcribed from the unmutated DNA. In contrast, a missense mutation occurs when a nucleotide substitution results in a codon that specifies a different amino acid. A nonsense mutation occurs if that new codon specifies a stop codon. A frameshift mutation occurs when a new nucleotide is inserted or an existing nucleotide is deleted. In the mRNA that is transcribed from DNA with a frameshift mutation, a change is created in all the codons that follow the point mutation.

27. **D.** There are no meiotic divisions during embryonic development. Meiosis is responsible for producing the gametes (sperm and eggs). Once fertilization of the egg occurs, development proceeds with mitotic divisions only. All of the other answers listed for the question contribute to differentiation among daughter cells.

28. **E.** As is the case with most insect behaviors, male courtship behaviors among fruit flies are inherited, or innate. They are not learned by conditioning, acquired through imprinting, or the result of insight.

29. **A.** In various endocrine cells, the smooth endoplasmic reticulum is responsible for the synthesis of steroid hormones (testosterone in the testes and estrogen in the ovaries, for example). A major function of the liver is the detoxification of harmful substances that it intercepts in the blood. The detoxification of these substances (including alcohol, antibiotics, and pesticides) occurs by the smooth ER. Also in liver cells, the smooth ER is responsible for allowing the release of glucose into the bloodstream after it is broken down from glycogen. The specialized smooth ER of skeletal muscle cells, the sarcoplasmic reticulum, initiates muscle contraction by releasing Ca^{2+} into the cytoplasm.

30. **E.** MHC (major histocompatibility complex) refers to a class of proteins produced by body cells. In a normal cell, these proteins display on the membrane surface and identify the cell as a "self" cell. In an infected or cancerous cell, the MHC proteins bind to antigens in the cell and display a "nonself" signature on the membrane surface, marking the infected cell for attack by T-cells. The MHC is not responsible for the secretion of interferons (proteins that stimulate other cells to prepare for viral infections) or for proteins of the complement system (that circulate in the bloodstream and promote destruction of foreign cells).

31. **C.** Root hairs are extended epidermal cells in the primary tissue of the root. Primary growth occurs only at the apical meristems (root and shoot tips) and is responsible for root and shoot elongation. As primary growth matures, it forms primary tissues (including root hairs, primary xylem, and primary phloem). Lateral growth, growth that increases the girth, or diameter, of roots and shoots is secondary growth. Secondary growth matures to form secondary tissues (including secondary xylem and secondary phloem). Wood, by definition, is secondary xylem. So heartwood, older xylem that no longer conducts water or stores food, and sapwood, newer xylem that may still be functional, are exclusively secondary tissues. Cork cambium is a secondary tissue that gives rise to the periderm (outer corky bark of a woody plant).

32. **E.** First assume that *CD* is on one chromosome and *cd* is on its homologous chromosome. If there is no crossing over, then, after meiosis is complete, one chromosome (with *CD*) ends up in one sperm and its homologue ends up in another sperm (with *cd*). But because there is 50 percent crossing over, half of the chromosomes will exchange a *C* on one chromosome with a *c* on its homologue (which has the same effect as exchanging a *D* with a *d*). As a result, 50 percent of the chromosomes will now be *Cd* and *cD*. The end result will be 50 percent *CD* and *cd* (or 25 percent each) and 50 percent *Cd* and *cd* (or 25 percent each). Another approach to this question is to assume that *Cd* and *cD* are the two homologous chromosomes instead of *CD* and *cd*. The end result is the same (25 percent each for *CD, Cd, cD,* and *cd*) if the crossing over frequency is 50 percent.

33. A. The sea otters are the keystone species because they were holding the community together. When the sea otter population declined, sea urchins proliferated and demolished many of the kelp beds. Without the kelp beds, fish populations decreased and shore erosion increased. The sea otters were maintaining a balance between predator and prey (sea urchins and kelp). With the sea otters gone, the kelp and fish populations crashed along with some of the habitat (shore erosion).

34. D. The nucleolus is an area in the nucleus were rRNA is actively being transcribed from DNA and where the rRNA and proteins are being assembled into small and large ribosomal subunits. No membrane encloses this area of activity.

35. E. Heterotrophs, including all animals and fungi, are organisms that cannot obtain energy or create carbohydrates from inorganic materials. Instead, they must acquire energy by eating other organisms. In contrast, algae and other photosynthetic organisms can obtain energy and produce carbohydrates from CO_2, H_2O, and sunlight. Similarly, certain prokaryotes called chemoautotrophs can obtain energy and produce carbohydrates from CO_2 and inorganic molecules such as NH_3, H_2S, and NO_2^-.

36. D. The taxon consisting of organisms that are more closely related than those in an order is a family. If cows, dogs, and whales are classified in different orders, they must be in different families and genera. If several different organisms were in the *same* order, they could be in the same family or in different families.

37. A. Testosterone stimulates the development of male reproductive structures and secondary male sex characteristics. Although female mammals, in general, produce some testosterone, it is usually at concentrations much lower than in males and at much lower concentrations than the female sex hormones (estradiol and progesterone). As a result, female characteristics in females prevail. In spotted hyenas, however, testosterone levels are so high in females that their sex organs mimic those of males and typical male behavior, such as aggression and dominance, is displayed by females.

38. C. Milk production is promoted by a *positive* feedback system. The more a baby nurses, the more milk the mammary glands of the mother are stimulated to produce. In a positive feedback system, feedback reinforces an activity. In contrast, a negative feedback system deters an activity. Blood glucose, for example, is controlled by negative feedback: when blood glucose increases, it is reduced by the hormone insulin, and when blood glucose decreases, it is increased by the influence of the hormone glucagon.

39. B. Imprinting is the acquisition of a behavior in response to a stimulus during a specific period of time (critical period) during development. Baby chicks will accept as their mother the first moving object they see after birth. The moving object usually *is* their mother, but if it is another animal or even a moving inanimate object, the chicks will follow it instead. The chicks must be exposed to the stimulus (moving object) within the first day or two of life (critical period) or no imprinting will occur.

40. A. An endosymbiont is an organism that lives within another organism. In endosymbiosis theory, a mutually beneficial symbiosis occurred when a prokaryotic cell engulfed another prokaryote. The foreign prokaryote ultimately became an organelle that shared cellular functions with the host cell. In a series of endosymbiotic events, mitochondria, chloroplasts and other plastids, flagella, and centrioles were introduced into the cells that became the eukaryotes. A note about charophyceans: They are a group of green algae from which land plants are believe to have evolved.

41. A. Gastrulation is the formation of the two-layer gastrula from the one-layer blastula stage. In frogs and sea urchins, this occurs in the blastula as a group of cells invaginate, forming a circular opening (blastopore) into a cavity (archenteron) that forms inside the gastrula. In birds, however, invagination occurs along a line (the primitive streak), and the blastopore is a crevice rather than a circular opening.

42. A. During the breakdown of glucose by respiration, CO_2 is *released*. In contrast, carbon (in the form of CO_2) is removed from the atmosphere and is incorporated into carbohydrates during photosynthesis. These carbohydrates and other hydrocarbon metabolites of plants form ocean sediments when marine organisms die. The organic remnants of other organisms are transformed to fossil fuels after burial deep underground for millions of years.

43. E. If A + T = 46%, then G + C = 54%. Since A = T and G = C, then A = T = 23% and G = C = 27%. Uracil only occurs in RNA.

44. A. Mycorrhizae are mutualistic relationships between fungi and plant roots. These relationships, which are common in angiosperms and gymnosperms, increase absorption of water and minerals into roots. In exchange, the fungi receive carbohydrates. Some of the other answers listed with this question describe additional symbiotic relationships. In a mutualistic relationship similar to mycorrhizae, nitrogen uptake by the roots of some plants (especially legumes) is increased by the presence of nitrogen-fixing bacteria in specialized root structures called nodules. Plants that live on other plants without harming them (commensalism) are called epiphytes.

45. B. The dominant generation of a fern is the leafy sporophyte. The gametophyte generation consists of a small, flat, and mostly one-cell thick prothallus. Fern sporophytes have true leaves. Because ferns do not produce seeds, but have vascular tissue (xylem and phloem), they are grouped in the category of seedless vascular plants.

46. B. Blood from the body returns to the right side of the heart (viewed from the perspective that it is your own heart), entering the right atrium (4), then the right ventricle (6), and exiting the heart through the pulmonary artery (2). The blood then travels to the lungs, where gas exchange occurs (oxygen diffuses into the blood and carbon dioxide diffuses out). It returns to the heart through the pulmonary veins (3), entering the left atrium (5), then the left ventricle (7). Blood leaves the heart through the aorta (1) and enters the systemic system (system of blood vessels throughout the body, excluding the lungs). The muscular ventricles are responsible for the pumping action of the heart, whereas the atria serve as a holding area for blood ready to enter the ventricles.

47. D. Helicase separates the double helix into two single strands. One of these two strands becomes the template for the leading strand, the other for the lagging strand.

48. C. The function of DNA polymerase is to *elongate* a new DNA strand by adding nucleotides in an order determined by the template strand. DNA polymerase cannot *begin* a new DNA strand. Instead, another enzyme, primase, begins a new strand by creating a short primer made of RNA nucleotides. The RNA nucleotides are added in the order determined by the template strand. After the primer is created, DNA polymerase takes over and continues the elongation of the new DNA strand by adding DNA nucleotides. Later, the RNA primer is removed and replaced with DNA nucleotides.

49. A. During the replication of DNA for the lagging strand, replication occurs in short segments away from the replication fork. As the replication fork advances, a new DNA segment begins again, each initiated by primase with an RNA primer. These DNA segments, called Okazaki fragments, are ultimately joined by DNA ligase.

50. E. During replication for the lagging strand, the RNA nucleotides of an RNA primer are replaced by DNA nucleotides. Normally, this occurs as follows. Assume that there are two adjacent Okazaki fragments, fragment 1 (attached to the lagging strand that extends in the direction away from the replication fork) and the next, more recently added, fragment 2 (closer to the replication fork) (see figure). Between these two fragments, there is an RNA primer attached to fragment 1. This was the primer that was needed to initiate the creation of fragment 1. In the first step to replacing the RNA primer, the primer itself is removed, creating a gap between fragments 1 and 2. Second, DNA polymerase attaches to the end of fragment 2 (its 3' end) and extends fragment 2 to fragment 1, filling the gap left by the primer. Third, ligase connects fragments 1 and 2. A problem develops, however, when the end of replication is reached and the primer that occupies the last region on the lagging strand is removed. There is no "next" fragment 2 (with a 3' end) for DNA polymerase to attach to and begin filling the gap created by the removal of the primer. Instead, telomerase attaches to the end of the template strand (with which the lagging strand is base-paired) and elongates the template strand with a short sequence of nucleotides in an order determined by its own "built-in" template. By elongating the template strand in this way, the lagging strand can then be extended the usual way (primers followed by DNA polymerase) as long as telomerase continues to elongate the template strand. Telomerase continues to elongate the template strand by adding a short sequence of DNA nucleotides over and over again. When the telomerase stops elongating the template strand (which it eventually does), DNA polymerase will still be unable to replicate the terminal section of the template strand where the primer is removed. However, the DNA at the end of the template strand is just repeating short segments of nucleotides (generated from the "built-in" template of telomerase) and merely acts to prevent the loss of the important coding DNA that precedes it.

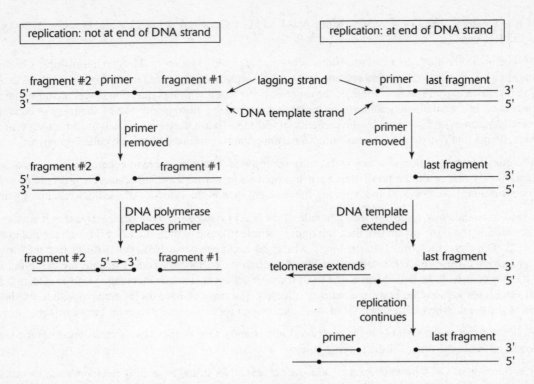

51. **E.** Thermoregulation is the maintenance of body temperature—a mechanism to cool the body when it is too hot is to dilate blood vessels (vasodilation), allowing more blood to enter regions with large surface-to-volume ratios (like ear lobes, fingers, and toes) where more heat is able escape.

52. **B.** Osmoregulation is the maintenance of correct concentrations of water and salts in cells and throughout the body.

53. **A.** A blastula is an early developmental stage of an embryo consisting of a single layer of cells that surrounds a fluid-filled cavity, the blastocoel. Gastrulation begins when some of the cells move inward (invaginate) into the blastocoel. As these cells invaginate, they create a second layer of cells. A third layer of cells forms between these two layers. The three layers, from outside to inside, are called the ectoderm, mesoderm, and endoderm, and each layer eventually leads to the development of specific parts of the body.

54. **C.** This is an example of adaptive radiation. When a single species is introduced into a new habitat that contains few other species, variation among individuals allows evolution of adaptations that increase survival and reproduction in many of the unoccupied niches. Eventually, the single species evolves into many species, each adapted to one of the many previously unoccupied niches.

55. **A.** This is an example of convergent evolution. All five species independently evolved spines in response to a common environmental pressure (probably predation).

56. **E.** This is an example of character displacement. When the species do not coexist, the range of ant sizes is wide. When the species do coexist, the range of ant size changes in each species so that size overlap and competition for food is minimized.

57. **B.** This is an example of divergent evolution. All three species share a common booby ancestor and, for various reasons, diverged for unknown reasons. There is no evidence that character displacement was the cause of this divergence because each of the three booby species exhibit the same feeding strategy in other parts of the world with or without interspecies competition.

58. **B.** Cohesion is the attraction between *like* substances. Because of the hydrogen bonding between them, water molecules stick to other water molecules.

59. **A.** Adhesion is the attraction between *unlike* substances. The polar regions of water molecules are attracted to oppositely charged polar regions of other molecules. This attraction, called capillary action, is responsible for water rising in tubing or creeping through filter paper.

60. E. Sweating is an effective mechanisms for cooling because water has a high heat capacity. Heat capacity is a measure of the amount of energy required for a substance to change temperature. As heat moves from the body into the water (sweat), the water temperature increases slowly. Eventually, the sweat reaches the temperature required to evaporate, and an even greater amount of heat is transferred when sweat is converted from liquid to vapor (heat of vaporization). For each molecule of water that is secreted and evaporated, a relatively large amount of body heat is lost.

61. B. The pancreas produces an inactive form of the enzyme trypsin and secretes it into the pancreatic duct, which delivers it to the duodenum, the first part of the small intestine. Once trypsin enters the small intestine, it is activated by another enzyme produced by cells of the intestinal wall. The pancreas also secretes other digestive enzymes (including chymotrypsin, for protein digestion, lipase, for fat digestion, and pancreatic amylase, for starch digestion) as well as sodium carbonate. Sodium carbonate provides an alkaline medium for the pancreatic juices, which neutralize the acidity of food arriving from the stomach.

62. D. The liver produces bile, a substance that emulsifies fats. Emulsify means to *physically* break down into smaller pieces, so bile breaks down fat into smaller fat particles. This creates a larger surface area for lipase to *chemically* (and enzymatically) break down bile into its chemical constituents, glycerol and fatty acid. Bile is a mixture of salts, bilirubin (a breakdown product of hemoglobin), and other substances.

63. C. Most nutrient absorption occurs in the small intestine (after the duodenum). This includes the absorption of monosaccharides, amino acids, glycerol, fatty acids, and nucleotides, molecules that are produced from the breakdown of carbohydrates, proteins, fats, and nucleic acids.

64. E. If *C* represents the allele for cleft chins, the man could be *CC* or *Cc*. His father was *cc* because he did not have a cleft chin, so the man must be *Cc*. Similarly, the woman (with a cleft chin) could be *CC* or *Cc*. Since she previously had a child without a cleft chin (*cc*), she must be *Cc* (the child had to get one of its *c* alleles from her). So the cross for this question is *Cc* × *Cc*. The probabilities for their offspring are ¼ *CC* + ½ *Cc* + ¼ *cc*. The probability for children with cleft chins (*CC* + *Cc*) is ¾.

65. C. From the answer to the previous question, the chance of having a child with a cleft chin is ¾. The chance of having a male child is ½. The chance of having a male child with a cleft chin is the product of the two probabilities, ¾ × ½ = ⅜.

66. D. Each child is a separate event, and the probabilities of inheritance apply to each birth separately. The chance for a child with a cleft chin for the first birth is ¾, and the chance for a similar child for the second birth is also ¾, so the chance of having both is ¾ × ¾ = ⁹⁄₁₆.

67. B. The primary tissue of a typical eudicot root is characterized by a multilobed core of xylem cells surrounded by phloem, mostly between the xylem lobes. In contrast, answer E illustrates a typical monocot root, where a ring of xylem cells is surrounded by phloem tissue.

68. C. The primary tissue of a typical monocot stem is characterized by bundles of cells scattered throughout ground tissue. Each bundle consists of xylem cells facing inward, toward the center of the stem, and phloem cells facing outward. In contrast, answer A illustrates the typical stem of most eudicots (and some gymnosperms), with vascular bundles arranged in a ring. Answer D shows the stem structure for some other dicots and some gymnosperms.

69. D. Process I is photolysis, splitting H_2O to form O_2 and H^+.

70. B. Acidity increases (H^+ concentration increases) when photolysis (the splitting of water) occurs inside the thylakoid releasing H^+ and also when H^+ follows electrons along the electron transport chain in the thylakoid membrane. Also, H^+ concentration decreases outside the thylakoid (in the stroma) when NADP and H^+ leave the stroma to enter the thylakoid membrane. The effect of all processes is to increase H^+ (increase acidity) inside the thylakoid and decrease H^+ in the stroma.

71. D. The higher concentration of H^+ inside the thylakoid compared to the stroma establishes an electrochemical H^+ (proton) gradient that drives the phosphorylation of ADP to ATP (Process II in figure) in the stroma. The enzyme ATP synthase catalyzes this reaction.

72. B. The production of ATP from ADP is generated by the enzyme ATP synthase. The activation energy for the reaction comes from the electrochemical H^+ (proton) gradient established by the higher concentration of H^+ inside the thylakoid compared to the stroma.

73. D. Process III is the Calvin cycle. The Calvin cycle generates the three-carbon sugar, G3P (glyceraldehyde-3-phosphate, or PGAL). Two molecules of G3P form glucose. The other product of the Calvin cycle is $NADP^+$ which, together with H^+ from the stroma, moves into the thylakoid.

74. C. Marine bony fish regulate their body ions and fluids to maintain an internal environment that is less salty than (and hypoosmotic to) their environment. By secreting salts (mostly through their gills), constantly drinking, and rarely urinating, the internal environment of these fish remains constant.

75. A. Isosmotic means that the concentration of ions and fluid in the body is the same as the environment. When the environment changes, the body conditions change in a like manner.

76. C. Whether salmon are in a marine or freshwater environment, the concentration of ions and fluid remains unchanged in their bodies. Relative to the changing concentration of ions in the surrounding environment, they are either hypoosmotic (when in the ocean) or hyperosmotic (when in fresh water).

77. E. Platyhelminthes are flat worms that have bilateral symmetry and are acoelomate. The figure places animals with these characteristics in group E.

78. C. Open circulatory systems characterize insects and most mollusks. Both groups have bilateral symmetry and have coeloms. Insects are segmented and mollusks are not segmented. Groups C and D fit these characteristics.

79. C. Nephridia are found in mollusks and annelid (segmented) worms. Both groups have bilateral symmetry and have coeloms. Annelid worms are segmented and mollusks are not segmented. Groups C and D fit these characteristics. Note that nephridia exemplify a tube-type system, with an opening inside the body that allows fluids to enter, to be filtered, and to pass out through an opening on the outside of the body (a pore). In contrast, the protonephridia of flatworms lack an internal opening. Instead, cilia inside specialized cells (flame cells) pull in body fluids that are filtered before passing out of the body through a pore.

80. B. Because the solution in the beaker turned blue-black, you know that the IKI diffused through the bag, into the solution in the beaker, and reacted with the starch. Because the contents of the bag did not turn blue-black, you know that the starch did not diffuse from the beaker into the bag. Thus you know the bag is permeable to IKI and not permeable to starch. Because no test for glucose was reported, no conclusion can be drawn for the bag's permeability to glucose.

81. E. In Figure VI, there are 4 haploid cells (each cell has one chromosome with two chromatids). In Figure VII there are 8 haploid cells (each cell has one chromatid). This is an example of mitosis because both parent and daughter cells have the same number of chromosomes. Note that a chromosome can consist of one or two chromatids.

82. C. Crossing over takes place during prophase of meiosis I, which occurs between figures III and IV. A description of the process that occurs between each figure follows:

I to II: mycelial fusion (plasmogamy) and pairing of nuclei from each strain (dikaryon)

II to III: fusion of nuclei from each strain (karyogamy)

III to IV: meiosis I

IV to V: meiosis II

V to VI: replication of second chromatid during "S" phase of cell cycle

VI to VII: mitosis

83. C. If no crossing over takes place, the arrangement of ascospores in the mature ascus will mirror the arrangement of the chromatids bearing the spore color genes in III, except that each chromatid will produce two (adjacent) spores. Such an ascus is illustrated in XI.

84. **A.** If B1 and T1 cross over, the ascus for VIII will be produced. In contrast, crossovers between B1 and T2 would produce the ascus in IX, crossovers between B2 and T1 would produce the ascus in XII, and crossovers between B2 and T2 would produce the ascus in Figure X. A crossover event occurs between homologous chromosomes, so answer E, which describes a crossover between sister chromatids, does not apply. Because each adjacent pair of ascospores consists of identical clones produced by mitosis, the ascus labeled XIII, with unlike adjacent pairs, cannot occur.

85. **A.** Plants with an *r*-selected life history are opportunistic, pioneer species that reproduce and mature quickly and produce many offspring. These species are usually the first species to invade a habitat when succession begins, when a previously uninhabited region becomes available, or after a climax community has been destroyed.

86. **E.** Hardwood trees are in greatest abundance in the climax stages of succession for a temperate forest community typical of the eastern United States.

87. **E.** The germinating seeds are obtaining energy from stored nutrients through respiration. The Krebs cycle of aerobic respiration releases CO_2. It is also true (but not listed as a possible answer) that CO_2 is released by fermentation, but most seeds are unlikely to germinate in the absence of oxygen because anaerobic respiration supplies too little energy.

88. **E.** Enzymes are generally effective only within a certain range of temperatures. Above a certain temperature, the secondary and tertiary structures of the enzymes (which are proteins) break down (denature) and become ineffective.

89. **B.** Each plot shows the accumulation of oxygen consumption as time passes. The slopes of the plots represent the *rates* of oxygen consumption (changes in O_2 with time, expressed as ml g^{-1} min^{-1}, or ml/g·min). Because the slopes are constant (straight lines), the respiratory rates are constant but different for the two temperatures. Oxygen production is recorded in ml/g, which means the amount of oxygen produced, in milliliters, is divided by the weight, in grams, of the hamster. As a result, oxygen production by hamsters of different sizes is averaged over their weights. Although these hamsters may indeed have different respiratory rates (due to size or even physiological differences), these differences are not detectable in the reported data.

90. **D.** In this experiment, time is an independent variable and respiratory rate is the dependent variable. Temperature is also an independent variable, but this variable was assigned two values (10 °C and 25 °C) for the purpose of examining how temperature affects respiratory rate over time. But within each chamber, the temperature must be constant (either 10 °C or 25 °C). Only time and respiratory rate are allowed to vary. Since respiratory rate is indirectly measured by changes in the quantity of oxygen consumed, the amount of oxygen in each chamber is allowed to change. Note that KOH was added to the animal chambers to absorb any CO_2 produced, thus maintaining a constant amount of CO_2 in the chambers.

91. **A.** The potato sections lost weight when in beakers with 0.6 M, 0.8 M, and 1.0 M solutions. Thus, water moved out of the potato sections and into the solutions in the beakers. Since water will move from areas of higher concentration of water to areas of lower concentration of water (which is the same as moving from areas of lower solute concentration to areas of higher solute concentration), the concentrations of solutes in the potato cores were lower than the concentrations of solutes in the surrounding solutions. Thus, the potato cores were hypotonic relative to the solutions in the beakers.

92. **D.** When there is no net movement of water between the potato section and the solution in the beaker, the concentration of solutes in both potato and solution is the same. This occurred when the concentration of the solution in the beaker was 0.4 M. Therefore, the potato section has a solute concentration of 0.4 M.

93. **D.** Divergence of species is indicated by horizontal changes. Nearly all of the horizontal changes and, thus, nearly all of the divergence occurs in the area indicated by IV.

94. **E.** This is an example of punctuated equilibrium, where long periods of stasis (no change, as in areas III and V) are punctuated with (interrupted by) short periods of rapid change (area IV).

95. **B.** Area III represents a period of time with little or no evolutionary change maintained by stabilizing selection.

96. **C.** Adaptive radiation can occur when a single species is introduced into an unoccupied area with many available niches. Rapid evolution of many species occurs as the available niches are exploited. After all the niches are filled, evolutionary rates decline.

97. B. Net productivity is the amount of fixed carbon produced from photosynthesis less the amount of fixed carbon consumed by respiration. Bottle 2 (light for 24 hours) is the sum of both of these processes.

98. A. Respiration (carbon utilization) in the absence of photosynthesis (carbon production) is determined by comparing bottle 3 (dark for 24 hours) to bottle 1 (initial measurement). So, 2.80 – 2.78 = 0.02.

99. C. The gross productivity is the total amount of carbon produced (before subtracting any consumed by respiration). By summing the net productivity (0.04, determined by comparing bottle 2 to bottle 1) and the carbon consumed by respiration (0.02, determined by comparing bottle 3 to bottle 1), the gross productivity is determined (0.04 + 0.02 = 0.06).

100. B. By measuring changes in O_2, the experiment was able to determine rates of photosynthesis (by how much O_2 was produced) and rates of respiration (by how much O_2 was consumed). The same rates can also be determined by measuring changes in the amount of CO_2 consumed (a measurement of photosynthetic rate) and the amount of CO_2 produced (a measurement of respiratory rate). A third way to measure productivity is by measuring changes in biomass.

Section II (Free-Response Questions)

Scoring Standards for the Essay Questions

To score your answers, award your essay points using the standards given. For each item listed that matches the content and vocabulary of a statement or explanation in your essay, add the indicated number of points to your essay score (to the maximum allowed for each section). Scores for each essay question range from 0 to 10 points.

Words appearing in parentheses in answers represent alternative wording.

Question 1 (10 points maximum)

Many different hypotheses are possible, and there are many ways to test each hypothesis. The answers provided are based on the cell respiration lab (Lab 5) described in the AP Lab Manual.

A. hypothesis statement (*2 points maximum*)

1 pt: Energy is obtained from aerobic respiration (or Krebs cycle).

1 pt: Energy is obtained from the breakdown of carbohydrates (or glucose, or $C_6H_{12}O_6$).

1 pt: Equation and associated explanation: $C_6H_{12}O_6 + O_2 \rightarrow H_2O + CO_2 + energy$ (or ATP).

1 pt: Glucose, or $C_6H_{12}O_6$, or starch is stored in endosperm or cotyledons.

B. description of experiment (*4 points maximum*)

1 pt: The independent variable is time.

1 pt: The dependent variable is O_2 uptake. (Alternately, for the hypothesis given in Section A, CO_2 release could be the dependent variable. Other dependent variables are possible depending on your hypothesis.)

1 pt: for each of the following three items (*2 points maximum*):

There are three treatments of the dependent variable:

1. Live seeds (peas, for example), soaked and beginning to germinate.

2. Dry (unsoaked) live seeds (or boiled seeds, or otherwise dead seeds).

3. Beads or other inanimate material to occupy the same amount of space/weight.

1 pt: The control variables (treatments) are the dry live seeds and the beads. (Note: The experimental treatment is the live seeds.)

1 pt: Provide a mechanism to deal with confounding factors. In the experiment described here (and in the AP lab), KOH is added to the apparatus in order to absorb released CO_2, which would otherwise make an accurate measurement of O_2 uptake impossible.

1 pt: Provide a brief description of the apparatus and procedure. For this example, respirometers are used to measure gas uptake. A respirometer is a vessel (or test tube) that can be sealed and has a device to measure changes in pressure inside (test tube with pipette sealed to opening with a rubber stopper).

C. expected results (*2 points maximum*)

1 pt: Experimental treatment: Pressure inside the vessel with the soaked, germinating seeds decreases.

1 pt: Control treatments: No change in the pressure inside the vessels enclosing the control treatments.

D. graphed data (see the example) (*2 points maximum*)

1 pt: Axes are labeled, units provided, and scale is linear (equal intervals anywhere on an axis represent the same amount of change in the variable) (or if scale is logarithmic, it is so identified).

1 pt: Independent variable is plotted on the *x*-axis and the dependent variable is plotted on the *y*-axis.

1 pt: A title to graph is provided.

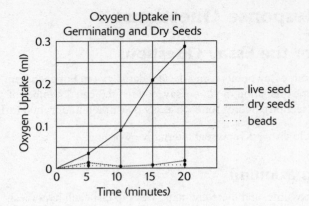

Oxygen Uptake in Germinating and Dry Seeds

— live seed
······ dry seeds
···· beads

E. alternate hypothesis (*1 point maximum*)

1 pt: The decrease in pressure in the experimental treatment (germinating seeds) could be the result of an uptake of gas other than oxygen. (A means to analyze the gas inside the vessels before and after the experiment is necessary.)

Question 2 (10 points maximum)

A. HIV structure (*2 points maximum*)

1 pt: Genome is diploid (consists of two copies of the RNA genome).

1 pt: Genome includes the enzyme reverse transcriptase.

1 pt: Virus includes a protein coat or capsid.

1 pt: Virus includes an envelope derived (partially) from the plasma membrane of the host.

1 pt: Virus includes viral glycoproteins on surface of envelope.

1 pt: Genome is positive-sense RNA (contains the same base sequence as the mRNA produced by the virus).

No points: Genome is single-stranded RNA (ssRNA), or is a retrovirus (stated in question).

B. how HIV enters a cell (*2 points maximum*)

1 pt: HIV glycoprotein (gp120) binds to a specific receptor molecule on plasma membrane of host cell.

1 pt: $CD4^+$ protein is marker for plasma membrane receptor molecule that is required for entry of HIV into host cell.

1 pt: Additional receptors/proteins on plasma membrane of host cell required for entry of HIV into host cell (CCR5, CXCR4).

C. stages of HIV infection from single-stranded RNA to provirus. (*3 points maximum*)

1 pt: Reverse transcriptase synthesizes an ssDNA from the HIV ssRNA creating a dsRNA/DNA.

1 pt: The HIV dsRNA/DNA is separated into an ssRNA and an ssDNA.

1 pt: The HIV ssDNA is replicated to form an dsDNA.

1 pt: The HIV dsDNA enters the host nucleus and inserts itself into host dsDNA (a provirus).

D. HIV replication (*3 points maximum*)

1 pt: HIV dsDNA is transcribed by DNA polymerase of host cell to produce HIV mRNA.

1 pt: Some HIV mRNAs are processed, or cut and rejoined with other HIV mRNAs in the nucleus.

1 pt: Some HIV mRNAs move to the cytoplasm of host cell for protein transcription.

1 pt: Some HIV mRNAs move to the cytoplasm to become new HIV genomes.

1 pt: Proteins assemble into capsids around mRNA genomes.

E. why disease is called AIDS (*2 points maximum*)

1 pt: Host cell is a T-cell that is normally involved in the immune response against viruses.

1 pt: HIV destroys T-cells (or CD4$^+$ T-cells); without T-cells, immune response is compromised (*immunodeficient*).

1 pt: Immunodeficiency is *acquired* as a result of HIV infection. (It is not an autoimmune deficiency, where the immune system attacks its body's own cells.)

1 pt: Illness and death usually occur with a group of symptoms (a *syndrome*), including cancers and opportunistic infections.

Question 3 (10 points maximum). Only three of the four parts to be scored.

A. thermoregulation in mammals (*4 points maximum*)

1 pt: Cooling occurs during sweating (or panting). Sweating (or panting) cools bodies when water molecules absorb energy and change from liquid to vapor (heat of vaporization).

1 pt: Warming occurs during shivering (contraction of skeletal muscles). Some energy obtained from ATP molecules for contraction is lost as heat.

1 pt: Warming or cooling occurs when blood vessels in the skin constrict or dilate, respectively. This especially occurs in hands (or toes, or ears) where a higher surface-to-volume ratio results in a greater heat loss.

1 pt: Thermoregulation is an example of a negative feedback mechanism. When the body gets too hot, cooling mechanisms are activated until normal temperatures return. When the body gets too cold, heating mechanisms are activated until normal temperatures return.

B. blood glucose regulation in humans (*4 points maximum*)

1 pt: Hormones are substances produced by cells in one part of the body to affect cells in another part of the body.

1 pt: Beta cells in the pancreas secrete the hormone insulin into the blood in response to high levels of glucose in the blood, such as after digesting a meal. Insulin stimulates the liver, muscle, and fat cells to absorb glucose, which lowers the amount of blood glucose.

1 pt: Alpha cells in the pancreas secrete the hormone glucagon into the blood in response to low levels of glucose in the blood, such as after exercise. Glucagon stimulates the liver to release glucose.

1 pt: Blood glucose regulation is an example of negative feedback. When blood glucose levels increase, insulin is secreted until levels return to normal. When blood glucose levels decrease, glucagon is secreted until levels return to normal.

C. osmoregulation in fish (*4 points maximum*)

1 pt: The problem for marine bony fish is that their normal internal environment is hypoosmotic (lower concentration of solutes) compared to their external environment. As a result, they constantly lose water by osmosis, which makes their internal environment saltier.

1 pt: The solution for marine bony fish is to secrete salts through their gills, constantly drink (to replace water lost to the environment by osmosis), and rarely urinate.

1 pt: The problem for freshwater fish is that their normal internal environment is hyperosmotic (higher concentration of solutes) compared to their external environment. As a result, they constantly gain water by osmosis, which makes their internal environment more dilute.

1 pt: The solution for freshwater fish is to absorb salts through their gills, rarely drink, and frequently urinate.

D. water deficit response in plant leaves (*4 points maximum*)

    1 pt: Water deficits in leaves can occur as a result of low environmental humidity, high temperatures, or low soil moisture.

    1 pt: Stomata close in response to high temperatures. When water diffuses out of the two guard cells that encircle a stoma, the cells lose turgor and collapse, closing the stomata. Water loss is reduced when stomata are closed.

    1 pt: Stomata close in response to low concentrations of water in leaves. When water concentrations are low in leaves and roots, as might occur because of low soil moisture, root cells and mesophyll cells secrete abscisic acid, which stimulates guard cells to close stomata.

    1 pt: Leaf abscission increases during water deficit conditions, causing the loss of leaves, the reduction in total leaf surface area, and the retention of more water.

    1 pt: In response to long-term, extreme water stress, epidermal cells may increase secretion of waxes, which results in a thickening of the cuticle.

Question 4 (10 points maximum). Only three of the four relationships to be scored.

Mycorrhiza

A. (*2 points maximum*)

    1 pt: A mycorrhiza is a symbiotic mutualistic association between a fungus and a plant.

    1 pt: Mycelia of the fungus penetrate individual cells of the outer cortex (or, alternatively, penetrate between the cells of the cortex) and extend out into the soil.

B. (*2 points maximum*)

    1 pt: The fungus increases the surface area of the roots, expanding their function by absorbing water and minerals.

    1 pt: The plant provides carbohydrates to the fungus.

Parasitoid

A. (*2 points maximum*)

    1 pt: A parasitoid is an insect that deposits its eggs into another insect or spider. When the eggs hatch, the larvae eat the inside of the living host. The host usually dies about the time the larvae pupate. Following metamorphosis, adult parasitoids fly away to repeat the life cycle.

    1 pt: Parasitoids are often small wasps, and their hosts are often caterpillars (larvae) of butterflies or moths.

B. (*2 points maximum*)

    1 pt: The parasitoid uses the host as food and shelter for its larvae.

    1 pt: The host gains nothing from the relationship and loses its life.

Mimicry

A. (*2 points maximum*)

    1 pt: In mimicry, two or more species resemble one another in appearance.

    1 pt: In Müllerian mimicry, two species, each of which has a defense mechanism, share a similar coloration.

    1 pt: In Batesian mimicry, two species, one with a defense mechanism and one without such a mechanism, share a similar coloration.

B. (*2 points maximum*)

    1 pt: In Mullerian mimicry, all mimic species benefit because their similar appearance is more easily learned by a predator than a unique appearance for each species.

    1 pt: In Batesian mimicry, the defenseless mimic gains protection from predators, yet does not need to use resources to produce or maintain the defense mechanism.

Camouflage

A. (*2 points maximum*)

    1 pt: A species uses camouflage to make its presence less apparent to another species.

    1 pt: Camouflage may be a color, pattern, shape, or behavior.

    1 pt for one example of camouflage, such as:

- Their beige color makes lions less visible against a savanna background.
- Their beige color makes gazelles less visible against a savanna background.
- A stick insect resembles the sticks or twigs of the plants it eats.

B. (*2 points maximum*)

    1 pt: Camouflage helps predators catch prey.

    1 pt: Camouflage helps prey escape predators.

Answer Sheet for Practice Exam 5

1 Ⓐ Ⓑ Ⓒ Ⓓ Ⓔ	26 Ⓐ Ⓑ Ⓒ Ⓓ Ⓔ	51 Ⓐ Ⓑ Ⓒ Ⓓ Ⓔ	76 Ⓐ Ⓑ Ⓒ Ⓓ Ⓔ
2 Ⓐ Ⓑ Ⓒ Ⓓ Ⓔ	27 Ⓐ Ⓑ Ⓒ Ⓓ Ⓔ	52 Ⓐ Ⓑ Ⓒ Ⓓ Ⓔ	77 Ⓐ Ⓑ Ⓒ Ⓓ Ⓔ
3 Ⓐ Ⓑ Ⓒ Ⓓ Ⓔ	28 Ⓐ Ⓑ Ⓒ Ⓓ Ⓔ	53 Ⓐ Ⓑ Ⓒ Ⓓ Ⓔ	78 Ⓐ Ⓑ Ⓒ Ⓓ Ⓔ
4 Ⓐ Ⓑ Ⓒ Ⓓ Ⓔ	29 Ⓐ Ⓑ Ⓒ Ⓓ Ⓔ	54 Ⓐ Ⓑ Ⓒ Ⓓ Ⓔ	79 Ⓐ Ⓑ Ⓒ Ⓓ Ⓔ
5 Ⓐ Ⓑ Ⓒ Ⓓ Ⓔ	30 Ⓐ Ⓑ Ⓒ Ⓓ Ⓔ	55 Ⓐ Ⓑ Ⓒ Ⓓ Ⓔ	80 Ⓐ Ⓑ Ⓒ Ⓓ Ⓔ
6 Ⓐ Ⓑ Ⓒ Ⓓ Ⓔ	31 Ⓐ Ⓑ Ⓒ Ⓓ Ⓔ	56 Ⓐ Ⓑ Ⓒ Ⓓ Ⓔ	81 Ⓐ Ⓑ Ⓒ Ⓓ Ⓔ
7 Ⓐ Ⓑ Ⓒ Ⓓ Ⓔ	32 Ⓐ Ⓑ Ⓒ Ⓓ Ⓔ	57 Ⓐ Ⓑ Ⓒ Ⓓ Ⓔ	82 Ⓐ Ⓑ Ⓒ Ⓓ Ⓔ
8 Ⓐ Ⓑ Ⓒ Ⓓ Ⓔ	33 Ⓐ Ⓑ Ⓒ Ⓓ Ⓔ	58 Ⓐ Ⓑ Ⓒ Ⓓ Ⓔ	83 Ⓐ Ⓑ Ⓒ Ⓓ Ⓔ
9 Ⓐ Ⓑ Ⓒ Ⓓ Ⓔ	34 Ⓐ Ⓑ Ⓒ Ⓓ Ⓔ	59 Ⓐ Ⓑ Ⓒ Ⓓ Ⓔ	84 Ⓐ Ⓑ Ⓒ Ⓓ Ⓔ
10 Ⓐ Ⓑ Ⓒ Ⓓ Ⓔ	35 Ⓐ Ⓑ Ⓒ Ⓓ Ⓔ	60 Ⓐ Ⓑ Ⓒ Ⓓ Ⓔ	85 Ⓐ Ⓑ Ⓒ Ⓓ Ⓔ
11 Ⓐ Ⓑ Ⓒ Ⓓ Ⓔ	36 Ⓐ Ⓑ Ⓒ Ⓓ Ⓔ	61 Ⓐ Ⓑ Ⓒ Ⓓ Ⓔ	86 Ⓐ Ⓑ Ⓒ Ⓓ Ⓔ
12 Ⓐ Ⓑ Ⓒ Ⓓ Ⓔ	37 Ⓐ Ⓑ Ⓒ Ⓓ Ⓔ	62 Ⓐ Ⓑ Ⓒ Ⓓ Ⓔ	87 Ⓐ Ⓑ Ⓒ Ⓓ Ⓔ
13 Ⓐ Ⓑ Ⓒ Ⓓ Ⓔ	38 Ⓐ Ⓑ Ⓒ Ⓓ Ⓔ	63 Ⓐ Ⓑ Ⓒ Ⓓ Ⓔ	88 Ⓐ Ⓑ Ⓒ Ⓓ Ⓔ
14 Ⓐ Ⓑ Ⓒ Ⓓ Ⓔ	39 Ⓐ Ⓑ Ⓒ Ⓓ Ⓔ	64 Ⓐ Ⓑ Ⓒ Ⓓ Ⓔ	89 Ⓐ Ⓑ Ⓒ Ⓓ Ⓔ
15 Ⓐ Ⓑ Ⓒ Ⓓ Ⓔ	40 Ⓐ Ⓑ Ⓒ Ⓓ Ⓔ	65 Ⓐ Ⓑ Ⓒ Ⓓ Ⓔ	90 Ⓐ Ⓑ Ⓒ Ⓓ Ⓔ
16 Ⓐ Ⓑ Ⓒ Ⓓ Ⓔ	41 Ⓐ Ⓑ Ⓒ Ⓓ Ⓔ	66 Ⓐ Ⓑ Ⓒ Ⓓ Ⓔ	91 Ⓐ Ⓑ Ⓒ Ⓓ Ⓔ
17 Ⓐ Ⓑ Ⓒ Ⓓ Ⓔ	42 Ⓐ Ⓑ Ⓒ Ⓓ Ⓔ	67 Ⓐ Ⓑ Ⓒ Ⓓ Ⓔ	92 Ⓐ Ⓑ Ⓒ Ⓓ Ⓔ
18 Ⓐ Ⓑ Ⓒ Ⓓ Ⓔ	43 Ⓐ Ⓑ Ⓒ Ⓓ Ⓔ	68 Ⓐ Ⓑ Ⓒ Ⓓ Ⓔ	93 Ⓐ Ⓑ Ⓒ Ⓓ Ⓔ
19 Ⓐ Ⓑ Ⓒ Ⓓ Ⓔ	44 Ⓐ Ⓑ Ⓒ Ⓓ Ⓔ	69 Ⓐ Ⓑ Ⓒ Ⓓ Ⓔ	94 Ⓐ Ⓑ Ⓒ Ⓓ Ⓔ
20 Ⓐ Ⓑ Ⓒ Ⓓ Ⓔ	45 Ⓐ Ⓑ Ⓒ Ⓓ Ⓔ	70 Ⓐ Ⓑ Ⓒ Ⓓ Ⓔ	95 Ⓐ Ⓑ Ⓒ Ⓓ Ⓔ
21 Ⓐ Ⓑ Ⓒ Ⓓ Ⓔ	46 Ⓐ Ⓑ Ⓒ Ⓓ Ⓔ	71 Ⓐ Ⓑ Ⓒ Ⓓ Ⓔ	96 Ⓐ Ⓑ Ⓒ Ⓓ Ⓔ
22 Ⓐ Ⓑ Ⓒ Ⓓ Ⓔ	47 Ⓐ Ⓑ Ⓒ Ⓓ Ⓔ	72 Ⓐ Ⓑ Ⓒ Ⓓ Ⓔ	97 Ⓐ Ⓑ Ⓒ Ⓓ Ⓔ
23 Ⓐ Ⓑ Ⓒ Ⓓ Ⓔ	48 Ⓐ Ⓑ Ⓒ Ⓓ Ⓔ	73 Ⓐ Ⓑ Ⓒ Ⓓ Ⓔ	98 Ⓐ Ⓑ Ⓒ Ⓓ Ⓔ
24 Ⓐ Ⓑ Ⓒ Ⓓ Ⓔ	49 Ⓐ Ⓑ Ⓒ Ⓓ Ⓔ	74 Ⓐ Ⓑ Ⓒ Ⓓ Ⓔ	99 Ⓐ Ⓑ Ⓒ Ⓓ Ⓔ
25 Ⓐ Ⓑ Ⓒ Ⓓ Ⓔ	50 Ⓐ Ⓑ Ⓒ Ⓓ Ⓔ	75 Ⓐ Ⓑ Ⓒ Ⓓ Ⓔ	100 Ⓐ Ⓑ Ⓒ Ⓓ Ⓔ

Practice Exam 5

Section I (Multiple-Choice Questions)

Time: 80 minutes

100 questions

Directions: Each of the following questions or statements is followed by five possible answers or sentence completions. Choose the one best answer or sentence completion.

1. Which of the following cellular bodies is involved in the processing of newly formed proteins, the attachment of carbohydrates to proteins to form glycoproteins, and the packaging of proteins within transport vesicles or lysosomes?

    A. smooth endoplasmic reticulum
    B. rough endoplasmic reticulum
    C. peroxisomes
    D. the nucleus
    E. Golgi complexes

2. In reference to a segment of DNA, which of the following molecules, if any, contains the *fewest* number of nucleotides?

    A. a single strand of the original DNA segment.
    B. a single strand of the original DNA segment after a point mutation.
    C. a single strand of complementary DNA (cDNA) made from the original DNA.
    D. the primary RNA transcript from the original DNA.
    E. All of the above contain the same number of nucleotides.

3. Prokaryotes include all of the following EXCEPT:

    A. photoautotrophs
    B. chemoautotrophs
    C. bacteria with flagella made with nine pairs of microtubules arranged in a circle surrounding two additional microtubules.
    D. cyanobacteria
    E. all species in the domain Archaea

4. An artery is any blood vessel that transports

    A. blood
    B. oxygenated blood
    C. deoxygenated blood
    D. blood away from the heart
    E. blood toward the heart

5. In peas, alleles for seed color are yellow (*Y*) and green (*y*), and alleles for seed shape are round (*R*) and wrinkled (*r*). If two parents, both green and round, are crossed and the offspring are ¾ green and round and ¼ green and wrinkled, what are the genotypes of the parents?

    A. *YyRr*
    B. *Yyrr*
    C. *yyRR*
    D. *yyRr*
    E. *yyrr*

6. All of the following are true about viruses EXCEPT:

    A. The genomes of RNA viruses are more likely to mutate than those of DNA viruses.
    B. Before entering a host cell, surface proteins of a virus bind to surface receptors of a specific host cell.
    C. All RNA viruses produce DNA as an intermediate molecule during the production of new RNA viruses.
    D. All DNA viruses produce RNA as an intermediate molecule during the production of new DNA viruses.
    E. All viruses require the use of ribosomes to produce new viruses.

GO ON TO THE NEXT PAGE

7. To which of the following groups would a bilateral animal without a coelom or pseudocoelom belong?

   A. Echinodermata
   B. Porifera
   C. Nematoda
   D. Rotifera
   E. Platyhelminthes

8. Male and female acorn woodpeckers live in groups that cooperate in food gathering, egg incubating, and chick rearing. The males are usually brothers and are unrelated to the females, who are usually sisters. Such group behavior

   A. increases the fitness of individuals as a result of their personal reproduction
   B. increases inclusive fitness
   C. increases sexual selection
   D. decreases survivability
   E. decreases total fitness

9. All of the following are mechanisms for communication between individuals of the same animal species EXCEPT:

   A. chemical signals
   B. visual signals
   C. acoustic signals
   D. tactile signals
   E. telepathic signals

10. Two species of rhea, an ostrich-like, flightless bird, occur in adjacent and overlapping areas in South America. Which of the following best explains why two species evolved and coexist?

   A. An earlier geographic barrier responsible for reproductive isolation was removed after speciation occurred.
   B. A mutation occurred in only one section of a larger, continuous ancestral population.
   C. There was selection for two different expressions of a trait within a larger, continuous ancestral population.
   D. The ancestral population experienced genetic drift.
   E. Gene flow between the two populations maintains reproductive isolation.

11. Contraction of the diaphragm and rib muscles in humans causes

   A. a decrease in the partial pressure of CO_2
   B. a decrease in the total pressure inside the lungs
   C. a decrease in the partial pressure of O_2
   D. an increase in the partial pressure of O_2
   E. air to be forced out of the lungs

12. A researcher wants to clone a human gene whose primary RNA transcript contains introns. A bacterial plasmid is used as a vector to transfer the gene into bacteria. To ensure success of the procedure, all of the following steps should be included in the process EXCEPT:

   A. Treat the plasmid and the human DNA with the same restriction enzyme.
   B. Use a restriction enzyme that does not produce sticky ends.
   C. Use the complementary DNA (cDNA) of the human gene.
   D. Provide suitable conditions (such as a calcium-rich growth medium) for transformation of the plasmid by the bacteria.
   E. Use DNA ligase to seal the human DNA in the plasmid.

13. Alternation of generations occurs in which of the following?

   A. mosses, only
   B. ferns and mosses, only
   C. all land plants, only
   D. all animals, only
   E. all plants and all animals

14. Children with DiGeorge syndrome are born without a thymus. To which of the following illnesses would these children be *least* susceptible?

   A. virus-infected cells
   B. cancerous cells
   C. intracellular fungal infections
   D. intracellular protozoan infections
   E. bacterial infections

15. Organisms in the Kingdom Fungi all share the following characteristics EXCEPT:

    A. Cell walls are made of chitin.

    B. Nutrients must be broken down before absorption by the fungus.

    C. Organisms are multicellular and form hyphae.

    D. Sexual and asexual reproduction produce haploid spores.

    E. They are heterotrophic.

16. During a viral infection, viral mRNA is translated. Where does this process occur within a eukaryotic host cell?

    A. in the lysosomes of the host cell

    B. in the cytoplasm of the host cell

    C. in the nucleolus of the host cell

    D. in the nucleus of the host cell, but not in the nucleolus

    E. outside of the host cell, before infection

17. Which of the following would most likely describe the fate of a vesicle formed as a result of phagocytosis?

    A. The vesicle merges with a mitochondrion.

    B. The vesicle merges with a lysosome.

    C. The vesicle is shuttled to the nucleus and its contents become part of the nucleolus.

    D. The vesicle is shuttled to the nucleus, where it interacts with the chromatin.

    E. The vesicle releases its contents to the cytoplasm to be digested.

18. All of the following occur during embryonic development in animals EXCEPT:

    A. formation of a gastrula

    B. formation of the endosperm

    C. cleavage

    D. mitotically dividing cells

    E. DNA synthesis

19. The secondary structure of a protein occurs as a result of

    A. hydrogen bonds

    B. disulfide bridges

    C. hydrophobic interactions

    D. hydrophilic interactions

    E. peptide bonds

20. A Y-linked allele is transmitted to

    A. all male offspring

    B. some male offspring depending upon whether the allele is dominant or recessive

    C. both male and female offspring if the allele is dominant

    D. both male and female offspring if the allele is recessive

    E. all offspring regardless of whether the allele is dominant or recessive

21. All of the following are examples of sexual selection EXCEPT:

    A. Male mule deer have antlers and females do not.

    B. An all-female, asexually reproducing whiptail lizard species reproduces by parthenogenesis, but females still engage in courtship behaviors with other females.

    C. Male marine iguanas are larger and more brightly colored than females.

    D. Male redwing blackbirds are black with red wing patches, while females are brown with streaks of pale yellow or orange.

    E. Male gray tree frogs who produce frequent and longer mating calls mate with more females than males who produce less frequent and shorter calls. Females, on the other hand, are unable to produce cells.

22. Polarity of eggs in many animals occurs because

    A. plant features appear at the top of the egg and animal features appear at the bottom of the egg

    B. cells divide more rapidly on one end of the embryo compared to divisions at the other end

    C. radial divisions occur at one end of the embryo and spiral divisions occur at the other end

    D. determinate divisions occur at one end of the embryo and indeterminate divisions occur at the other end

    E. the concentration of cytoplasmic substances among cells varies from one end of the embryo to the other

GO ON TO THE NEXT PAGE

23. Holes in plant leaves that allow for the diffusion of CO_2 into the leaf are called

    A. petioles
    B. meristematic cells
    C. stomata
    D. guard cells
    E. sieve tubes

24. All of the following are learned behaviors EXCEPT:

    A. trial-and-error
    B. association
    C. conditioning
    D. instinct
    E. habituation

25. In humans, the water-insoluble products of fats are absorbed from the

    A. small intestine and passed into the lymphatic system
    B. small intestine and passed into the bloodstream
    C. large intestine and passed into the bloodstream
    D. stomach and passed into the bloodstream
    E. liver and passed into the bloodstream

26. The major reservoirs for phosphorus are

    A. plants and animals
    B. detritus and decomposing microorganisms
    C. rain and fresh water
    D. terrestrial rocks and ocean sediments
    E. volcanic activity and the atmosphere

27. During development of a seed from a megasporangium, all of the following occur in angiosperms EXCEPT:

    A. production of cells by mitosis and meiosis
    B. formation of a triploid endosperm
    C. formation of an embryo sac
    D. formation of a coelom
    E. fertilization of one haploid egg and two haploid polar nuclei

28. Which of the following colors of light, if used alone, would produce the slowest rate of photosynthesis?

    A. violet
    B. blue
    C. green
    D. orange
    E. red

29. Which of the following characteristics is TRUE for all lipids?

    A. They contain carbon rings.
    B. They are relatively insoluble in water.
    C. They are polymers.
    D. They have at least one peptide bond.
    E. They have at least one hydrocarbon chain.

30. All of the following occur in primary tissues of plants EXCEPT:

    A. cork cambium
    B. apical meristems
    C. palisades mesophyll
    D. spongy mesophyll
    E. leaf primordia

31. Following muscle contraction, relaxation of the muscle fibers occurs when

    A. Ca^{2+} is released from the sarcoplasmic reticulum
    B. Ca^{2+} binds to troponin
    C. an action potential travels along the T-tubule system
    D. ATP is converted to $ADP + P_i$
    E. ATP binds to myosin heads and Ca^{2+} is withdrawn into the sarcoplasmic reticulum

32. Which of the following molecules contributes to the ability of cells to change shape?

    A. tubulin
    B. hemoglobin
    C. immunoglobulin
    D. collagen
    E. actin

33. All of the following are associated with nervous system development EXCEPT:

    A.   the neural plate

    B.   the neural tube

    C.   neural crest cells

    D.   the notochord

    E.   the ectoderm

34. Which of the following is *most likely* to initiate an action potential in a postsynaptic membrane of a neuron?

    A.   a neurotransmitter that causes some gated K^+ channels to open

    B.   a neurotransmitter that causes some gated Na^+ channels to open

    C.   several neurotransmitters that open both K^+ and Na^+ gated channels but together cause depolarization to exceed the threshold potential

    D.   several neurotransmitters that open both K^+ and Na^+ gated channels but together cause hyperpolarization

    E.   several neurotransmitters arriving at the postsynaptic membrane in rapid succession that cause K^+ gated channels to open

35. Current evidence suggests that the first genetic material in protobionts or the earliest living things was probably

    A.   fats

    B.   proteins

    C.   carbohydrates

    D.   DNA

    E.   RNA

36. All of the following would be good areas to search for mitotically dividing cells EXCEPT:

    A.   root tips of plants

    B.   stem tips of plants

    C.   whitefish blastulas

    D.   anthers of plants

    E.   early cleavages of the fertilized egg of a roundworm

37. Which of the following would increase the concentration of solutes in the collecting duct of a mammalian nephron?

    A.   an increase in the concentration of water in the bloodstream

    B.   an increase in the concentration of water in body cells

    C.   an increase in the release of aldosterone into the bloodstream

    D.   an increase in the release of ADH into the bloodstream

    E.   an increase in the amount of angiotensin II in the bloodstream

38. Digger wasps dig holes in the ground to serve as nests for their eggs and larvae. If nearby landmarks, such as pinecones or rocks, are moved, the wasp is unable to find the nest to deliver food to her larvae. This behavior indicates that the wasp is using which of the following to locate her nest?

    A.   imprinting

    B.   insight

    C.   spatial learning

    D.   operant conditioning

    E.   classical conditioning

39. All of the following help prevent the temperature of an animal from getting too warm EXCEPT:

    A.   muscle contractions

    B.   dilation of blood vessels

    C.   sweating

    D.   panting

    E.   bathing

40. In a multicellular organism, some cells become nerve cells, while others become muscle cells or skin cells. What is responsible for making different cell types in an individual? Cell types are determined by

    A.   mutations

    B.   transposons

    C.   which genes are present in the genome

    D.   which genes in the genome are expressed

    E.   random activation of chromosomes

GO ON TO THE NEXT PAGE

41. All of the following are found in plant cells EXCEPT:

    A. plasmodesmata

    B. mitochondria

    C. central vacuole

    D. plasma membrane containing cholesterol

    E. cell wall containing cellulose

42. All of the following are true for the ascent of water from roots to leaves of tall trees EXCEPT:

    A. Movement of water up the stem occurs by bulk flow.

    B. Movement of water up the stem occurs within xylem cells.

    C. Adhesion of water molecules to the walls of transporting cells supports the water column.

    D. Cohesion of water molecules by hydrogen bonding maintains water movement.

    E. Air bubbles aid in the movement of water.

43. Which of the following is a correct description for starch, glycogen, cellulose, chitin, and peptidoglycans?

    A. They are all polymers.

    B. They are all proteins.

    C. They are all polysaccharides containing α-glucose.

    D. They can all be found in a plasma membrane.

    E. They all contain nitrogen atoms.

44. A population consists of individuals all heterozygous for a particular locus. Which of the following is true for this population with reference to this locus?

    A. The population is in Hardy-Weinberg equilibrium.

    B. p is fixed.

    C. q is fixed.

    D. $p = 0.5$ and $q = 0.5$.

    E. p and q both equal 0.

Questions 45–46 refer to the genetics of corn seeds.

45. In corn seeds (kernels), the P allele produces a purple seed and p produces a red seed. Which of the following correctly describes all genotypes of a purple seed?

    A. PP only

    B. Pp only

    C. pp only

    D. PP and Pp

    E. PP and pp

46. What is the genotype of each parent if an ear of corn has 200 purple kernels and 200 red kernels?

    A. PP and Pp

    B. PP and pp

    C. Pp and Pp

    D. Pp and pp

    E. pp and pp

Question 47 refers to the following figure.

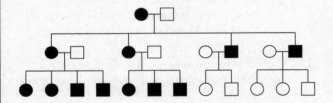

47. The preceding pedigree describes the inheritance of a human muscle disease. Circles indicate females, and squares indicate males. A horizontal line connecting a male and female indicates that these two individuals produced offspring. Offspring are indicated by a descending vertical line that branches to the offspring. A filled circle or filled square indicates that the individual inherited the muscle disease trait.

Which of the following is the most likely mode of inheritance for this trait?

    A. autosomal recessive

    B. autosomal dominant

    C. X-linked recessive

    D. X-linked dominant

    E. mitochondrial DNA

Question 48 refers to the following figure.

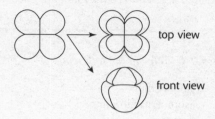

top view

front view

48. The preceding figure shows early cleavages in a four-cell embryo. Which of the following describes the developmental pattern illustrated in the figure?

A. protostome development with spiral cleavages

B. deuterostome development with radial cleavages

C. deuterostome development with spiral cleavages

D. triploblastic development with spiral cleavages

E. diploblastic development with radial cleavages

Questions 49–51 refer to the following.

A. 12
B. 24
C. 48
D. 96
E. 184

The genome of chimpanzees consists of 48 chromosomes ($2n = 48$). For the following questions, assume that no mutations occurred during DNA replication.

49. How many DNA molecules are in the genome of a chimpanzee cell before it begins meiosis?

50. How many unique DNA molecules are in this genome of a chimpanzee cell?

51. How many DNA molecules have a unique set of genes (but not necessarily alleles)?

GO ON TO THE NEXT PAGE

Directions: Questions that follow consist of a phrase or sentence. Each question is preceded by five lettered choices. Select the one lettered choice that best matches the phrase or sentence. Each lettered choice may be used once, more than once, or not at all.

Questions 52–55 refer to the following.

    A. follicle
    B. oviduct
    C. ovary
    D. uterus
    E. corpus luteum

52. Contains one oocyte *A*

53. Primary secretion is estrogen *A*

54. Secretes both estrogen and progesterone *E*

55. Location where fertilization occurs *B*

Questions 56–59 refer to the following.

    A. chitin
    B. cutin
    C. gibberellin
    D. secretin
    E. suberin

56. Forms a water-impenetrable barrier on the surface of leaves *B*

57. Forms a water-impenetrable barrier in the roots of plants

58. Promotes cell growth in plants *C*

59. Stimulates the secretion of bicarbonate by the pancreas *D*

Questions 60–63 refer to the following.

    A. realized niche
    B. resource partitioning
    C. parasitism
    D. mutualism
    E. commensalism

60. In parts of Africa, grazing animals pass through grasslands, one species at a time. First, the zebras eat the upper parts of the grass, followed by wildebeests, who eat more of the grass, followed by gazelles, who are able to pick out the best of what remains. *B*

61. Follicle mites live among the follicles of human hairs, where they consume oils secreted by sebaceous glands, but cause no harm to the human host. *E*

62. On the Galápagos Islands, two species of seabirds, the blue-footed booby and the masked booby, nest on the ground in coastal sites when the other species is absent. When both species are present, the blue-footed booby nests further inland. *A*

63. Pollen from flowers of plants in the genus *Yucca* are collected by *Tegeticula* moths. The moths roll the pollen into a ball, carry it to another *Yucca* plant, and deposit it on the stigma of a flower. The moths then deposit their eggs into some of the flower's ovules. When the larvae hatch from the eggs, they eat about a third of the flower's seeds before exiting the flower ovary. *D*

Directions: Questions that follow involve data from experiments or laboratory analyses. In each case, study the information provided. Then choose the one best answer for each question.

Questions 64–66 refer to the following.

Two populations of a species of water snake live in and around Lake Erie. One population is colored *gray,* lives on rocky islands, and basks in the sun while lying on gray rocks. A second population is *banded,* lives on the mainland, and basks in the sun among vegetation along the shore.

64. Which of the following could explain the difference in coloration between the two populations of snake?

   A.   camouflage
   B.   Müllerian mimicry
   C.   Batesian mimicry
   D.   aposematic coloration
   E.   realized niche

65. On the rocky islands, *young* water snakes are either gray or banded, but among adults, only gray snakes are found. This could be explained by which of the following?

   A.   artificial selection
   B.   directional selection
   C.   disruptive selection
   D.   stabilizing selection
   E.   sexual selection

66. If all adult snakes on the rocky islands are gray, how can the occasional appearance of banded young snakes be explained?

   A.   mutation
   B.   sexual selection
   C.   gene flow
   D.   genetic drift
   E.   founder effect

Questions 67–69 refer to the following.

An X-linked recessive allele is responsible for a human disease whose symptoms include loss of teeth and loss of sweat glands. When males have the disease, they are toothless and have no sweat glands.

67. What is the probability that a male will inherit the disease if his mother is heterozygous and his father had the disease?

   A.   0%
   B.   25%
   C.   50%
   D.   75%
   E.   100%

68. Females who are heterozygous are often missing some teeth and have some areas of skin lacking sweat glands. Which of the following best explains why heterozygous females express the trait in this manner?

   A.   epistasis
   B.   pleiotropy
   C.   polygenic inheritance
   D.   incomplete dominance
   E.   X-inactivation

69. How will the disease be inherited in identical female twins heterozygous for this trait?

   A.   The entire body of one twin will lack sweat glands while the other twin will be normal.
   B.   Both twins will express the disease and the areas of the body where sweat glands are absent will be exactly the same in both twins.
   C.   Both twins will express the disease but areas of the body where sweat glands are absent will be different in each twin.
   D.   The entire body of both twins will lack sweat glands.
   E.   Neither twin will express the disease because heterozygous females must inherit two copies of the recessive allele in order to express the disease.

GO ON TO THE NEXT PAGE

Questions 70–71 refer to the following figure.

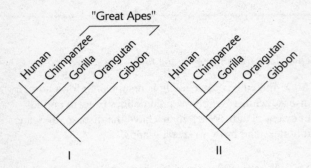

70. In cladogram I, the group "Great Apes" consisting of chimpanzees, gorillas, and orangutans

    A. is monophyletic
    B. is paraphyletic
    C. is polyphyletic
    D. is an outgroup
    E. contains taxa for which hair is a shared derived character

71. In cladogram II, which of the following groups is monophyletic?

    A. humans and chimpanzees
    B. humans, chimpanzees, and gorillas
    C. chimpanzees, gorillas, and orangutans
    D. chimpanzees, gorillas, orangutans, and gibbons
    E. orangutans and gibbons

Questions 72–73 refer to the following figure that shows variation in stomatal aperture, CO_2 assimilation, and pH of plant leaves with time of day.

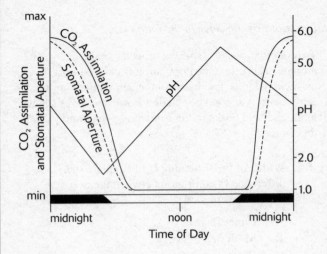

72. Which of the following is correct for the activities that occur *during the day*?

    A. CO_2 assimilation is maximum, stomata are open, and acidity increases.
    B. CO_2 assimilation is maximum, stomata are closed, and acidity decreases.
    C. CO_2 assimilation is minimum, stomata are open, and acidity increases.
    D. CO_2 assimilation is minimum, stomata are closed, and acidity increases.
    E. CO_2 assimilation is minimum, stomata are closed, and acidity decreases.

73. The activities occurring in these leaves as indicated in the figure are consistent with which of the following?

    A. C_3 photosynthesis
    B. C_4 photosynthesis
    C. CAM photosynthesis
    D. Calvin cycle occurring at night
    E. photophosphorylation occurring at night

Questions 74–76 refer to the following graph that shows hourly measurements of glucose concentration in the blood. One hour of moderate and sustained exercise begins at 9 A.M. and a meal is eaten at 1 P.M.

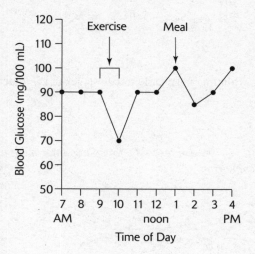

74. The decrease in blood glucose between 1 P.M. and 2 P.M. is caused by the secretion into the blood of

A. epinephrine
B. glucagon
C. insulin
D. testosterone
E. thyroxin

75. Which hormone is mostly likely responsible for the change in blood glucose following exercise between the hours of 10 A.M. and 11 A.M.?

A. ADH
B. testosterone
C. insulin
D. glucagon
E. thyroxin

76. Which of the following is the source of glucose for restoring blood glucose after exercise?

A. liver
B. pancreas
C. spleen
D. muscle tissue
E. adipose tissue

GO ON TO THE NEXT PAGE

Question 77 refers to the following figure.

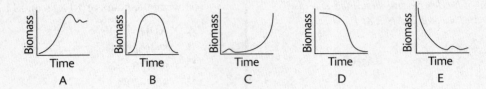

77. Which of the preceding correctly shows how biomass changes with time from early to late stages of ecological succession?

Question 78 refers to the following ecological pyramid.

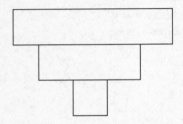

78. If the preceding figure illustrates a pyramid of *biomass*, which of the following would best explain the relative sizes of the trophic levels?

   A. The pyramid represents a marine community where phytoplankton multiplies as fast as it is eaten.

   B. The pyramid represents a subalpine community during the winter.

   C. The pyramid represents a desert community where little or no rain has fallen for over a year.

   D. The pyramid represents the ecological state of a late successional stage.

   E. The pyramid construction is in error because the bottom trophic level in a pyramid of biomass must always have a greater biomass than the level above it.

Questions 79–81 refer to the following diagram of a mitochondrion.

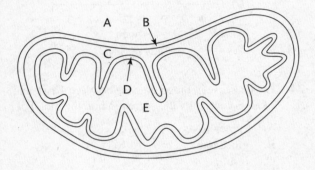

79. In what area of the figure does the Krebs (citric acid) cycle occur?

80. In what area of the figure are the proteins that remove electrons from NADH and $FADH_2$ located?

81. In what area of the figure is the pH lowest?

Questions 82–84 refer to the following.

Salmon lay thousands of eggs at the summit of streams. For the few eggs that survive, the baby salmon swim downstream to the ocean, where they spend several years maturing. They return to the streams of their birth to lay or fertilize eggs and then die.

82. Which of the plots in the following figure describes this survivorship pattern?

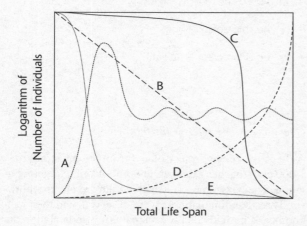

83. Which of the following describes this reproductive strategy?

   A.   iteroparous
   B.   semelparous
   C.   redundant reproduction
   D.   *K*-selection life history
   E.   logistic growth

84. In general, in what kind of environments is the salmon reproductive strategy successful?

   A.   freshwater environments
   B.   marine environments
   C.   extreme environments
   D.   stable, unchanging environments
   E.   unpredictable or variable environments

Questions 85–86 refer to the following figure that shows the relationship between body temperature and environmental temperature.

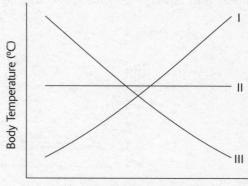

   A.   I
   B.   II
   C.   III
   D.   I and II
   E.   I and III

85. Assuming the organism remains stationary, which of the plots could represent the body temperature of an ectothermic organism?

86. Which of the plots could represent the body temperature of an endothermic organism?

GO ON TO THE NEXT PAGE

Questions 87–89 refer to the following.

An experiment designed to evaluate the importance of chloroplasts and light on photosynthetic activity uses DPIP as a substitute for NADP⁺. Oxidized DPIP is blue, and reduced DPIP is clear. The graph that follows shows the results of the experiment using healthy chloroplasts, boiled chloroplasts, or no chloroplasts in the presence or absence of light.

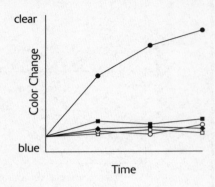

- I   healthy chloroplasts + light
- II   healthy chloroplasts + no light
- III   boiled chloroplasts + light
- IV   no chloroplasts + light
- IV   no chloroplasts + no light

87. A color change in DPIP from blue to clear is a measurement of energized electrons produced by which of the following?

  A. Calvin cycle
  B. photolysis
  C. photosystem I
  D. photosystem II
  E. ATP synthase

88. Which combination of plots in the figure best supports the hypothesis that chloroplasts and light are required for photosynthesis?

  A. I and II
  B. I and III
  C. I, II, and IV
  D. I, II, and V
  E. I, II, III, and IV

89. Which combination of plots in the figure best supports the hypothesis that heating chloroplasts disrupts membrane proteins that are necessary for photosynthesis?

  A. I and II
  B. I and III
  C. III and IV
  D. I, III, and IV
  E. I, II, III, and IV

Questions 90–91 refer to the following.

A digestive enzyme was isolated from the intestines of 1,000 cockroaches selected randomly from a large population. The enzyme was evaluated with gel electrophoresis. Three banding patterns were observed, and the number of individuals for each pattern is indicated in the figure.

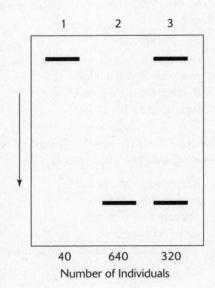

90. What are the allele frequencies for the gene locus coding for this enzyme?

  A. 0.04, 0.32, and 0.64
  B. 0.36 and 0.98
  C. 0.34 and 0.64
  D. 0.4 and 0.6
  E. 0.2 and 0.8

91. Is this population in Hardy-Weinberg equilibrium for this locus?

A. Yes.
B. No, because $p^2 + 2pq + q^2$ is not equal to 1.
C. No, because $p + q$ is not equal to 1.
D. No, because $p + q + r$ is not equal to 1.
E. Not enough information is provided to determine if this population is in Hardy-Weinberg equilibrium.

Questions 92–95 refer to the following diagram, which illustrates the laboratory procedure PCR (polymerase chain reaction).

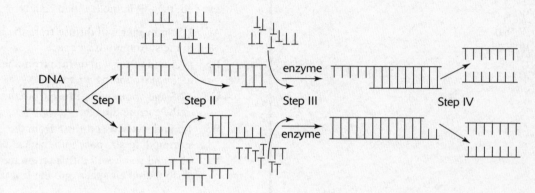

92. The purpose of this procedure is to

A. transcribe DNA (to make mRNA)
B. translate mRNA
C. make copies of a specific polypeptide
D. make copies of an entire chromosome
E. make copies of a specific DNA fragment

93. Step I is accomplished by

A. adding helicase and topoisomerase
B. adding restriction enzymes
C. denaturation using a weak acid
D. vigorous agitation
E. denaturation using heat

94. In Step II, which of the following is added to the mixture?

A. short single-stranded DNA molecules to function as primers
B. small nuclear ribonucleoproteins (snRNPs) to initiate RNA processing
C. restriction fragment length polymorphisms (RFLPs) to act as gene probes
D. complementary DNA (cDNA) to serve as a template for replication
E. mRNA to serve as a template for translation

95. In Step III, what enzyme is added?

A. DNA ligase
B. DNA polymerase
C. RNA polymerase
D. a restriction enzyme
E. a digesting enzyme

GO ON TO THE NEXT PAGE

Questions 96–98 refer to water potential, Ψ, as expressed by the formula

$$\Psi = \Psi_P + \Psi_s$$

where

Ψ_P = pressure potential and

Ψ_s = osmotic (or solute) potential.

96. Which of the following is correct for the inside of a normally hydrated spongy mesophyll leaf cell?

    A. $\Psi > 0$

    B. $\Psi_P = 0$

    C. $\Psi_P < 0$

    D. $\Psi_s < 0$

    E. $\Psi_s > 0$

97. Which of the following is correct for air spaces inside the leaf surrounding spongy mesophyll cells where relative humidity is 100 percent and atmospheric pressure is typical of sea level?

    A. $\Psi = 0$

    C. $\Psi < 0$

    D. $\Psi > 0$

    B. $\Psi_P < 0$

    E. $\Psi_s > 0$

98. If $\Psi_s = -2.0$ MPa and $\Psi_P = 0.5$ MPa inside a leaf cell and if the relative humidity is 98 percent and $\Psi = -2.7$ MPa in the air spaces surrounding the leaf cell, then Ψ in the leaf cell equals

    A. 1.5 and water will diffuse from the leaf cell to the surrounding air space

    B. −1.5 and water will diffuse from the leaf cell to the surrounding air space

    C. −2.5 and water will diffuse from the leaf cell to the surrounding air space

    D. 1.5 and water will diffuse from the surrounding air space into the leaf cell

    E. −1.5 and water will diffuse from the surrounding air space into the leaf cell

Questions 99–100 refer to the following.

Mitochondria isolated from cells can be induced to carry out respiration if an appropriate substrate is provided and a low temperature is maintained to prevent enzyme degradation. The following experiment uses isolated mitochondria in this manner to investigate respiration.

During the Krebs cycle, succinate is oxidized to fumarate as electrons are transferred to FAD for its reduction to $FADH_2$ (see figure). In this experiment, DPIP is provided as a substitute electron acceptor for FAD. DPIP, which is blue in its oxidized state, accepts electrons from succinate. After accepting the electrons, DPIP turns clear, its reduced state. A spectrophotometer is used to quantify the degree of color change by measuring the amount of light that is transmitted through a cuvette. A cuvette with a higher transmittance percentage indicates a solution with more reduced DPIP.

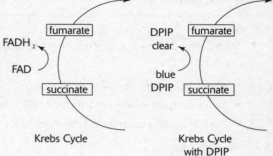

Three cuvettes are prepared at low temperatures with an appropriate buffer. The contents of a fourth cuvette are similarly prepared except that the mitochondrial suspension is first preheated to 100°C and then returned to a low temperature. A summary of the contents of the cuvettes follows.

Cuvette 1: 0.2 ml succinate added to isolated mitochondria

Cuvette 2: 0.1 ml succinate added to isolated mitochondria

Cuvette 3: 0 ml succinate added to isolated mitochondria

Cuvette 4: 0.1 ml succinate added to isolated mitochondria *preheated* to 100°C

Transmittance in each cuvette is measured every 10 minutes. The results of the experiment are summarized in the following graph.

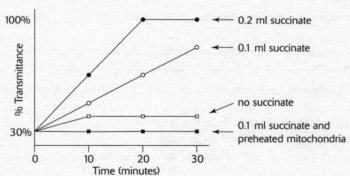

99. The results of the experiment indicate that the respiratory *rate* increases as

A. the concentration of substrate increases

B. the concentration of DPIP increases

C. the concentration of enzyme increases

D. the time increases

E. the temperature of the mixture increases

100. Which of the following is true with respect to the availability of electrons from other steps of the Krebs cycle?

A. No other steps of the Krebs cycle are involved in the reduction of electron acceptors.

B. Only one step of the Krebs cycle provides electrons for reducing an electron acceptor such as DPIP.

C. Electrons from other steps could also reduce DPIP, but the substrates for these steps are consumed before succinate is added.

D. FAD is the only electron acceptor for the Krebs cycle.

E. NAD^+ is the only electron acceptor for the Krebs cycle.

GO ON TO THE NEXT PAGE

Section II (Free-Response Questions)

Reading Time: 10 minutes (for organizing your thoughts and outlining your answers)
Writing Time: 90 minutes

1. Hydrogen bonding is essential for the structure and function of numerous molecules. For each of the molecules listed, describe

   - the structure of the molecule.
   - two examples with a description of their functions.
   - how hydrogen bonding is important to its function.

   A. proteins
   B. DNA
   C. RNA
   D. prions

2. There is much variation in traits among individuals in a population.

   A. Explain how each of the following contributes to variation in sexually reproducing, diploid organisms.
      - mutation
      - meiosis
      - diploidy
      - haploid gametes
   B. Describe mechanisms in prokaryotes that generate variation.

3. Communication is an essential mechanism for living organisms. It can occur within cells, between cells, or between organisms. Describe THREE of the following communication processes.

   A. Describe the *trp* operon OR the *lac* operon in its role as a feedback mechanism that regulates protein production.
   B. Describe signaling in embryonic cells during development.
   C. Describe how a neuron signals a muscle cell to contract.
   D. Give two examples of chemical communication between individuals of a species. Explain the purpose of each.

4. Bears living in their natural habitats often enter campgrounds, where they break into cars to obtain food. The following data show the number of such encounters over a period of two years.

Year	Jan	Feb	Mar	Apr	May	Jun	Jul	Aug	Sep	Oct	Nov	Dec	Total
2004	10	10	25	20	20	25	50	55	60	40	20	15	350
2005	20	20	30	35	40	40	90	130	150	85	50	30	720

   A. Plot the preceding data using the axes provided.
   B. Propose a hypothesis that could explain the pattern of behavior demonstrated by these bears for the year **2004.**
   C. Propose a hypothesis that could explain the increase in the number of bear encounters observed in the year 2005 compared to 2004.
   D. Describe an experiment to test the hypothesis in **part B of this question.** Include an identification of independent and dependent variables.

E. Describe the results you would expect to obtain if the experiment were performed.

F. Graph your expected results on the axes provided.

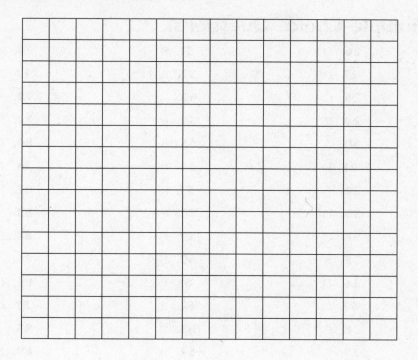

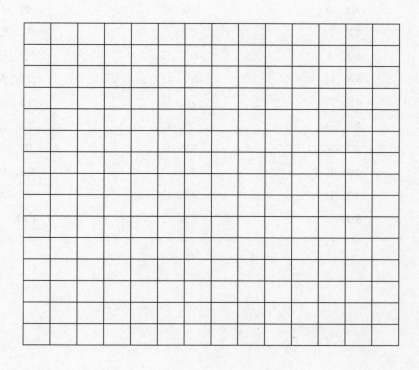

Answer Key for Practice Exam 5

Section I (Multiple-Choice Questions)

1. B	26. D	51. B	76. A
2. C	27. D	52. A	77. A
3. C	28. C	53. A	78. A
4. D	29. B	54. E	79. E
5. D	30. A	55. B	80. D
6. C	31. E	56. B	81. C
7. E	32. E	57. E	82. E
8. B	33. D	58. C	83. B
9. E	34. C	59. D	84. E
10. A	35. E	60. B	85. A
11. B	36. D	61. E	86. B
12. B	37. D	62. A	87. C
13. C	38. C	63. D	88. C
14. E	39. A	64. A	89. D
15. C	40. D	65. D	90. E
16. B	41. D	66. C	91. A
17. B	42. E	67. C	92. E
18. B	43. A	68. E	93. E
19. A	44. D	69. C	94. A
20. A	45. D	70. B	95. B
21. B	46. D	71. B	96. D
22. E	47. E	72. E	97. A
23. C	48. B	73. C	98. B
24. D	49. D	74. C	99. A
25. A	50. C	75. D	100. C

Scoring Your Practice Exam

Section I (Multiple-Choice Questions)

Number of questions you answered correctly: _____ × 1 = _____

Number of questions you answered wrong: _____ × ¼ = _____ *

Number of questions you left unanswered: _____ × 0 = ____0___

TOTAL for Section I (0–100 points): = _____ **

(subtract number wrong from number correct)

Round to nearest whole number.
** *If less than zero, enter zero.*

Section II (Free-Response Questions)

For each correct and relevant piece of information you include in your answers to the free-response questions, you earn one point. Refer to the scoring standards that follow the multiple-choice explanations.

Score for essay 1 (0–10 points): _____

Score for essay 2 (0–10 points): _____

Score for essay 3 (0–10 points): _____

Score for essay 4 (0–10 points): _____

Combined Score (Sections I + II)

Total for Section I (from above): _____ × 0.6 = _____

(60% of 100 points = 60 points maximum)

Total for Section II (from above): _____ × 1.0 = _____

(100% of 40 points = 40 points maximum)

Combined Score (Add Sections I and II)_____

(0–100 points possible)

Probable AP Grade		
61–100	5	
47–60	4	
39–46	3	
30–38	2	
0–29	1	

Answers and Explanations for Practice Exam 5

1. **B.** Because of its association with ribosomes (which are responsible for making proteins), the rough endoplasmic reticulum is heavily involved in processing proteins. The rough ER modifies *newly formed* proteins by adding carbohydrates to them (to form glycoproteins) and packaging the proteins into transport vesicles. Many of these transport vesicles merge with the plasma membrane to release their contents for export or fuse with the Golgi complex (or Golgi apparatus) for further modification before export. Some vesicles become lysosomes, bodies that contain hydrolytic enzymes for the breakdown of food, aging organelles, or foreign invaders. In contrast, smooth endoplasmic reticulum is not involved in the processing of proteins (because "smooth" defines ER as ER without ribosomes). Similar to the rough ER, the Golgi complex is also involved with modifying and packaging proteins, but the proteins that are delivered to the Golgi complex have already been partially modified by the rough ER.

2. **C.** The cDNA lacks the introns found in the original DNA segment and contains only the exons necessary for making mRNA. The number of nucleotides in the introns of a primary RNA transcript varies dramatically, from hundreds to hundreds of thousands of nucleotides. The intron nucleotides are removed by snRNPs during RNA splicing (processing of RNA while still in the nucleus), thus reducing the length of the final RNA considerably. A DNA segment with a point mutation (a single nucleotide replaced, added, or deleted) will differ from the original DNA segment by, at most, only one nucleotide. The primary RNA transcript, containing both introns and exons, will contain the same number of nucleotides as the original DNA segment.

3. **C.** The flagella of bacteria consist of the protein flagellin. The flagellin proteins are not arranged in a "9+ 2" pattern characteristic of eukaryotic flagella. Prokaryotes include photoautotrophs (bacteria that obtain their energy from light, such as cyanobacteria), chemoautotrophs (bacteria that obtain their energy from inorganic molecules such as H_2S or NH_3), and heterotrophs. The domain Archaea consists of the archaebacteria, a group of prokaryotes that lack peptidoglycans in their cell walls and have ribosomes that resemble those of animals more than those of bacteria.

4. **D.** An artery transports blood, oxygenated or deoxygenated, away from the heart. The pulmonary arteries transport deoxygenated blood from the heart to the lungs. All other arteries transport oxygenated blood away from the heart and through the systemic system.

5. **D.** Because both parents are green, they must both be *yy,* and because they are both round, they could be either *RR* or *Rr.* Therefore, each parent must be either *yyRR* or *yyRr.* Because some of the offspring are wrinkled (*rr*), both parents must be able to donate an *r* allele. That means both parents must be *yyRr.* You can confirm the frequencies by working out a Punnett square for the cross $Rr \times Rr.$

6. **C.** All viruses produce RNA sometime in their replication cycle in order to generate proteins for their capsids. Only certain RNA viruses, the retroviruses, produce DNA as an intermediate molecule. When a retrovirus enters a cell, it uses the enzyme reverse transcriptase to make dsDNA (double-stranded DNA). The dsDNA then enters the nucleus, where it integrates with the host's DNA. In this state, the viral DNA is a provirus. The provirus becomes active when it is transcribed by host enzymes to produce mRNA. The virus that causes AIDS (HIV) is an example of a retrovirus. The RNA genome of RNA viruses that are not retroviruses either produces mRNA or acts directly as mRNA when it enters a cell.

7. **E.** Platyhelminthes is a bilateral animal without a coelom. Echinodermata, Nematoda, and Rotifera are bilateral animals with a coelom or pseudocoelom. Members of the Porifera lack symmetry.

8. **B.** Fitness is a measure of the relative number of genes an individual leaves to the next generation. The number of offspring an individual produces is one source of those genes. But because relatives share a portion of their genes, an individual can increase his or her fitness by helping relatives survive and produce offspring. Inclusive fitness is a measure of genes left to the next generation that includes genes in an individual's offspring and the genes he or she shares with the offspring of his or her relatives. For the acorn woodpeckers, woodpeckers increase their inclusive fitness by helping their brothers or sisters survive and produce offspring.

9. **E.** There is no evidence that communication occurs between animals by means other than by using the five senses of smell, sight, sound, touch, and taste. Male moths use the sense of smell to detect chemical signals, or pheromones, released by females to signal that they are ready to mate. Male lampyrid beetles (fireflies) produce

flashes of light as visual signals to attract mates. Birds use songs as auditory signals to attract mates or deter competitors from entering their territories. Honeybees use their tactile sense to receive signals from workers whose dances indicate the location of food.

10. **A.** In order for the two species to have evolved, some kind of reproductive barrier must have existed at some time in the past. During that period of reproductive isolation, natural selection, mutations, or genetic drift occurred, changing the populations sufficiently so that when the reproductive barrier was removed, the two populations could no longer intermate.

11. **B.** Contraction of the diaphragm and rib muscles causes the lungs to expand. As a result, air pressure in the lungs drops. Because gases move from areas of higher pressure to areas of lower pressure, air from outside the body (at atmospheric pressure) rushes into the lungs (this is bulk flow). In contrast, the partial pressures of O_2 and CO_2 are important for diffusion into and out of the blood stream: after inhalation, the partial pressure of O_2 is higher in the lungs than in the blood inside capillaries, so O_2 diffuses from the lungs through the alveolar walls and into the bloodstream; CO_2 diffuses in the opposite direction because the partial pressure of CO_2 in the blood is higher than in the lungs. Note that inhalation and exhalation occur by bulk flow, whereas gas exchange between the lungs and bloodstream occurs by diffusion.

12. **B.** Sticky ends are single-stranded extensions at ends of DNA after they are cut with certain restriction enzymes. Not all restriction enzymes produce sticky ends. However, sticky ends are necessary if the DNA fragments are to be successfully joined using DNA ligase. If both the human gene and bacterial plasmids are treated with the same restriction enzyme, DNA ligase will join fragments of each where the sticky ends base pair. A complementary DNA copy of the human gene is necessary because the cDNA lacks the introns that the bacteria would otherwise be unable to remove. The absorption of foreign DNA and its incorporation into the genome (transformation) occur naturally in bacteria but usually only for specially recognized DNA. Various environmental conditions, such as a growth medium with a high concentration of Ca^{2+}, help induce bacteria to absorb unrecognized DNA.

13. **C.** Alternation of generations occurs when *both* generations are multicellular. All land plants have a reproductive cycle that alternates between generations that are multicellular haploid and multicellular diploid. Animals have a haploid and diploid generation, but only the diploid is multicellular (the haploid generation, sperm and eggs, is unicellular). Some algae also have alternation of generations.

14. **E.** T-cells mature in the thymus. In the absence of a thymus, few T-cells exist. Therefore, there is no cell-mediated immune response and any cell that displays nonself MHC molecules (cancerous cells and intracellular infections from viruses, protozoans, or fungi) cannot be attacked and eliminated. In contrast, B-cells mature in the bone marrow and so are unaffected by the absence of a thymus. Thus, the humoral immune response is functional, and B-cells actively recognize antigens (bacteria and toxins) and produce plasma-cell daughter cells that produce antibodies. These antibodies neutralize or help eliminate the antigens. In addition, phagocytic leukocytes (such as macrophages and neutrophils), also unaffected by the absence of a thymus, engulf bacteria and their toxins (antigens).

15. **C.** Although most fungi are multicellular and form hyphae, some do not. Some chytrids (chytridiomycetes) and yeasts (ascomycetes) are unicellular with a round or oval shape.

16. **B.** Translation of the viral mRNA must occur in the cytoplasm of the eukaryotic host cell because that is where the ribosomes are located. Ribosomes, along with tRNA and amino acids, carry out the process of translation.

17. **B.** Vesicles that form by phagocytosis usually merge with a lysosome, and their contents are digested by the hydrolytic enzymes inside the lysosome.

18. **B.** An endosperm is a nutritive tissue in embryos of plants.

19. **A.** The secondary structure of a protein forms as a result of hydrogen bonding between amino acids. Hydrogen bonding causes the protein to form a helix (alpha helix) or a folded surface (beta pleated sheet). The primary structure of the protein is the string of amino acids linked by peptide bonds. A tertiary structure results when disulfide bridges form between two cysteine amino acids and when hydrophobic amino acids group together toward the inside of the protein and hydrophilic amino acids group together toward the outside of the protein. A quaternary structure occurs in some proteins when two or more individual proteins cluster together.

20. A. In order for an offspring to be a male, he must inherit a Y chromosome. So all males inherit all of the alleles that are on their father's Y chromosome whether those alleles are dominant or recessive. The concepts of dominance and recessiveness really don't apply here because, normally, only one copy of a Y-linked gene is inherited (by the males). That one allele is the allele that is expressed, regardless of whether it could be dominant or recessive.

21. B. Sexual selection is responsible for the differences between males and females that are not necessary for reproduction. These differences are called secondary sex characteristics. Because there are only females in the asexually reproducing whiptail lizards, there is no sexual selection.

22. E. The polarity of eggs is created by an uneven distribution of cytoplasmic material. Denser material, comprising stored food (yolk), concentrates in the lower region, or vegetal pole, of the egg and is destined to occur, in varying proportions, in subsequent daughter cells from this region. The upper region, or animal pole, contains less yolk, and cleavages in this region produce daughter cells with a cytoplasm similar to this region.

23. C. Stomata are holes in the epidermis that allow for the diffusion of CO_2 into the leaf. Each stoma (or stomate) is flanked by two guard cells. When water diffuses into the guard cells, they form kidney shapes that create an opening, the stoma, between them. When water diffuses out, the kidney shape collapses and the stoma closes. Open stomata not only allow CO_2 to diffuse in but permit water to evaporate (transpiration). So stomata strongly influence photosynthetic activity by controlling the availability of CO_2 and H_2O.

24. D. Instinct is an inherited behavior (innate). Associative learning occurs when an animal learns that two or more events are connected. This includes classical conditioning, when an animal learns to respond to a substitute stimulus, and trial-and-error learning (operant conditioning). Habituation is a learned behavior to ignore a meaningless stimulus.

25. A. Pancreatic lipase breaks down fats (triglycerides or triacylglycerols) into water-insoluble fatty acids and monoglycerides (glycerols with one fatty acid). These products, mixed with bile salts to form micelles, are absorbed by cells lining the small intestine. The fat products are then mixed with cholesterol and proteins (forming chylomicrons) and passed to lymphatic capillaries.

26. D. Most of the phosphorus in the biosphere occurs as ocean sediments (mostly from the accumulation of dead organisms) and terrestrial rocks (from geologic uplifting of ocean basins). Phosphorous becomes available in the various ecosystems as organisms die or as streams deliver the phosphorous eroded from terrestrial rocks. Although phosphorous is plentiful in the biosphere, most is inaccessible to living things and, as a result, phosphorus may be a limiting factor to population growth. Hence, most commercial fertilizers contain phosphorus.

27. D. The coelom is a fluid-filled cavity in the mesoderm tissue of animals. Sexual reproduction in angiosperm plants begins with meiosis in the anther or ovary. In the ovary, a megaspore mother cell divides by meiosis to produce four haploid daughter cells. One surviving daughter cell divides by mitosis three times to produce eight daughter nuclei, all enclosed within the cell membrane of the original daughter cell (forming the embryo sac). One of the eight daughter nuclei, the ovum, is fertilized by a sperm cell that is delivered by the pollen tube, and two other of the eight daughter nuclei, the polar nuclei, are fertilized by a second sperm cell (delivered by the same pollen tube) to form a triploid endosperm.

28. C. Relatively little green light is absorbed by plant pigments. Instead, green light is reflected, giving leaves their green color.

29. B. Triglycerides (triacylglycerols, or fats), phospholipids, steroids, and waxes are classified together as lipids because they are generally hydrophobic. Phospholipids are amphipathic, that is, they have both hydrophobic (insoluble) and hydrophilic (soluble) regions. Because of their amphipathic properties, phospholipids are the integral part of a plasma membrane, where two layers of phospholipids are arranged so that the hydrophobic, hydrocarbon fatty acid tails face each other and the hydrophilic, phosphate heads face the inside and outside of the cell.

30. A. Cork cambium is a secondary tissue. Secondary tissues are those that expand the girth of shoots and roots and are the source of woody tissues. The cork cambium produces a layer of cork that is the protective layer that covers the outside of woody stems and roots.

31. E. When a new ATP binds to a myosin head, the cross bridge between the myosin and actin breaks. When Ca^{2+} is withdrawn into the sarcoplasmic reticulum, tropomyosin recedes into the actin binding sites, blocking the attachment of myosin heads to these sites. After the myosin heads can no longer attach to the actin, the muscle relaxes.

32. **E.** The microfilament actin is responsible for various kinds of cytoplasmic movements inside the cell, which often lead to changes in cell shape and cell movement. Actin is responsible for the amoeboid movement that results when the cytoplasm moves toward one end of the cell, forming a pseudopod. Such changes in cell shape are observed in various cells including amoebas (protists) and macrophages (a kind of white blood cell). Actin filaments are also responsible for the constriction of the plasma membrane during cleavage furrow formation and the subsequent separation of daughter cells at the conclusion of cytokinesis in animal cells.

33. **D.** During neurulation, outer ectoderm cells in an area called the neural plate invaginate and form the neural tube, which later becomes the brain and spinal cord. Cells along the edges of the neural plate, the neural crest cells, migrate elsewhere to form various tissues, including nerve cells. The notochord, unrelated to the nervous system, develops from mesoderm cells to form a supporting rod in lower chordates.

34. **C.** Depolarization occurs when Na^+ channels open, producing an excitatory postsynaptic potential (EPSP). However, only if the threshold potential is exceeded is an action potential actually generated. Opening some gated Na^+ channels does not guarantee an action potential (answer B). If several neurotransmitters open a combination of K^+ and Na^+ channels and depolarization exceeds the threshold potential (answer C), then an action potential is guaranteed. In contrast, if a neurotransmitter stimulates the opening of K^+ channels (answers A and E) or more K^+ than Na^+ channels (answer D), then the postsynaptic membrane becomes more polarized (hyperpolarized), producing an inhibitory postsynaptic potential (IPSP) and making it more difficult to generate an action potential.

35. **E.** RNA is believed to be the first genetic material because of its many applications in cells living today. RNA can act as heredity information (mRNA and tRNA hold the information for making proteins) and can function as an enzyme (as it does in ribosomes, ribozymes, and snRNPs). Also, its basic single-stranded structure gives RNA the flexibility that allows it to form different three-dimensional shapes with multiple functions (unlike DNA, which is restricted to a double-helix).

36. **D.** Mitotically dividing cells are found in areas of growth. Examples include dividing embryos, areas of growth or cell replacement in animals, and the tips of roots and shoots in plants. In contrast, the anthers of plants are sites of gamete (pollen) production and would be good sites to search for meiotically dividing cells.

37. **D.** ADH, produced in the hypothalamus and released by the posterior pituitary, causes the collecting duct to become more permeable to water. Because the surrounding medium is hyperosmotic to the filtrate in the duct, water diffuses out of the duct, concentrating the urine. In contrast, when the body is well hydrated, ADH production decreases and the urine retains more water. Aldosterone leads to more diluted urine by increasing the reabsorption of Na^+ from the distal convoluted tubule. Angiotensin II stimulates an increase in aldosterone and causes vasoconstriction. In response to blood loss (from injury), increases in angiotensin II would help maintain blood volume and blood pressure (and glomerular filtration rate).

38. **C.** Spatial learning occurs when relative positions of physical features are used to modify behavior.

39. **A.** Muscle contractions such as those that occur during shivering generate heat and are a mechanism to keep animals warm in cold environments, not cool in hot environments.

40. **D.** Because all cells of a multicellular organism contain the same set of chromosomes with the same genes, the different cell types of an organism are produced by differential expression of its genes. Each cell type has a different array of genes that are active, while the remaining genes are turned off. Various factors are responsible, including cytoplasmic influences, the presence or absence of neighboring cells, and the effect of neighboring cells (induction).

41. **D.** There is no cholesterol in the plasma membranes of plants. The plasma membrane of all cells contain phospholipids and proteins. The fluidity of the membrane is influenced by the kinds of phospholipids that are present. When phospholipids contain more unsaturated fatty acids, the membrane is more fluid because the double covalent bonds in unsaturated fatty acids create bends that keep the phospholipids from packing too tightly. Cholesterol, also, influences the fluidity of the membrane, keeping it more firm at higher temperatures but more fluid at lower temperatures. In contrast, the plasma membranes of plant cells obtain additional support from the cell wall.

42. E. Water is transported by bulk flow through xylem cells (tracheids and vessel elements). Cohesion (attraction between *like* substances) of H_2O molecules produces a column of water from roots to leaves. The H_2O column is lifted each time an H_2O molecule is removed by transpiration. Water molecules ultimately exit the leaf through stomata. Energy for the process is supplied by the sun. The water column is also supported by the adhesion (attraction between *unlike* substances) of H_2O molecules to the hydrophilic cell walls of xylem cells. When an H_2O column breaks, which may occur during freezing conditions, an air bubble forms (a process called cavitation), preventing any future movement of water through the area of bubble formation.

43. A. These are all polysaccharides (polymer carbohydrates). In particular, starch and glycogen are polymers of α-glucose, cellulose is a polymer of β-glucose, chitin is a polymer of a β-glucose modified with a nitrogen-containing group, and peptidoglycan is a mixed polymer, consisting of alternating units of two different nitrogen modified glucoses. Most of these molecules can be found in cell walls or the extracellular matrix but not typically in plasma membranes. Only chitin and peptidoglycans contain nitrogen.

44. D. An individual who is heterozygous possesses one copy of each allele at the locus being described. If all individuals are heterozygous, all individuals possess one copy of each allele, so $p = 0.5$ and $q = 0.5$. Clearly, if there are no individuals who are homozygous dominant or homozygous recessive, the population cannot be in Hardy-Weinberg equilibrium.

45. D. Because purple (P) is the dominant allele, seeds a with genotype PP or Pp will be purple.

46. D. The cross $Pp \times pp$ produces ½ Pp + ½ pp, or half purple and half red.

47. E. *All* females who have the trait pass it to *all* of their offspring. *No* males who have the trait pass the trait to their offspring. This pattern of inheritance is characteristic of traits inherited in the DNA of mitochondria. All the mitochondria (and the mitochondrial DNA) of individuals are inherited from their mothers (except for rare exceptions).

48. B. The figure shows a radial pattern of cleavages, characteristic of deuterostomes. Spiral cleavages, characteristic of protostomes, are rotated slightly (about half the width of a cell) so that the top layer of cells is not directly above the bottom layer.

49. D. The chimpanzee has 48 chromosomes, and each chromosome consists of two sister chromatids (each a DNA molecule), making a total of 96 DNA molecules.

50. C. Because sister chromatids are identical (assuming no mutations), the 48 chromosomes represent 96 DNA molecules, but only 48 are unique DNA molecules.

51. B. The 48 chromosomes in a chimpanzee cell consist of 24 homologous pairs. The two chromosomes of a homologous pair contain the same genes (coding for the same traits), so there are only 24 chromosomes with a unique set of genes. On the other hand, there could be as many as 48 chromosomes with a unique set of *alleles* if the genes in each chromosome of every homologous pair contain different alleles.

52. A. Numerous follicles occur in the ovary, each follicle containing one primary oocyte.

53. A. Under the influence of follicle stimulating hormone (FSH) from the anterior pituitary, the follicle grows and secretes estrogen. At ovulation (stimulated by a sudden increase in FSH and LH, luteinizing hormone), the oocyte ruptures from the follicle and enters the oviduct. The follicle, now without the oocyte, is now the corpus luteum.

54. E. The function of the corpus luteum (previously the follicle when it enclosed the oocyte) is to continue the secretion of estrogen and in addition, the secretion of considerable amounts of progesterone. This activity is maintained by luteinizing hormone (LH) from the anterior pituitary. Estrogen and progesterone stimulate the thickening of the uterine wall in preparation for the implantation of a fertilized egg.

55. B. After the oocyte leaves the follicle, it enters the oviduct, where fertilization usually occurs, if sperm are present. The fertilized egg (zygote) continues through the oviduct and into the uterus, where it implants on the uterine wall. The uterine wall, or endometrium, is thickened with nutrient-rich tissue and blood vessels as a result of growth stimulated by estrogen and progesterone from the corpus luteum.

56. B. The epidermis of leaves and other aerial portions of the plant is covered by the waxy material cutin.

57. E. The endodermis is a cylinder of cells that surrounds the vascular cylinder in plant roots. The waxy material suberin forms a ring around each endodermal cell, restricting the passage of water to pathways through the cell rather than between the cells. This water-impenetrable barrier is called the Casparian strip.

58. C. Gibberellins are a group of plant hormones that promote cell growth. The group consists of various gibberellic acids that promote stem elongation (especially together with auxin), seed germination, and fruit development.

59. D. Secretin is a hormone produced by cells of the duodenum in response to the presence of acidic chyme (partially digested food mixed with digestive juices). Secretin stimulates the release of bicarbonate into the duodenum, which serves to neutralize the acid previously introduced by the stomach. In the stomach, acid was necessary to help physically break down foods and to activate the protein-digesting enzyme pepsin.

60. B. Resource partitioning occurs when species divide a resource in such a way that it minimizes competition. Each grazing species in this question is specialized to eat a slightly different grass with respect to grass species or size.

61. E. Commensalism is a living-together relationship (symbiosis) where one species benefits and the second species neither benefits or is harmed.

62. A. In the absence of a competitor, each booby species occupies its fundamental niche. When both species are present, each species occupies its realized niche. For the masked booby, the fundamental and realized niches are the same. For the blue-footed booby, the realized niche is further inland than its fundamental niche.

63. D. Mutualism is a living-together relationship (symbiosis) where both species benefit. The relationship between the *Yucca* and pollinating moths is an extreme example of mutualism because not only do they benefit each other, but they depend upon each other for survival. If one species becomes extinct, the other species will follow.

64. A. Gray snakes are well camouflaged when they sun themselves while lying on the gray rocks of the rocky islands. Similarly, banded snakes are well camouflaged while lying in the vegetation.

65. D. On the rocky islands, there is selection *for* gray snakes and *against* banded snakes. This kind of selection, selection that maintains the traits of an existing population, is stabilizing selection.

66. C. The simplest explanation for the appearance of young snakes is that snakes from the mainland migrate to the islands and mate with the island snakes. Offspring that are banded are eliminated by predators before they reach reproductive age.

67. C. If N is used to represent the normal allele and n is the allele that expresses the disease, then the cross for this question is $X^N X^n \times X^n Y$. The offspring will be $\frac{1}{4} X^N X^n + \frac{1}{4} X^n X^n + \frac{1}{4} X^N Y + \frac{1}{4} X^n Y$. Half the offspring will be males and of those, half the males will have the disease ($X^n Y$).

68. E. Because males have one X chromosome and females have two, the expression of X-linked genes in females is potentially twice that of males. In order to compensate for this inequality, one of the female chromosomes is inactivated, leaving only one chromosome to produce transcripts. This is called X-inactivation. Which of the two X chromosomes that is inactivated is determined randomly and independently in each cell early in embryonic development. After inactivation occurs, all descendents of the cell have the same chromosome inactivated. The result produces groups of cells all with the same X chromosome inactivated, adjacent to other groups of cells with a different X chromosome inactivated. For the trait in this question, the disease in heterozygous females is expressed as patches of skin without sweat glands as well as missing some teeth.

69. C. Because selection of one of the two X chromosomes that becomes inactivated occurs randomly and independently in early embryonic cells, each female twin will have different X chromosomes inactivated in different parts of her body. The areas over each twin's body that are lacking sweat glands will be different, and different teeth will be missing. (See answer to previous question for an explanation of X-inactivation.)

70. B. A paraphyletic group excludes one or more descendents of the most recent ancestor of the group. The group "Great Apes" omits humans, a descendent of the most recent ancestor of the "Great Apes."

71. B. Humans, chimpanzees, and gorillas make a monophyletic group because it contains the most recent ancestor and all of its descendents. A group consisting of humans and chimpanzees, as in answer A, is paraphyletic because it excludes one of the descendents (gorillas) of the most recent ancestor. Answers C, D, and E are also paraphyletic.

72. E. According to the figure, CO_2 assimilation is minimum, stomata are closed, and pH increases (acidity decreases) during daytime hours (the middle portion of the graph).

73. C. Clearly, this is not normal photosynthesis. All three recorded variables (CO_2 uptake, stomata opening and closing, and leaf pH) are typical of CAM photosynthesis. In CAM, the stomata are closed during the day to minimize water loss. During the night, the stomata open, allowing CO_2 to enter. The CO_2 is fixed by PEP carboxylase (instead of the rubisco typical of C_3 photosynthesis), which leads to the formation of malic acid, which is stored in the cell vacuole. Malic acid accumulation accounts for the decrease in pH (increase in acidity) during the night. During the day, the stomata close, and C_3 photosynthesis occurs. But the source of CO_2 is from malic acid when it is converted to pyruvate.

74. C. Insulin, secreted by the beta cells of the pancreas, stimulates muscle, liver, and adipose cells to absorb glucose from the blood. It also stimulates the liver to convert the absorbed glucose to glycogen.

75. D. Glucagon, produced by alpha cells of the pancreas, stimulates the liver to secrete glucose into the blood when blood glucose concentration drops after exercise or during fasting. Negative feedback mechanisms maintain homeostasis of blood glucose by the antagonistic action of two hormones -- glucagon (which increases blood glucose) and insulin (which decreases blood glucose).

76. A. Glucagon stimulates the liver to secrete glucose. The liver obtains the glucose by breaking down its stored glycogen (glycogenolysis) and by synthesizing new glucose (gluconeogenesis) from amino acids, lactate, and glycerol.

77. A. Biomass increases as succession progresses from early stages to middle successional stages. As the climax-community stage approaches, fewer new species are introduced (diversity stabilizes), and fewer new individuals of established species are able to become established (abundance stabilizes). As a result, biomass stabilizes.

78. A. In some aquatic communities, the individuals in lower tiers of a pyramid of biomass are eaten almost as fast as they reproduce. As a result, most of the biomass is concentrated in the upper tiers. For example, large predatory fish (top tier) feed on small fish (middle tier), which feed on plankton (bottom tier).

79. E. The enzymes for the Krebs cycle reside in the matrix, inside the inner membrane that forms the cristae. Here, in the matrix, the Krebs cycle generates 3 NADH, 1 $FADH_2$, and 1 ATP from 1 pyruvate. This ATP is generated by substrate-level phosphorylation, that is, not a product of the electron transport chain and oxidative phosphorylation.

80. D. The inner mitochondrial membrane folds inward into the matrix to form cristae. Here, in the cristae, four protein complexes form the electron transport chain through which the flow of electrons removed from NADH and $FADH_2$ occurs. During the process, protons (H^+) are pumped from the matrix, across the cristae, and into the inner membrane space (labeled C in the diagram).

81. C. The area labeled C in the figure is the inner membrane space (between the inner membrane that forms the cristae and the outer mitochondrial membrane). As electrons from NADH and $FADH_2$ pass along the electron transport chain in the cristae, protons (H^+) are pumped from the matrix, across the cristae, and into this area C. An increase in H^+ decreases the pH (makes it more acidic). When H^+ returns to the matrix via the ATP synthase in the cristae, the flow of H^+ powers the phosphorylation of ADP to form ATP.

82. E. Because few of the eggs survive, the survivorship pattern is best described with the plot that shows a sharp decline in population size early in the life.

83. B. Semelparity is a "big-bang" reproductive strategy where individuals culminate their lives with a single reproductive effort that produces many offspring. Such a strategy is characteristic of r-selected species. In iteroparity, individuals repeat their reproductive effort seasonally or annually, at least several times during their lifetime.

84. E. When environments are unpredictable or variable and few offspring are likely to survive, the best strategy is to produce lots of offspring, each requiring little or no care. In stable environments, where competition is likely to be high, the best strategy is to produce few offspring, providing them with parental care to help them meet competitive challenges. Effective parental care limits the number of offspring that can be produced, so the strategy requires that the reproductive effort is repeated several times during the life of the individual.

85. A. An ectotherm is an animal that is dependent upon its surroundings for its source of heat. As a result, its body temperature closely follows the temperature of its environment. However, ectotherms are not necessarily passive recipients of environmental conditions. Lizards, for example, can adjust their body temperatures by moving from shade to sun or by raising and lowering their bodies (movements that look like "pushups") to regulate the cooling effect of moving air.

86. B. An endotherm is an animal that generates its own heat to maintain its body temperature. As a result, the animal is able to maintained a constant body temperature.

87. C. $NADP^+$ is the recipient of energized electrons from photosystem I. When reduced by these electrons from photosystem I, DPIP turns from blue to clear.

88. C. Light (present or absent) and chloroplasts (present, boiled, or absent) are two independent variables in this experiment. Treatment I establishes that photosynthesis occurs (DPIP turns clear) when light and healthy chloroplasts are present. Removing light (Treatment II) tests if light is necessary for photosynthesis, and removing chloroplasts (Treatment IV) tests if chloroplasts are necessary. Treatment III tests for the effect of heat on chloroplasts, which is not part of the hypothesis being investigated in this question. Furthermore, the boiled-chloroplasts treatment (III) is a poor substitute for the no-chloroplasts treatment (IV) because alternative hypotheses are introduced. For example, one could argue that byproducts from boiling chloroplasts and not disabled chloroplasts are responsible for the decrease in photosynthetic activity.

89. D. Treatments I, III, and IV test the effect of heat on chloroplasts, which supports the hypothesis that heat disrupts membrane proteins. Additional investigations, however, are necessary to eliminate alternative hypotheses. For example, parts of the chloroplast other than the proteins may be disabled and responsible for the decrease in photosynthesis. Treatments I and III alone do not adequately test for this hypothesis because Treatment IV is also necessary to establish that healthy chloroplasts are required for photosynthesis. Treatment II is unnecessary because it tests for the necessity of light, a variable not investigated in the hypothesis for this question (so the variable of light should remain constant for this question).

90. E. The data from the electrophoresis banding patterns represent phenotypic frequencies of an enzyme trait, that is, p^2, $2pq$, and q^2. If $q^2 = 0.04$, then $q = 0.2$, and if $p^2 = 0.64$, then $p = 0.8$. Note that $p + q = 1$.

91. A. The population is in Hardy-Weinberg equilibrium if $p^2 + 2pq + q^2 = 1$ and $p + q = 1$.

92. E. PCR is a process that makes multiple copies of a specific DNA fragment in a very short amount of time.

93. E. Heating the double-stranded DNA fragment to about 95°C causes the DNA to "melt," or separate into two strands of single-stranded DNA.

94. A. In step II, primers (short single-stranded DNA molecules) are added and the temperature is reduced. The primers attach to the single-stranded DNA fragment to be copied.

95. B. Once the primers are in place (step II in the figure), a heat-stable DNA polymerase is added. DNA polymerase attaches to the primers and begins replication of the DNA fragment.

96. D. The osmotic water potential, Ψ_s, is always negative because the presence of solutes in water decreases Ψ (makes it more negative than pure water whose $\Psi = 0$); the greater the concentration of solutes, the smaller the value of Ψ_s. The value of Ψ_P is 0 unless a force is applied and because the cell wall is applying a force, $\Psi_P > 0$.

97. A. The value of $\Psi = 0$ for pure water because $\Psi_s = 0$ (no solutes) and Ψ_P is 0 (no pressure applied).

98. B. Inside the leaf cell, the value of $\Psi = \Psi_P + \Psi_s = 0.5 + (-2.0) = -1.5$ MPa. Water moves from higher to lower values of water potential, so water moves out of the cell (-1.5 is greater than -2.7).

99. A. The graph shows that the cuvette with the higher concentration of substrate (succinate) has a higher rate of respiration. The vertical axis of the graph records the percent transmittance of the solution. The greater the transmittance, the more reduced DPIP in the cuvette, and the greater amount of respiration. Because the y-axis represents respiration and the x-axis represents time, the respiratory *rate* is the slope of a plotted line. (Note that *rate* means a change in a variable with time, or $\Delta y/\Delta t$, graphically represented by the slope of a plotted line.)

100. C. Pyruvate, the product of glycolysis, is the initial substrate for the Krebs cycle. All of the steps of the Krebs cycle that normally reduce NAD^+ to NADH can also reduce DPIP if NAD^+ and pyruvate are continuously provided. However, only succinate is provided, so only succinate can contribute electrons (normally for the reduction of FAD to $FADH_2$).

Section II (Free-Response Questions)

Scoring Standards for the Essay Questions

To score your answers, award your essay points using the standards given. For each item listed that matches the content and vocabulary of a statement or explanation in your essay, add the indicated number of points to your essay score (to the maximum allowed for each section). Scores for each essay question range from 0 to 10 points.

Words appearing in parentheses in answers represent alternative wording.

Question 1 (10 points maximum)

A. proteins (*4 points maximum*)

- structure of the molecule (*2 points maximum*)

    1 pt: Proteins are polymers of amino acids (or a labeled figure showing this).

    1 pt: The structure of an amino acid consists of a central carbon with four groups attached: an amino group, a carboxyl group, a hydrogen atom, and a variable group (represented by R).

    OR

    A drawing of the structure of an amino acid with groups labeled, as follows (either one).

amino group   carboxyl group   amino group   carboxyl group

    1 pt: The R group of an amino acid varies among amino acids and determines which amino acid it is.

    1 pt: A protein takes on three-dimensional shapes as a result of hydrogen bonding and other interactions between amino acids.

    1 pt: Additional detail of tertiary and quaternary protein structures.

- function of the molecule (*2 points maximum*)

    1 pt: Proteins function as enzymes, such as the enzyme maltase, which splits maltose into two glucose molecules.

    1 pt: Proteins function as structural components of organisms, such as collagen, which is a major component of connective tissues.

    1 pt: Proteins function as hormones, such as insulin, which regulates blood glucose.

    1 pt: Proteins function as transport molecules, such as hemoglobin, which transports O_2 through blood vessels.

    1 pt: Proteins function as contractile fibers, such as actin, which is a major component of muscle cells.

    1 pt: Any other protein function with an example.

- importance of hydrogen bonding (*2 points maximum*)

    1 pt: Hydrogen bonding contributes to the three-dimensional shape of the protein that is essential to its function.

    1 pt: Hydrogen bonding is responsible for the (alpha) helix form of the secondary structure of the protein.

1 pt: Hydrogen bonding is responsible for the (beta) pleated-sheet form of the secondary structure of the protein.

1 pt: Hydrogen bonds form between the (positive) hydrogen of the amino group of one amino acid and the (negative) oxygen of the carboxyl group of a nearby amino acid.

B. DNA (*4 points maximum*)

- structure of the molecule (*2 points maximum*)

  1 pt: DNA is a polymer of four different nucleotides.

  1 pt: The structure of a DNA nucleotide consists of the sugar deoxyribose, to which a phosphate and a nitrogen base are attached.

  1 pt: Each DNA nucleotide is named after one of four bases: adenine, thymine, guanine, and cytosine.

  1 pt: DNA takes the form of a double helix where two polymers of DNA nucleotides form hydrogen bonds between bases.

  1 pt: Base pairing always occurs between an adenine and a thymine or between a guanine and a cytosine.

- function of the molecule (*2 points maximum*)

  1 pt: DNA holds the hereditary information of the cell.

  1 pt: DNA contains the genes for making polypeptides (proteins or enzymes).

  1 pt: Bacterial plasmids are small, circular DNA molecules that carry genes not normally essential to the functioning of the bacterium.

- importance of hydrogen bonding (*1 point maximum*)

  1 pt: The double-stranded structure allows for semiconservative replication of the hereditary information (DNA).

  1 pt: Hydrogen bonds occur between nitrogen bases of adjacent DNA polymers (base pairing) and hold the two strands of DNA together to form the double helix.

C. RNA (*4 points maximum*)

- structure of the molecule (*2 points maximum*)

  1 pt: RNA is a polymer of four different nucleotides.

  1 pt: The structure of an RNA nucleotide consists of the sugar ribose, to which a phosphate and a nitrogen base are attached.

  1 pt: Each RNA nucleotide is named after one of four bases: adenine, uracil, guanine, and cytosine.

  1 pt: When base pairing occurs, it occurs between adenine and uracil or between guanine and cytosine.

  1 pt: There are three kinds of RNA: messenger RNA (mRNA), ribosomal RNA (rRNA), and transfer RNA (tRNA).

- function of the molecule (*3 points maximum*)

  1 pt: The function of mRNA is to provide a template for the amino acid sequence of proteins during protein synthesis.

  1 pt: The function of rRNA is to form ribosomes (or ribosomal subunits) (along with proteins) which assemble amino acids during protein synthesis.

  1 pt: The function of tRNA is to deliver amino acids to the ribosomes during protein synthesis.

- importance of hydrogen bonding (*1 point maximum*)

  1 pt: Hydrogen bonding occurs between mRNA and tRNA during protein synthesis.

  1 pt: Hydrogen bonding occurs within each tRNA to form its (cloverleaf-like) shape that is essential to its function of attaching to amino acids and to ribosomes.

1 pt: Hydrogen bonding (base-pairing) occurs between rRNA and tRNA at binding sites on the rRNAs in the ribosome during protein synthesis.

C. prions (*2 points maximum*)

- structure of the molecule (*1 point maximum*)

    1 pt: Prions are abnormally folded versions of proteins.

- function of the molecule (*1 point maximum*)

    1 pt: Prions stimulate normal proteins to assume the same abnormal folding as that of the prions, thus converting the normal proteins to prions, which then cause disease in the tissues where these proteins occur (usually nerve tissue, especially brain).

- importance of hydrogen bonding (*1 point maximum*)

    1 pt: Incorrect hydrogen bonding converts normal proteins to disease-causing proteins.

Question 2 (10 points maximum)

A. genetic variation in sexually reproducing organisms (*6 points maximum*)

- mutation (*1 point maximum*)

    1 pt: Mutations introduce new variations into the gene pool.

    1 pt: New variations introduced by mutations may produce advantageous or disadvantageous variations (traits).

- meiosis (*3 points maximum*)

    1 pt: Genetic recombination occurs during meiosis and creates new gene combinations in gametes.

    1 pt: Genetic variation is generated when crossing over occurs during prophase I of meiosis.

    1 pt: Crossing over is the exchange of genetic material between homologous chromosomes.

    1 pt: Independent assortment of homologous chromosomes during anaphase I of meiosis contributes to new combinations of genes (genetic variation) in daughter cells.

- diploidy (*1 point maximum*)

    1 pt: Diploidy preserves genetic variation because recessive alleles are hidden from natural selection when they are inherited with a dominant allele.

    1 pt: When a diploid individual inherits two alleles in the heterozygous condition, the recessive allele is not expressed and is hidden from the effects of natural selection.

- haploid gametes (*1 point maximum*)

    1 pt: Fertilization is required to generate a diploid organism from haploid gametes.

    1 pt: Random union of male and female gametes generates new combinations of genes (genetic variation).

B. genetic variation in prokaryotes (*4 points maximum*)

1 pt: Mutations introduce new variations into the genome of daughter cells.

1 pt: Genetic variation is introduced by transformation, the process of absorption of DNA from the environment followed by the assimilation of the DNA into its genome.

1 pt: Genetic variation is introduced by transduction, the process of assimilating DNA that is introduced by viruses carrying bacterial DNA from a previous infection.

1 pt: Genetic variation is introduced by conjugation, the process of exchanging DNA (chromosomal or plasmid) through connecting appendages called pili.

Question 3 (10 points maximum). Only three of the four parts to be scored.

A. feedback mechanisms that regulate protein production (*4 points maximum*)

- *trp* operon

    1 pt: In prokaryotes, when tryptophan is present in the environment surrounding the prokaryotic cell, it activates a repressor protein that blocks the transcription of proteins (enzymes) that synthesize tryptophan. When tryptophan is absent, the repressor protein is inactive, and enzymes to synthesize tryptophan are transcribed.

    1 pt: The *trp* operon is a repressible operon; it is normally turned on and a repressor protein must be activated to turn the operon off.

    1 pt: The *trp* operon is a section of DNA that includes a promoter region to which RNA polymerase attaches to begin transcription, an operator region which when occupied by a repressor protein blocks the attachment of RNA polymerase to the promoter, and a region occupied by the structural genes for manufacturing the proteins (enzymes) necessary for tryptophan synthesis.

    1 pt: When present, tryptophan binds to and activates a repressor protein. The activated repressor protein then binds to the operator in the promoter region of the operon, which, in turn, represses transcription for the enzymes that synthesize tryptophan.

    1 pt: When tryptophan is unavailable, the repressor protein remains inactive, and the operator allows transcription.

- *lac* operon

    1 pt: In prokaryotes, when lactose is present, it is metabolized to generate ATP. Normally, the genes that code for the enzymes that metabolize lactose are not being transcribed. To activate transcription of these genes, a byproduct of lactose inactivates a repressor protein that blocks this transcription. As a result, transcription occurs, enzymes are produced, and lactose is metabolized. When lactose is not present, the repressor remains active and transcription is repressed.

    1 pt: The *lac* operon is an inducible operon; it is normally turned off and a repressor protein must be deactivated to turn the operon on.

    1 pt: The *lac* operon is a section of DNA that includes a promoter region to which RNA polymerase attaches to begin transcription, an operator region which when occupied by a repressor protein blocks the attachment of RNA polymerase to the promoter, and a region occupied by the structural genes for manufacturing the proteins (enzymes) to metabolize lactose.

    1 pt: When lactose is present, one of its breakdown products binds to and inactivates a repressor protein. An inactivated repressor cannot bind to the operator region of the operon and block RNA polymerase access to the promoter region. As a result, RNA polymerase can bind to the promoter region and begin transcription.

    1 pt: When lactose and its breakdown product are absent, the repressor is active, binds to the operator, blocks RNA polymerase from the promoter region, and thus represses transcription.

B. embryonic signaling (*4 points maximum*)

    1 pt: In the embryonic development of some organisms, cytoplasmic substances (developmental signals or determinants) are unequally distributed to daughter cells, leading to different developmental fates for the cells.

    1 pt: In induction, embryonic cells influence (induce) developmental changes in nearby cells by secreting signaling proteins.

    1 pt: Organizers are groups of embryonic cells that secrete signal proteins to influence the development of adjacent tissues.

    1 pt: Cell-to-cell contact between adjacent cells provides signals that influence growth.

1 pt: Signal substances directly or indirectly turn on or off genes that code for enzymes that influence development.

1 pt: Signal substances may influence the transcription of genes that code for transcription factors, proteins that turn on other genes that influence development.

C. neuron-muscle communication (*4 points maximum*)

1 pt: Acetylcholine is a neurotransmitter secreted by the neuron to signal the muscle to contract.

1 pt: When an action potential along a neuron reaches the neuromuscular junction, synaptic vesicles in the neuron release acetylcholine, a neurotransmitter.

1 pt: Acetylcholine diffuses across the synaptic cleft (space between neuron and muscle).

1 pt: Acetylcholine depolarizes the muscle cell, causing an action potential to spread along the surface of the transverse tubule (T-system), a system of invaginations into the plasma membrane.

1 pt: The action potential stimulates the sarcoplasmic reticulum (endoplasmic reticulum) of the muscle cell to release Ca^{2+}.

1 pt: Ca^{2+} stimulates the contraction of muscle fibers when ATP is present.

1 pt: When Ca^{2+} binds to the troponin complex on actin, tropomyosin changes its position such that binding sites for myosin cross-bridges are exposed. Myosin attaches and contraction results.

D. chemical communication between individuals (*4 points maximum*)

(*Two points for each example with purpose*)

2 pt: Female elephants secrete a pheromone (a chemical released into the environment) into their urine to communicate to males their readiness to mate.

2 pt: During mating season, male elephants secrete from their temporal glands two pheromones, the ratio of which changes as elephants age. Pheromone ratios secreted by older elephants are more attractive to females and drive away younger males.

2 pt: Ants secrete pheromones to mark trails that guide other ants to food.

2 pt: Queen ants (termites, bees) secrete pheromones eaten by workers that prevent development of reproductive ability.

2 pt: Mammals (wolves, cats) spray urine to mark their territories, securing for themselves an area to feed and mate.

2 pt: Female moths release pheromones into the air that signal to males their readiness to mate.

2 pt: Any other example with an explanation for what the communication accomplishes.

Question 4 (10 points maximum)

A. plot data (*3 points maximum*)

1 pt: Axes are labeled, units provided, scale is linear (equal intervals anywhere on an axis represent the same amount of change in the variable), and graph is titled.

1 pt: For 2004, the independent variable (time or months) is plotted on the *x*-axis and the dependent variable (bear encounters) is plotted on the *y*-axis.

1 pt: For 2005, same as above.

1 pt: The two plots (2004 and 2005) are drawn with different line styles (solid and dash) and labeled (or a legend provided).

B. hypothesis for year 2004 (*1 point maximum*)

Only a sample of the many possible hypotheses is provided. Your hypothesis must be testable.

The number of bear encounters with campgrounds results from variations in

1 pt: the ease of obtaining food.

1 pt: the weather (temperature, precipitation).

1 pt: mating frequency.

1 pt: interspecific competition for food.

1 pt: associative learning (classical conditioning).

1 pt: taxis.

C. hypothesis for the increase from 2004 to 2005 (*1 point maximum*)

Only a sample of the many possible hypotheses is provided. Your hypothesis must be testable.

The increase in bear encounters from 2004 to 2005 resulted from

1 pt: an increase in bear population size.

1 pt: associative learning (classical conditioning).

1 pt: the ease of obtaining food.

1 pt: the weather (temperature, precipitation).

1 pt: mating frequency.

1 pt: interspecific competition for food.

D. description of experiment for hypothesis in B (*5 points maximum*)

Hypothesis: Bear encounters with campgrounds are related to the ease with which food can be obtained.

1 pt: for an explanation of each variable or treatment

1 pt: This experiment compares the number of bear encounters with food availability in campsites. Availability of food in campsites varies with the method of storing food. Some campsites are equipped with storage lockers to store food, while in others, visitors hang their food from tree limbs in an attempt to make their food less accessible to bears. In other campgrounds, visitors store their food in their tents and cars.

1 pt: There are two independent variables: time and food availability.

1 pt: There are three treatments (manipulations) of the independent variable.

- campgrounds where food is stored in cars or tents
- campgrounds where food is stored in trees
- campgrounds where food is stored in lockers that bears cannot open.

1 pt: The dependent variable is the number of bear encounters per visitor. Dividing the number of bear encounters by the number of visitors minimizes the effect that the number of visitors (and the quantity of food) that occupies each campground has on the dependent variable.

E. (*1 point maximum*)

1 pt: The number of bear encounters will be greatest in the campsites where food is stored in cars or tents and least in campsites where food is stored in lockers.

F. (*2 points maximum*)

1 pt: Axes are labeled, units provided, and scale is linear (equal intervals anywhere on an axis represent the same amount of change in the variable).

1 pt: Each treatment is plotted as a separate line and identified with treatment (line style and label or legend).

Bear Encounters in 2004 and 2005

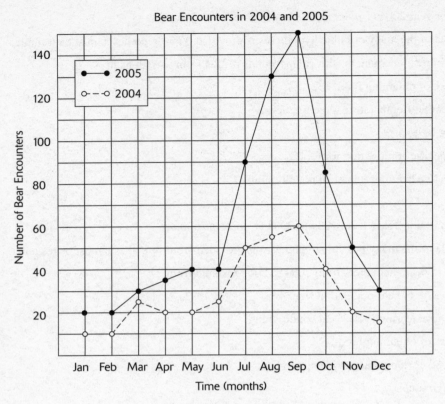

Bear Encounters and Food Availability

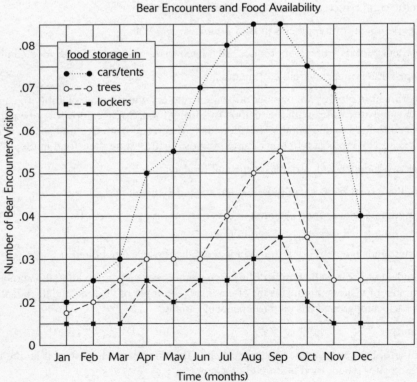